My Samsung® Galaxy S® III

Steve Schwartz

800 East 96th Street
Indianapolis, Indiana 46240 USA

My Samsung® Galaxy S® III

Copyright © 2013 by Pearson Education

ISBN-13: 978-0-7897-4963-5
ISBN-10: 0-7897-4963-7

Library of Congress Cataloging-in-Publication Data is on file.

Printed in the United States of America

First Printing: November 2012

Trademarks

All terms mentioned in this book that are known to be trademarks or service marks have been appropriately capitalized. Que Publishing cannot attest to the accuracy of this information. Use of a term in this book should not be regarded as affecting the validity of any trademark or service mark.

All S III images are provided by Samsung Mobile.

Warning and Disclaimer

Every effort has been made to make this book as complete and as accurate as possible, but no warranty or fitness is implied. The information provided is on an "as is" basis. The author and the publisher shall have neither liability nor responsibility to any person or entity with respect to any loss or damages arising from the information contained in this book.

Bulk Sales

Que Publishing offers excellent discounts on this book when ordered in quantity for bulk purchases or special sales. For more information, please contact

U.S. Corporate and Government Sales

1-800-382-3419

corpsales@pearsontechgroup.com

For sales outside of the U.S., please contact

International Sales

international@pearsoned.com

Editor-in-Chief
Greg Wiegand

Acquisitions Editor
Michelle Newcomb

Development Editor
Charlotte Kughen

Managing Editor
Kristy Hart

Project Editor
Anne Goebel

Copy Editor
Krista Hansing

Indexer
Tim Wright

Proofreader
Paula Lowell

Technical Editor
Christian Kenyeres

Editorial Assistant
Cindy Teeters

Cover Designer
Anne Jones

Compositor
Tricia Bronkella

Contents at a Glance

Table of Contents

9 Sending and Receiving Email   239

About the Author

Steve Schwartz got an early start as a computer industry writer and author. Immediately after buying an Apple II+ in 1978, he began writing regularly for the computer magazines of the day. Since then, he has written hundreds of articles for major publications, including *Macworld, PC World, InfoWorld,* and *Computerworld.* He is also the author of more than 60 books on game and computer topics, including guides to business/productivity software (Microsoft Office, Access, and FileMaker Pro), Internet software (Internet Explorer, Outlook Express, Entourage, and Gmail), and graphics/image-editing software (Picasa, Picture It!, Digital Image Suite, and CorelDRAW).

Before becoming a full-time writer in 1990, Steve served as editor-in-chief for *Software Digest* and technical services director for Funk Software. He also authored the first trade paperback on the then-new Nintendo phenomenon: *Compute!'s Guide to Nintendo Games.*

Steve has a Ph.D. in psychology, consults on game and database design issues, and lives in the fictional town of Lizard Spit, Arizona. You can see the complete list of his published books at http:// www.siliconwasteland.com/ misc.htm.

Dedication

To the millions of people who buy smartphones thinking, "I can figure this out. This will be easy!"

Acknowledgments

I'd like to extend my special thanks to the following individuals:

- Carole Jelen of Waterside Productions
- The talented editorial and production team at Que: Michelle Newcomb, Anne Goebel, Charlotte Kughen, and Krista Hansing.
- Mieshel and Dane Thompson

We Want to Hear from You!

As the reader of this book, *you* are our most important critic and commentator. We value your opinion and want to know what we're doing right, what we could do better, what areas you'd like to see us publish in, and any other words of wisdom you're willing to pass our way.

We welcome your comments. You can email or write to let us know what you did or didn't like about this book—as well as what we can do to make our books better.

Please note that we cannot help you with technical problems related to the topic of this book.

When you write, please be sure to include this book's title and author, as well as your name and email address. We will carefully review your comments and share them with the author and editors who worked on the book.

Email: feedback@quepublishing.com

Mail: Que Publishing
ATTN: Reader Feedback
800 East 96th Street
Indianapolis, IN 46240 USA

Reader Services

Visit our website and register this book at quepublishing.com/register for convenient access to any updates, downloads, or errata that might be available for this book.

Status bar

Widget

Google
Quick
Search bar

Apps

Primary
shortcuts

Home
screen
page
indicator

In this chapter, you become familiar with the basics of setting up and operating your new phone. Topics include the following:

→ Familiarizing yourself with the phone hardware, operating system, interface, and customization options

→ Charging the battery

→ Turning the phone on and off

→ Restoring a dark display

→ Adjusting the volume

→ Using a headset or headphones

→ Setting up voicemail

→ Creating and registering a Gmail account

→ Creating a Samsung account

→ Connecting to Wi-Fi, 3G, and 4G

1

Galaxy S III Essentials

Welcome to *My Samsung Galaxy S III*. In this chapter and Chapter 2, "Understanding the Android/TouchWiz Interface," you become familiar with the fundamentals of operating and interacting with your new Android-based phone.

The Galaxy S III Hardware

To create a powerful, flexible smartphone, Samsung equipped the Galaxy S III with the following features:

- 1.5GHz dual core processor, running the Android 4.*x* operating system

- HD Super AMOLED, 1280 × 720–pixel, 4.8" touchscreen display

- 1.9-megapixel front-facing camera; 8-megapixel rear-facing camera with HD video recording

- 16, 32, or 64GB internal memory; support for up to 64GB of additional memory with a microSDHC card

- GPS (global positioning system)

- Wi-Fi and Bluetooth connectivity

The following are the key hardware components of the Galaxy S III:

Proximity and ambient light sensors

Earpiece

Microphone

Status or indicator light

Front camera

Volume control

Power button

Touchscreen

Home key

Menu key

Back key

USB Power/ Accessory connector

Microphone

Rear camera

Headset jack

Flash

External
speaker

Power button   Press the power button to turn the phone on or off and to manually darken (lock) or restore the screen.

Volume control   Press this context-sensitive hardware control to raise (top part) or lower (bottom part) the volume of the current activity, such as conducting a call or playing music.

Microphone   Speak into the bottom microphone when participating in a call, giving voice commands, or using the phone's speech-to-text feature. The top microphone is used for noise cancellation and stereo recording.

Earpiece   When you're not using a headset, call audio is transmitted through this front speaker. The external speaker on the back of the phone is used to play music, ringtones, and other audio.

Headset jack   Port for connecting a compatible 3.5mm wired headset or headphones; enables 5.1 channel sound when playing media.

Front camera   Low-resolution (1.9-megapixel), front-facing camera for taking self-portraits and participating in video chats.

Rear camera   High-resolution (8-megapixel), rear-facing camera for taking pictures and high-definition movies.

Flash   Illuminate photos shot with the rear-facing camera (unless you've disabled it for the shot).

Touchscreen   Touch-sensitive screen; displays information and enables you to interact with the phone.

Menu, Home, and Back keys   Press these hardware keys to interact with the operating system and installed applications.

USB Power/Accessory connector   Enables the phone to be connected with the supplied USB cable to a computer (for file transfers) or to the charger head and a wall outlet (to charge the phone's battery).

Status or indicator light   Displays a flashing or steady light to indicate that the phone is performing its startup sequence, denoting notifications (such as newly received email or text messages), or showing the charging status.

Ambient light and proximity sensor   The ambient light sensor allows the screen's brightness to adjust to current lighting conditions. The proximity sensor detects how close an object is to the phone. During calls, it senses when your face is pressed to the screen and locks the keypad to prevent accidental key presses.

The Android Operating System and TouchWiz

Just like a computer, every smartphone has an *operating system* that controls virtually every important activity that the phone can perform, as well as the ways in which you interact with it. On the Galaxy S III, the operating system is Android 4.*x*.

Like many of the other major cellphone manufacturers, Samsung has custom-
ized the Android operating system to differentiate its phones from those of
competitors. Samsung's TouchWiz touch interface is that operating system
customization. Even though phones from other manufacturers run Android
4.x, TouchWiz ensures that Galaxy S III phones operate in a similar—but never
identical—fashion to such phones.

Note that operating system updates are periodically made available to
phones through the carrier.

The Galaxy S III Interface

Other than using the hardware controls described earlier in the chapter,
much of what you do with the phone involves using its touchscreen. The
main *(Home)* screen consists of seven customizable pages. On it, you can
place shortcuts to the applications *(apps)* that you use most often, as well as
small applications *(widgets)* that run directly on the Home screen. To interact
with the touchscreen, you tap app icons to launch programs, flick up or down
to scroll through lists, pinch and spread your fingers to change the current
magnification, and so on. Chapter 2 explains in detail how to work with the
touchscreen interface.

Customization

One of the main reasons for buying a smartphone such as the Galaxy S III is that you can do considerably more with it than you can with an ordinary telephone or cellphone. Much as you can do with a computer, you can customize your phone by populating the Home screen with custom arrangements of widgets and application icons, change the Home screen's background *(wallpaper),* install additional useful applications, and set preferences (called *settings*) for the system software and applications. When you're comfortable with the phone's basic operations and are ready to start customizing it, read Chapter 17, "Customizing Your Phone."

Settings screen

CHANGING SYSTEM SETTINGS

To change certain operating system features (such as choosing a new Wi-Fi network), you need to access the Settings screen. There are several ways you can do this:

• From any Home screen page, press the Menu key and tap Settings in the pop-up menu that appears.

Settings————

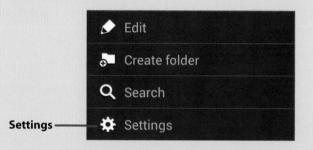

• Tap a Settings shortcut icon. (It's a default icon on the third Home screen page.)

Settings shortcut

Home screen page 3

• Open the Notifications panel by dragging the status bar downward and then tap the Settings icon.

Settings icon

Charging the Battery

The Galaxy S III includes a two-piece wall charger that consists of a special USB cable and a charger head. You charge the phone's battery by connecting the assembled wall charger to the phone and a standard wall outlet. It's recommended that you fully charge the phone before its first use.

It isn't necessary to wait until the battery is almost fully discharged before charging. In fact, the phone's manual recommends that you *not* wait because repeatedly letting the battery completely drain can reduce its capability to store a charge.

Connecting to a Computer

The battery also charges while the phone is connected to a computer by the USB cable. See "Transferring Files over USB," in Chapter 13, "Transferring and Sharing Files," for instructions on making the connection.

1. Plug the large end of the USB cable into the charger head.

2. Plug the small end of the USB cable into the bottom of the phone.

3. Plug the charger head into a wall outlet. The LED indicator light is red while the phone is charging.

4. When the LED changes color, the phone is fully charged. Disconnect the USB cable from the wall outlet and phone.

Charging While the Phone Is On

If you need to complete a call or use apps when the battery is almost drained, you can continue to use the phone while it charges.

Powering On/Off

Although many people prefer to simply leave their phone on, you can turn it off whenever you like—to conserve the battery, for example:

- To turn on the phone, press and hold the power button until the phone begins its normal startup sequence (approximately 3 seconds).

Power button

- To turn off the phone, press and hold the power button for 1–2 seconds. In the Device Options menu that appears, tap Power Off.

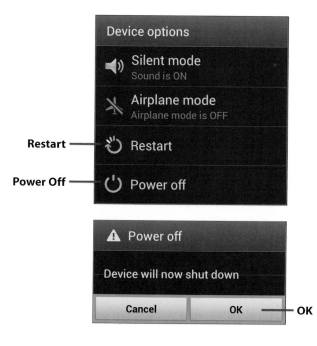

Restart

Power Off

OK

- Tap OK in the Power Off dialog box to confirm that you want to shut down your phone.

Restarting the Phone

Note that you can also restart the phone from the Power Off dialog box. If you've been running the phone continuously for several days, periodically restarting clears memory fragmentation—enabling you to start again with a clean slate.

>>>Go Further

ON-DEVICE SETUP WIZARD

The first time the phone is turned on, the On-Device Setup Wizard automatically launches and displays its Welcome screen. You can respond to its prompts to set up some essential services, such as creating or signing in to a Google account. The sections in this chapter shows you how to establish these basic settings manually—without the wizard's assistance.

**On-Device Setup Wizard
opening screen**

Darkening and Restoring the Display

Depending on the *screen timeout* setting, the display automatically turns off during periods of inactivity. In addition to waiting for this timeout to occur, you can manually darken the display to conserve the battery or maintain privacy.

Restoring a Dark Display

1. To restore the display, press the Power button on the right side of the phone to make the *lock screen* appear. (The lock screen also appears when you turn on the phone.)

Dimmed, Not Dark

The display automatically dims for a brief period before it turns black. To restore a dimmed display, tap any blank spot on the touchscreen.

2. Swipe in any direction to dismiss the lock screen.

Working with a Locked Phone

You can secure the phone by assigning a password, PIN, or pattern, for example, to require more than a simple finger swipe to dismiss the lock screen. See "Securing the Phone" in Chapter 17 for instructions.

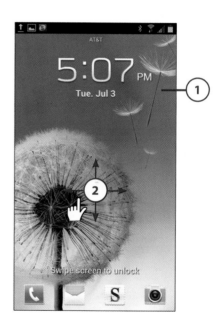

Manually Darkening the Display

To instantly darken the display, press the Power button on the right side of the phone.

Setting the Screen Timeout Interval

1. On the Home screen, press the Menu key and then tap Settings.

2. On the Settings screen, tap Display.

3. On the Display screen, tap Screen Timeout.

4. In the Screen Timeout dialog box, select a new timeout interval or tap the Cancel button to retain the current setting.

It's All About Tradeoffs

Substantial juice is needed to power the Galaxy S III's gorgeous display, so the sooner it dims during idle periods, the longer the current charge will last. The key is to select a screen timeout that enables the phone to sit idle as long as possible before dimming and still have sufficient charge to meet your daily calling and app requirements.

To avoid timeouts when you're reading or viewing material onscreen, you can enable *Smart Stay* (found in Display Settings). If the front-facing camera detects that you're looking at the screen, it prevents the normal timeout from occurring.

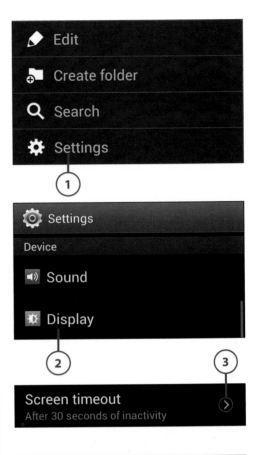

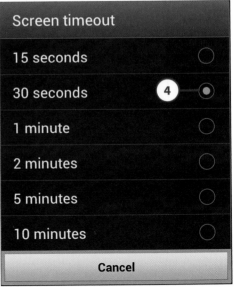

>>>Go Further

LOCK SCREEN OPTIONS

You can perform certain actions on the lock screen—in addition to simply clearing the screen. If you flick one of the four app icons upward (Phone, Messaging, S Memo, or Camera), the lock screen clears and the app launches. And if the lock screen presents a new message indicator, you can flick the indicator to the left in order to clear the lock screen, launch Messaging, and display the relevant conversation.

Adjusting the Volume

You can press the volume control on the left side of the phone to adjust voice volume during a call, media playback volume, or ringer volume (when you're neither playing media nor participating in a call). The volume control is context sensitive instead of being a general volume control; what is affected when you press the control depends on what you're doing.

1. To change the volume, press the volume control. A context-sensitive control appears.

2. To raise or lower the volume, drag the slider. You can also press the top part of the hardware volume control to raise the volume or press the bottom part to lower the volume.

3. *Optional:* To adjust other common volume settings, tap the Settings icon and drag the sliders that appear.

Adjust Everything at Once

If you want, you can set multiple volumes simultaneously. On the Home screen, press the Menu key, and—in order—tap Settings, Sound, and Volume. Adjust the Volume sliders by dragging, and then tap the OK button.

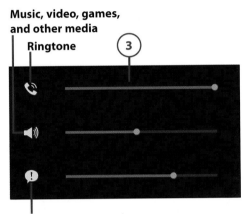

Music, video, games, and other media

Ringtone

Notifications

Volume dialog box

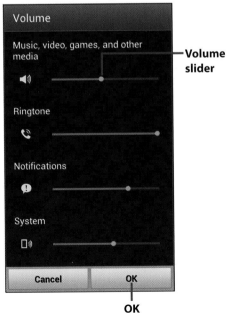

Volume slider

OK

Using a Headset or Headphones

By connecting the headset that's included with the Galaxy S III (or any other compatible 3.5mm wired headset or headphones), you can improve the phone's audio quality. For example, the Music Player app supports 5.1 channel sound when a headset is connected. And a wired or a wireless (Bluetooth) headset is handy for making hands-free calls.

Wired Headset or Headphones

1. Plug any compatible headset or headphones into the jack at the top of the phone.

2. Adjust the volume for whatever you're currently doing (taking a call, playing media, and so on) using the phone's or the headset's volume control. For instructions on the former, see "Adjusting the Volume," earlier in this chapter.

Bluetooth Headset

Although a few Bluetooth headsets support stereo (making them suitable for listening to music), most are mono devices intended primarily for hands-free phone calls. With a maximum range of 30 feet, using a Bluetooth headset enables you to place the phone nearby and conduct a conversation. Unlike using a speakerphone, the audio is routed directly to your ear and the headset's microphone won't pick up as much ambient noise.

Working with a Bluetooth headset involves two steps: pairing the headset and phone (a one-time procedure) and using the headset for calls. The procedures for pairing and answering calls are specific to your headset and are explained in the headset's instructions. As an example, the following step lists illustrate how to use a Jabra EasyGo Bluetooth headset with the Galaxy S III.

Pairing the Headset with the Phone

1. On the Home screen, press the Menu key and tap Settings.

2. In the Wireless and Network section of the Settings screen, enable Bluetooth (if it's off) by dragging the slider to the On position, turn the Bluetooth headset on, and then tap Bluetooth.

Check Your Headset's Manual

Your Bluetooth headset may require more than simply turning it on to enter pairing mode. With the Jabra EasyGo, for example, you must hold down the answer button for 5 seconds to initiate any new pairing after the initial one.

3. *Optional:* If the headset doesn't appear in the Available Devices list, tap the Scan button.

4. Tap the headset's name to pair it with the phone.

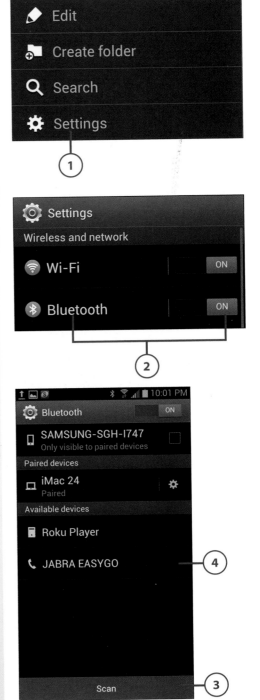

5. A confirmation appears when pairing is successful.

Using the Headset for Calls

1. Turn on the headset and place it in your ear. If Bluetooth isn't currently enabled, open the Notifications panel by touching the status bar and dragging downward. Tap the Bluetooth icon to enable it.

When the Headset Won't Connect

If your previously paired Bluetooth headset refuses to connect to the phone, open the Notifications panel and disable and then re-enable Bluetooth.

2. To place a call, dial using any of the methods supported by the phone (see "Placing Calls" in Chapter 6, "Placing and Receiving Calls").

3. To receive an incoming call, tap the headset's answer/end button or drag the green Accept Call icon to the right.

Adjusting the Volume

While on a call, you can adjust the volume by pressing the volume control on the left side of the phone or on your headset.

4. To end the call, tap the headset's answer/end button or tap the End Call icon on the phone. If you're done using the headset, you can remove it from your ear and turn it off.

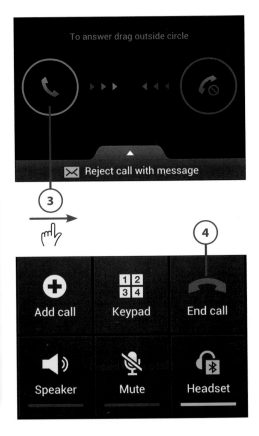

>>>Go Further

IN-CALL OPTIONS

Your headset may support a variety of other in-call options. For example, you can also use the Jabra EasyGo to reject incoming calls, redial the last number, mute the microphone, and place the current call on hold to switch between two conversations (if you have call waiting). Refer to your headset manual for instructions.

Setting Up Voicemail

After your phone is activated, one of the first things you should do is set up voicemail. Doing so identifies the phone number as yours and ensures that callers have an opportunity to leave a message when you're unavailable.

Note that the exact process of setting up and using voicemail is provider-specific. As an example, the following steps show how to set up AT&T's voice-mail. (See "Using Voicemail" in Chapter 6 for instructions on accessing voice-mail and changing your settings.)

1. On any Home screen page, tap the Phone icon.

2. On the Phone keypad, press and hold **1** (the speed dial number reserved for voicemail) or tap the voicemail icon.

3. When prompted, record your name, enter a password, and select or record a greeting. When you've finished reviewing voice-mail options, tap the End Call icon.

Gmail and Your Phone

Your phone runs on Android, the Google operating system. To use and connect to any Google service (such as Google Play, the source for Android apps that run on your phone), you must have a Gmail account, Google's free email service. If you don't have an account, you should create one now. The final step is letting your phone know your Gmail account username and password, enabling it to access Google services.

Do It the Easy Way

Although you can create a Gmail account using your phone, a lot of typing is required. It's easier to use your computer's web browser (as described next).

Creating a Gmail Account

1. On your PC or Mac, launch your web browser: Internet Explorer, Safari, Firefox, or Chrome, for example. Type www.gmail.com in the address box and press Enter/Return.

2. Click the Create an Account button in the page's upper-right corner.

3. Enter the requested registration information on the Create a New Google Account page.

ACCOUNT-CREATION TIPS

The most common, desirable Gmail usernames are taken. To get one based on your name or your company's name, try adding numbers at the end (**sschwartz972**), separate words with periods (**steve.schwartz**), or combine two or more unusual words (**hamstringwarrior**). Your username can be any combination of letters, numbers, and periods.

Your password must contain at least eight characters and can be any combination of uppercase letters, lowercase letters, and numbers. The Password Strength rating indicates how secure the password is. If possible, resist the temptation to use your ISP (Internet service provider) account password for Gmail, too. If you use one password everywhere on the Internet and someone learns it, all your accounts could be compromised. The most secure passwords combine uppercase letters, lowercase letters, and numbers (such as **hA73rTv91**).

Registering Your Gmail Account

1. On the Home screen, tap the Apps icon.

2. In the Apps pages, locate and tap the Gmail icon.

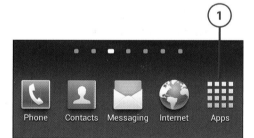

3. On the Add a Google Account screen, tap the Existing button. (If you don't have a Google/Gmail account, tap New and follow the onscreen prompts or perform the steps in "Creating a Gmail Account.")

4. On the Sign In screen, enter your Gmail username and password. Tap the Sign In button.

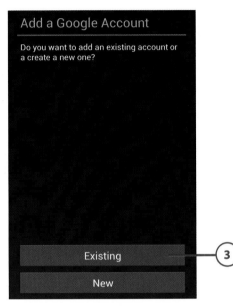

5. On the Backup and Restore screen, the check box determines whether important phone data will be routinely backed up to your Gmail account. Ensure that the box is checked or unchecked according to your preference, and tap the Next button.

6. A sync is performed and your Gmail account's Inbox is displayed. Press the Home key when you're ready to exit from Gmail.

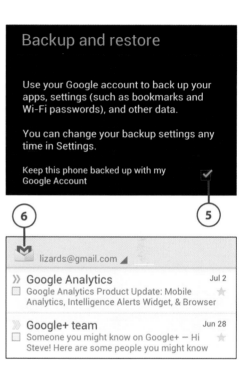

Creating a Samsung Account

Certain Samsung applications that are supported on the Galaxy S III, such as ChatOn, Music Hub, and SamsungDive, require you to sign up for a free Samsung account. You can create the account now or the first time you use an application that requires it.

About SamsungDive

If your phone disappears, SamsungDive (Find My Mobile) enables you to remotely locate, lock, or delete the contents of the phone. To learn more about SamsungDive, visit http://www.samsungdive.com/ and click the Help link.

1. From the Home screen, press the Menu key and tap Settings.

2. In the Personal section of Settings, tap Accounts and Sync.

3. At the bottom of the Accounts and Sync screen, tap Add Account.

4. On the Add Account screen, tap Samsung Account.

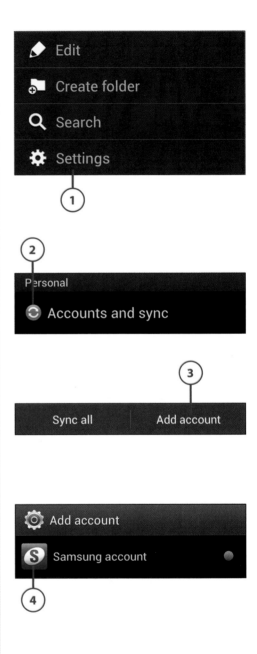

5. On the Samsung Account screen, tap Create Account.

6. Review the Terms and Conditions, tap the I accept all the terms above check box, and then tap the Agree button.

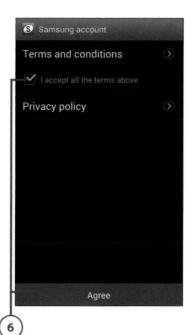

7. Create the account by entering an email address and password to use for the account, as well as your birthdate, country, and ZIP Code. Tap the Sign Up button.

8. To activate the account, open the verification email and visit the provided link. (If you've added the email account specified in step 7 to your phone, tap Go to Mailbox. Otherwise, check for the email on your computer.) To complete the process, tap the Activate Account button.

9. Tap Confirm in the Information dialog box that appears.

⑦ Samsung account

Email
resident@hotmail.com

Password
••••••

Confirm password
••••••|

☐ Show password

Date of birth
5/21/1951

Why we ask for your date of birth ⓘ

Country
United States

Zip code

Cancel   Sign up

⑦

Samsung account

resident@hotmail.com

This account has not been activated yet. Check your email and follow the verification link to activate your account

Check email in Mailbox?

Go to Mailbox

Already verified email address?

Activate account

⑧

Cannot find the verification email?

Information

Your account has been activated successfully. Now you can enjoy all benefits we offer

Confirm

⑨

10. The Samsung account is marked with a green dot on the Add Account screen, indicating that it's now recorded on your phone.

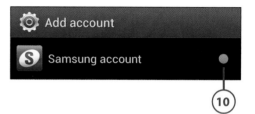

Working with Data

Any activity that transmits data to and from your phone over 3G or 4G counts toward your plan's data limit. The same data transmitted over Wi-Fi, on the other hand, doesn't count. By tapping icons in the Notifications panel, you can manually control the method by which data transmissions occur, ensuring that the least expensive and fastest method is used. In this section, you learn how to enable and disable Wi-Fi, 3G, and 4G, as well as how to connect your phone to a wireless (Wi-Fi) network.

Connection Methods

At any given time, only Wi-Fi or 3G/4G can be the active data connection method. When Wi-Fi is enabled and you're connected to a network, 3G/4G is automatically disabled. When Wi-Fi is disabled or unavailable and you perform a data-related activity, 3G or 4G is automatically used.

Note that you can also use Bluetooth to exchange data directly between the phone and any Bluetooth-capable computer or laptop. For instructions on working with Bluetooth, see Chapter 13.

Manually Setting a Connection Method

1. Reveal the Notifications panel by touching the status bar at the top of the screen and dragging downward.

2. The Wi-Fi icon toggles between a Wi-Fi and 3G/4G data connection. Wi-Fi is enabled when the icon is green; 3G/4G is enabled when the Wi-Fi icon is dim. Tap the Wi-Fi icon to toggle its state.

Which Wi-Fi Network?

When you enable Wi-Fi, a notification shows the network to which you're connected.

3. Close the Notifications panel by touching the bottom of the panel and dragging upward.

Monitoring Data Usage

If your data plan isn't unlimited, you can use the Data Usage setting to monitor your usage and warn when you're close to the limit. See "Managing Talk Time and Data Usage" in Chapter 19 for details.

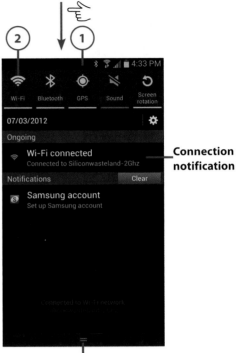

Connection notification

Connecting to a New Wireless Network

Because it's free and often a faster connection than using 3G or 4G, it's advantageous to use a Wi-Fi connection whenever it's available. After you've successfully connected to a given network (such as your home network or one at a local coffee shop), your phone can reconnect without requesting the password again.

1. On the Home screen, press the Menu key and tap Settings.

2. In the Wireless and Network section of the Settings screen, enable Wi-Fi (if it's off) by dragging the slider to the On position, and then tap the Wi-Fi text.

3. A list of nearby networks appears. If a network to which you've previously connected is found, the phone automatically connects to it. If no network is automatically chosen or you want to connect to a *different* network, tap the name of the network to which you want to connect.

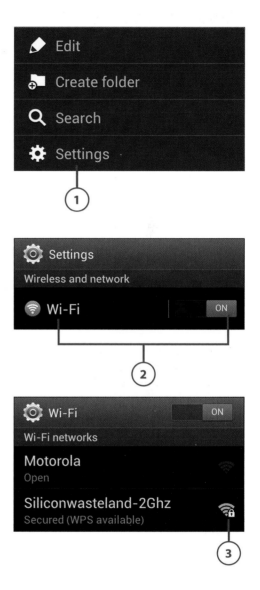

4. Do one of the following:

    - If the network is unsecured (open), tap the Connect button.

    - If the network is secured (pass-word protected), enter the requested password and then tap the Connect button.

Show Password

When entering a lengthy or complex password, you may find it helpful to tap the Show Password check box. Otherwise, each character in the password is visible only as you type it and is immediately covered by a bullet (•) character.

5. If successful, the screen shows you're connected to the network. While you're connected, this infor-mation is also displayed in the Notifications panel.

Unsecured network

Motorola

Signal strength
Weak

Security
None

☐ Show advanced options

| Cancel | Connect |

Secured network

Siliconwasteland-2Ghz

Password

```
••••••••••••|
```

☐ Show password

☐ Show advanced options

| Cancel | Connect |

Show password

Siliconwasteland-2Ghz
Connected

Switching Networks

If you're in range of several networks to which you've previously
connected, the phone automatically connects to one of them
whenever you enable Wi-Fi and
are within range. You can switch
to a different listed network by
performing steps 1–3, tapping the
desired network, and then tapping the Connect button in the
dialog box that appears.

To *forget* a network to which
you've previously connected,
press and hold the network name
in the Wi-Fi networks list and then
tap Forget Network.

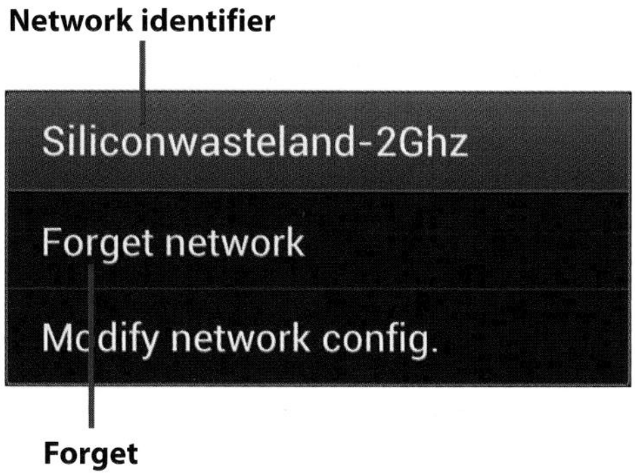

Network identifier

Siliconwasteland-2Ghz

Forget network

Modify network config.

Forget

Recording

In this chapter, you learn about the Samsung Galaxy S III interface and how to interact with it. Topics include the following:

→ Using the Home screen
→ Using the three hardware keys below the touchscreen
→ Working with the Notifications panel
→ Tapping and using other motions to interact with touchscreen elements
→ Using the onscreen keyboard and voice input to enter and edit text

Understanding the Android/TouchWiz Interface

The Galaxy S III has a touch-sensitive screen (or *touchscreen*) that can detect location, pressure, and motion on its surface. The Android operating system and Samsung's TouchWiz modifications to it determine how the phone and its apps react to the various touches. Even if you've previously owned an Android phone or another touch-sensitive device, such as an iPod touch or a tablet, you need to be familiar with the information in this chapter. Read on for the essential methods of interacting with the touchscreen and the hardware keys below it, as well as the techniques for entering and editing text.

The Home Screen

The Home screen is Command Central for your phone. You launch *apps* (applications) from this screen, view the latest information presented on widgets (such as the local weather from AccuWeather.com), and initiate phone calls and texting sessions.

The important parts of the Home screen include the status bar, the main area (equivalent to a PC or Mac's desktop), Home screen indicator, and icons for five primary shortcuts (Phone, Contacts, Messaging, Internet, and Apps).

Status bar

Main area

Home screen indicator

Primary shortcuts

The Status Bar

The status bar at the top of the screen serves two functions. First, icons on the right side of the status bar show the active communication features (such as Wi-Fi, 3G, 4G, Bluetooth, and GPS) and display status information (such as the current battery charge and Wi-Fi signal strength). Second, the left side of the status bar displays notification icons for important events, such as new email, new text messages, and missed calls.

Notification icons

Service status icons

Although it might be tempting to do so, you can't interact with the status bar; tapping its icons does nothing. To change the active features or respond to notifications, you use the Notifications panel (described later in this chapter).

Main Area

The Home screen is yours to embellish as you like. As you can see, you can place widgets and shortcuts wherever you want, as well as choose a custom *wallpaper* (background) for it, as explained in Chapter 17, "Customizing Your Phone."

Pandora Internet Radio widget

Wallpaper

Folder shortcut

App shortcuts

Home screen indicator

Extended Home Screen

The Home screen actually consists of seven different screens or pages, each represented by a Home screen indicator. As with the center Home screen page, you can add different widgets and shortcuts to each page. To move from one page to another, do any of the following:

- Press the Home key to go directly to the center Home screen page.

- Tap the Home screen indicator of the page that you want to view.

- Swipe left or right to flip to the desired page.

- Drag a Home screen indicator to the left or right to see a visual and numeric representation of each Home screen page.

Although you can rearrange the Home screen pages and delete unwanted ones (see Chapter 17), you cannot create additional pages beyond the seven.

Other Screen Indicators

The dots in Apps and Widgets work in the same manner as they do on the Home screen pages. Each dot represents a screen of icons and the lit dot indicates the screen that you're viewing.

Primary and Other App Shortcuts

Beneath the indicator dots on every Home screen page are icons for Phone, Contacts, Messaging, Internet, and Apps. These are known as the *primary shortcuts*. With the exception of the Apps shortcut, you are free to remove, reorder, or replace the first four. If, for example, you seldom use Messaging, you can replace its shortcut with one for Email, Settings, or another app that you constantly use, such as Angry Birds or Facebook. See "Repositioning and Removing Home Screen Items" in Chapter 17 for instructions.

Note that another set of app shortcuts appear just *above* the Home screen indicator dots on the second, third, and fourth pages. Like the primary short-cuts—as well as other shortcuts that you add to any Home screen page, you can freely remove, reorder, or replace these shortcuts.

Using the Hardware Keys

There are three ever-present hardware *keys* located directly below the touch-screen: Menu, Home, and Back. When pressed, each key performs a context-sensitive function related to the operating system (when viewing the Home screen) or the application that you're currently using.

Menu   Home   Back

Menu Key

As its name implies, when you press the Menu key, a menu of options or commands may appear. When you press the Menu key on the Home screen, the menu displays options for creating a folder, setting preferences, and so on. When you press the Menu key within an application, the menu's contents are set by the developer and frequently vary depending on the part of the app that's active.

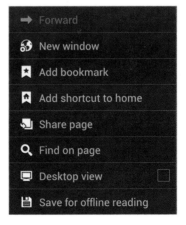

Menu (Home screen)   **Menu (Internet app)**

Home Key

The Home key has multiple functions (depending on whether you're on the Home screen or using an app). You can also use it in combination with the power button to take screen shots (as described next).

Within an app. Press the Home key to exit the app and return to the most recently viewed Home screen page. Press and hold the Home key to display a list of recently run and active applications. You can tap any app thumbnail to launch or switch to that app.

Recently run and active apps

On the Home screen. When you press the Home key while viewing the Home screen, it displays the center (fourth) Home screen page. Press and hold the Home key to display a list of recently run and active applications. You can tap any thumbnail to launch or switch to that app or system component. If you double-press the Home key, S Voice is activated. See Chapter 17 for information about using S Voice.

Within an app or on the Home screen. If you press and hold the Home key and power button, the phone performs a *screen capture,* creating a graphic image of the entire screen. All captures are saved in the Pictures/Screenshots folder and can be viewed in Gallery. (You can also perform a screen capture by dragging the side of your hand across the screen.)

— **Number of items**

**Pictures/Screenshots
folder**

Back Key

The Back key is used within apps to return to the previous screen or, if on the app's initial screen, to exit to the Home screen.

Within an app. Press the Back key to return to the previous screen. If you press it on the app's initial screen, you exit the app and return to the most recently viewed Home screen page.

Within Internet. Press Back to display the previous web page. The Back key has the same function as pressing Backspace (Windows) or Delete (Mac) when using a web browser.

Within a dialog box or an options menu. Similar to pressing the Escape key in many computer programs, you can press Back to exit a dialog box or options menu without making a choice.

When typing. Press Back to dismiss the onscreen keyboard.

Within the Notifications panel. Press Back to dismiss the panel.

The Notifications Panel

When new notifications appear in the status bar announcing received email, text messages, software updates, and the like, you can display the Notifications panel and optionally respond to the notifications or clear them.

1. Open the Notifications panel on the Home screen and within most apps by touching the status bar and dragging downward.

2. Tap a listed notification to respond to or interact with it. For example, tapping a New Email notification launches Email and displays the Inbox. When you respond to a notification, it's removed from the Notifications panel.

3. To remove a notification without responding to it, drag it off the screen to the left or right. To simultaneously remove *all* notifications, tap the Clear button.

4. To close the Notifications panel, touch the gray bar at the bottom and drag upward.

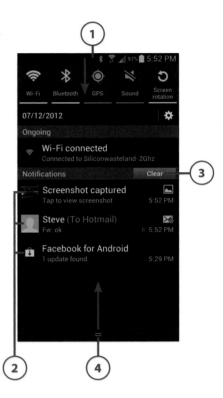

Interacting with the Touchscreen

Your phone has a touch-sensitive screen that you interact with by tapping, touching, and making other motions with your fingers. In addition, within many apps, the phone recognizes and responds to the angle at which it's being held.

Using Your Fingers

You can interact with the touchscreen by doing any of the following:

- *Tap*. To launch an app, open a document, choose a menu command, select an item in a list, activate a button, or type characters on the onscreen keyboard, tap the item lightly with your fingertip. (A tap is equivalent to a mouse click on a computer.)

**Tap a thumbnail to view a photo
(Gallery)**

- *Touch and hold.* You can interact with some items by touching and holding them. For example, touching and holding a person's record in Contacts causes a contextual menu to appear that enables you to do something with the record, such as edit or delete it. To move or delete a Home screen item, you can touch and hold the item (such as a shortcut or widget).

Touch and hold a song in Music Player...

Can I Get A Witness
Share music via
Set as
Add to playlist
Add to quick list
Delete

...to display this menu

- *Flick.* Scroll up or down through a lengthy menu or any vertical list of items (such as a message list in Email) by making light, quick vertical strokes.

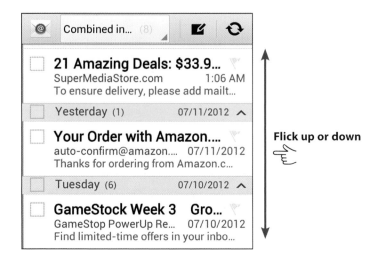

Flick up or down

- *Swipe.* A swipe is the horizontal equivalent of a flick. Swipe to flip through images in a Gallery folder, view different Home screen pages, and move through the pages of icons in Apps and Widgets.

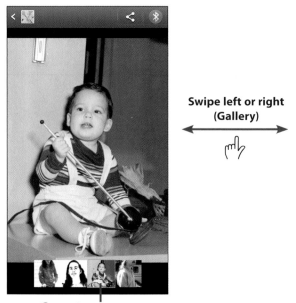

Swipe left or right (Gallery)

Current page or screen

- *Drag.* To move an item (such as a widget or app icon on the Home screen), press and hold the item, and don't release it until it's in the desired position—on the current screen page or a different one.

Drag a Home screen item to change its position

- *Spread/pinch.* To zoom in or out (increasing or decreasing the magnification) when viewing a photo or web page, place two fingers on the screen and spread them apart or pinch them together, respectively.

Try a Double Tap

In certain apps (Gallery and Internet, for example), you can also double-tap the screen to zoom in or zoom out. Spreading and pinching, however, give you control over the amount of magnification.

Rotating the Screen

In many apps, you can rotate the screen to change from portrait to landscape orientation and vice versa. It's extremely useful when viewing photos in Gallery that were shot in landscape orientation, when reading web pages in the Internet app, and when you need to type on the onscreen keyboard, for example.

Portrait   **Landscape**

USING MOTIONS

In addition to tapping, flicking, swiping, and pinching, you can perform certain actions using *motions*, such as shaking or tilting the phone. As you use the built-in apps, special screens introduce you to some of the supported motions and their effects. For instance, in Email or Contacts, you can double-tap the top of the phone to scroll to the top of the current list.

After mastering the basics of controlling the phone and apps via touch, you should explore the motion-control options (see "Enabling Motion Settings" in Chapter 17) and determine which motions, if any, that you find helpful and want to enable.

>>>Go Further

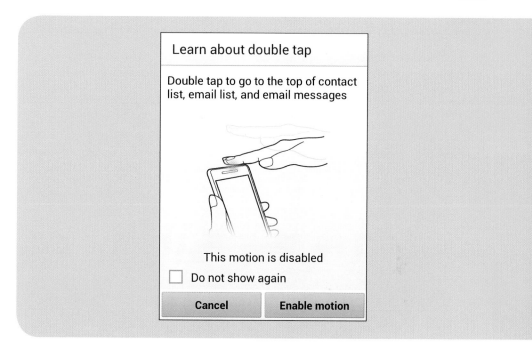

Entering Text

In addition to simply viewing and listening to content on your phone, much of what you do involves entering text. You can enter text using the onscreen keyboard or by speaking into the phone.

Using the onscreen keyboard, there are two methods of typing. You're familiar with the first one in which you tap letter, number, and punctuation keys as you would on a computer keyboard or a typewriter. The second uses software known as *T9 Trace*, in which you drag your finger over the keyboard—touching the characters needed to spell each word.

Using the Keyboard: Tapping

1. Tap to select a text field or box, such as the Internet address box or the message area of a text message. The onscreen keyboard appears. A blinking text insertion mark shows where the next typed character will appear.

2. Tap keys to type.

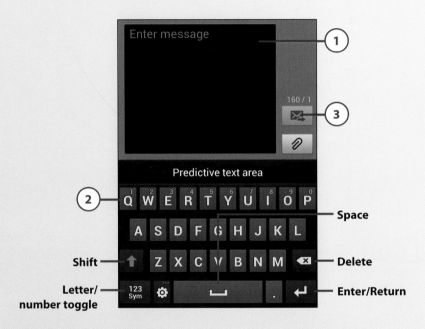

Accessing the Non-alphabetic Characters

Tap the 123 SYM key. The key above it is now labeled 1/3 and the layout displays numbers and common punctuation. Repeatedly tap this key to cycle through the symbol (2/3) and emoticon layouts (3/3). To return to the alpha-betic layout, tap the ABC key.

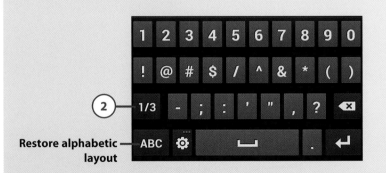

Restore alphabetic layout

3. To dismiss or hide the keyboard, perform the action necessary to complete your typing (such as tapping the Send icon) or press the Back key. To restore the keyboard after pressing Back, tap in the text box or window again.

Capitalization

When you begin entering text into a field or are starting a new sentence, the first character is usually capitalized automatically. Subsequent capitalization is determined by the state of the Shift key. Tap the Shift key to toggle it among its three states: lowercase, capitalize next letter only, and capitalize all letters.

Lowercase

Capitalize next letter

Uppercase

Using the Keyboard: T9 Trace

1. Tap to select a text field or box, such as the message area of a text message. The onscreen keyboard appears.

2. To type each word, drag over its letters—in order. Complete the word by briefly lifting your finger from the screen and then dragging over the letters needed to form the next word. A space is automatically inserted between each pair of words. Tap punctuation where it's needed.

Duplicate Letters

If a letter is repeated in a word, such as *l* in *follow*, make a loop over the letter or scribble over it to indicate that it's repeated.

TYPING TIPS

>>>Go Further

Although the basics of typing are relatively straightforward, the following information and tips will help you fine-tune what can be a difficult process.

- *Use landscape mode.* To use a larger version of the keyboard, simply rotate the phone to landscape orientation. (For this to work, the phone's *auto-rotate* feature must be enabled. From the Home screen, press the Menu key, tap Settings, tap Display, and then ensure that Auto-Rotate Screen is checked.)

Landscape keyboard

- *Change the input method.* The phone supports typed or traced text input (Samsung Keyboard) and voice input (Google Voice Typing). To switch from the current input method to the other while entering text, open the Notifications panel, tap Select Input Method, and select the alternate method in the dialog box that appears.

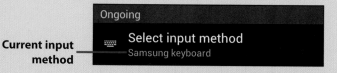

Current input method

- *Explore the Language and Input settings.* Take time to browse the Language and Input settings. You can configure Google Voice Typing (described in the next section) and set options for the Samsung Keyboard (tapping and T9 Trace), such as whether to display predictive text or support handwriting.

Alternate keyboards

- *Use Predictive Text.* As you type or trace, the phone presents a scrolling list of suggestions (*predictive text*) for the word it thinks you're typing. If you spot the correct one, tap it to use it as a replacement for the current word. You can also tap the down-arrow icon on the right to view other possible replacement words.

Predictive text ——— Where | Weber | Webber | Ever ⌄ ——— **More options**

Fine-tuning Predictive Text

Predictive text isn't just an on or off feature. When enabled, there are many settings that determine how it works. When working in a text box, tap the Settings key (or press the multi-mode icon to the left of the spacebar and select Settings), tap Predictive Text, and review the various options.

- *Character preview.* You can type certain secondary characters (such as the numbers above the top row of keys) without leaving the main alphabetic keyboard. If you press and hold any key, its secondary characters, if any, appear. (If you press and hold *g*, for example, *G* appears.) Release the key to insert the secondary character into your text. If you press and hold longer on a key, every associated character, number, and symbol for the key appears in a pop-up menu. Tap the one that you want to insert. Note that different sets of characters are available for lowercase and uppercase keys.

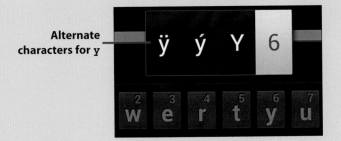

Alternate characters for **y**

- *Other input options.* When entering text, you can switch input methods at any time, using any combination that you find convenient. To change methods, press and hold the multi-mode icon and select the desired input method. Options include voice input (described in the next section), handwriting, and inserting material from the Clipboard.

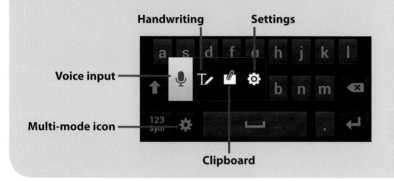

Handwriting   **Settings**

Voice input

Multi-mode icon

Clipboard

Using Voice Input

If you're abysmal at using the onscreen keyboard and are unwilling to take the time to master it, voice input (also called *voice typing*) may be more to your liking. You speak what you want to type, and it's translated into text.

1. To enable voice input, press and hold the multi-mode icon and select voice input—the microphone. If the multi-mode icon already displays the microphone, simply tap it.

Switch Using the Notifications Panel

As explained earlier in the chapter, you can also switch input methods by opening the Notifications panel, tapping the Select Input Method item, and selecting Google Voice Typing in the dialog box.

2. A recording indicator appears. Speak the text, saying punctuation (such as *comma* and *period*) where it's needed.

3. When you're finished recording, tap the Done button. The text is transcribed, and it appears at the text insertion mark.

4. Any instance of questionable transcribing is automatically underlined. To view and select a possible correction, tap the underlined text.

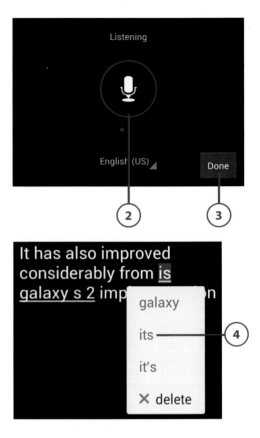

It's Not All Good

Excellent, but Not Perfect

Voice input is great for converting straightforward, common speech to text. It has also improved considerably from its Galaxy S II implementation. For example, it now understands web addresses and more punctuation. However, it still has some drawbacks that necessitate after-the-fact editing:

- Although you can speak most punctuation (comma, period, exclamation point, semicolon, and colon, for example), voice input doesn't always recognize what you're saying as being punctuation. Sometimes it simply spells out the word.

- When voice input doesn't understand a word, it frequently breaks it up into several short words that it *does* know, resulting in total gibberish.

To determine if voice input will work for you, you have to test it. Say some normal text and try reading a few sentences from a book or magazine. Whether it's a winner for you will be decided by how accurate it is and the amount of cleanup you need to do.

Editing Text

Typos, missing capitalization and punctuation, and bad guesses in T9 Trace are common in entered text. Instead of just tapping Send and hoping your message recipient will *know* what you mean, you can edit the text by doing any of the following:

- At the blinking text insertion mark, you can type or paste new text or press the Delete key to delete the character to the left.

- To reposition the text insertion mark for editing, tap in the text. If the text insertion mark isn't positioned correctly, carefully drag the blue marker to the desired spot.

Marker —— What are you doing for dinner? How does meatloaf sound? I'm not exactly sure how to make it, but I suspect I can fake it. B-)

- To select a single word for deletion or replacement, double-tap the word or long-press the word. To delete it, tap the Delete key; to replace it, type over it.

- To select a specific text string (a word, sentence, or paragraph, for instance), start by selecting a word at the beginning or end of the text that you want to select. Drag the selection handles to highlight the desired text. Then select a command from the menu at the top of the screen, press the Delete key, or overtype the selected text.

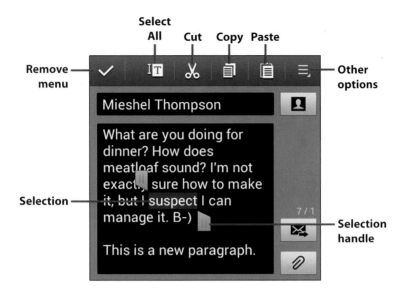

Select All — Cut — Copy — Paste

Remove menu — Other options

Selection — Selection handle

- To paste the most recently copied or cut text into a text box, set the text insertion mark, tap the marker, and then tap Paste in the pop-up that appears.

Paste — Marker

Pasting Other Material

If you select Clipboard from the pop-up rather than Paste, you can paste *other* material (images, for example) that you recently copied or cut.

Copying Text from a Web Page

You can use the same technique to copy text from a web page. On the page, select the material that you want to copy. In the menu above the page, tap Copy to copy the material to the Clipboard so that you can paste it elsewhere or tap Share to copy the material directly into a new email, text message, or Facebook post, for example.

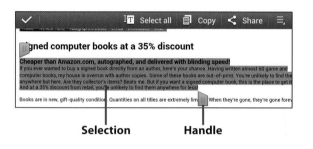

Selection   **Handle**

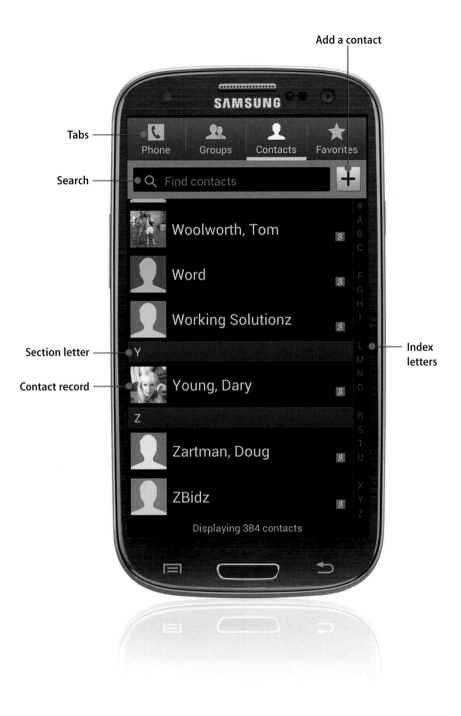

Add a contact

Tabs

Search

Phone   Groups   Contacts   Favorites

Q Find contacts   +

Woolworth, Tom

Word

Working Solutionz

Section letter   Y

Contact record   Young, Dary

Z

Zartman, Doug

ZBidz

Displaying 384 contacts

Index
letters

In this chapter, you learn how to use the Contacts app to create and manage your business and personal contacts. Topics include the following:

→ Understanding the Contacts interface

→ Creating, viewing, and editing contact records

→ Defining and working with contact groups

→ Backing up your contacts to the SIM card, built-in memory, or a memory card

→ Exporting Outlook 2010 (Windows) and Address Book (Mac) contacts and importing them into Google Contacts

→ Setting display options

Managing Contacts

Contacts is the Galaxy S III's built-in address book app. It's populated by contact records created on the phone, in your Google Contacts account on the web, and in other information sources that you sync to it, such as Facebook, LinkedIn, and Exchange Server accounts. The Contacts app links to Phone for dialing numbers, Email for selecting email recipients, and Messaging for selecting text and multimedia message recipients.

The Contacts Interface

Contacts has four sections, each represented by a tab at the top of the screen. Here's what you can do in each section:

- *Phone.* Tap Phone to switch to the Phone app to make a call. (Phone and Contacts are linked; you can quickly switch between them by tapping the appropriate tab. Chapter 6, "Placing and Receiving Calls," covers the Phone app.)

- *Groups. Groups* are contact record subsets with some common element. Some groups are pre-defined or automatically created as you use the Galaxy S III and its apps. You can also define your own groups, such as members of your bowling team or a commit-tee on which you're serving. To see the members of any group, tap the Groups icon and then tap the group name. To learn more about using and creating groups, see "Working with Contact Groups," later in the chapter.

- *Contacts.* This is the default Contacts tab. It displays a scrolling list of your contact records. You can tap a person's name to view his or her contact record. This sec-tion is also displayed by Phone, Email, and Messaging when selecting a call, email, or message recipient. The Contacts section is discussed throughout this chapter.

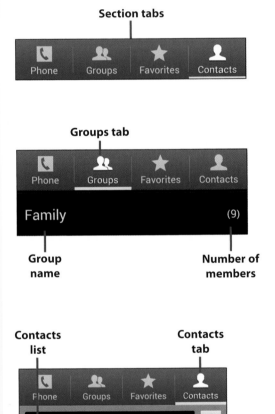

Section tabs

Groups tab

Group name   **Number of members**

Contacts list   **Contacts tab**

• *Favorites.* Tap this tab to view a list of only those contact records that you've marked as favorites. To add or remove someone as a favorite, open the person's record for viewing in any list and then tap the star icon beside his or her name. Beneath your favorites are other people and companies that you frequently call. Although not officially favorites, these automatic listings make it easy for you to place calls to them. For more information about favorites, see "Marking Contacts As Favorites," later in this chapter.

Grid Versus List View

If you've added photos to your contacts, press the Menu key and tap Grid View to display a grid of favorite contact photo thumbnails. (To restore the normal scrolling list, tap List View.)

Favorites list   Favorites tab

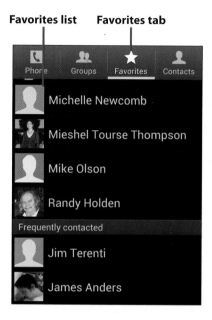

List View or Grid View

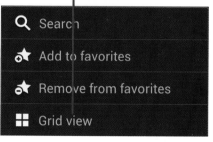

Creating a Contact Record

In addition to creating contacts in Google Contacts or another address book utility that you're syncing with your phone, you can create new contact records directly on the phone.

1. To launch Contacts, tap its Home screen icon or select it in Apps.

2. If it isn't automatically selected, tap the Contacts tab. To create a new contact record, tap the plus (+) button beside the search box.

3. The Create Contact screen appears, ready for you to enter the person's contact information.

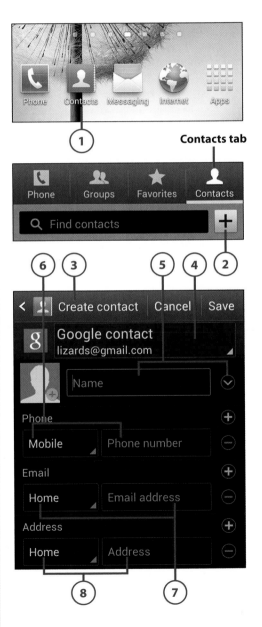

Contacts tab

4. The top line shows where the contact will be stored and shared. To change this setting, tap its text. Select Phone for a contact that will reside only on the phone. Tap Google, Microsoft Exchange ActiveSync, or Samsung Account to share this record with the specified contact list. (These options appear only after you add accounts of these types.) Tap SIM to store the contact on your SIM card; only the name, email address, and phone number are stored.

5. Enter the person's name. You can type the full name in the Name field or—to enter more detailed name information, such as a pre-fix, suffix, or middle name—tap the expand/collapse icon beside the field. When you're done enter-ing the name components, you can collapse the name by tapping the same icon.

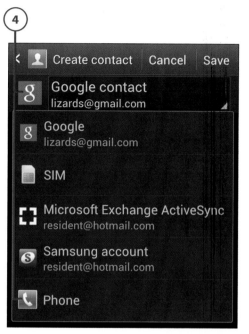

Expand/collapse

6. Enter a phone number for the person in the first Phone field. If the label (such as Mobile) is incorrect, tap the label and select the correct one from the drop-down list. (Select Custom if you want to create your own label.)

To add more numbers, tap the Phone field's plus (+) icon. To remove an unwanted or blank number, tap its minus (–) icon.

Text Messaging

If you intend to send text or multimedia messages to this person, you must record at least one number that's designated as Mobile.

7. Use the method described in step 6 to add one or more email addresses to the contact record. As with phone numbers, you can select a label for each email address from the drop-down list.

Remove number **Add number**

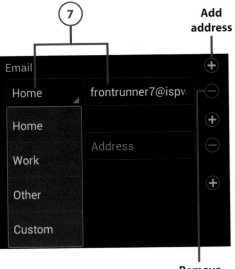

Add address

Remove address

8. If desired, you can record one or more physical addresses for the person (Address). Use the same method that you used to enter Phone and Email information. Note that Address is a single field rather than multiple fields for address, city, state, and ZIP.

9. *Optional:* To add dates of important annual events, such as the person's birthday or anniversary, tap the plus (+) icon for Events.

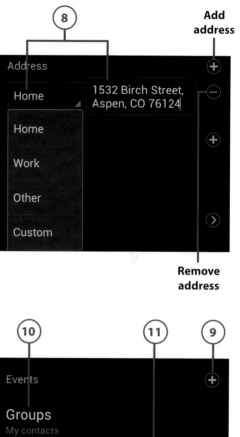

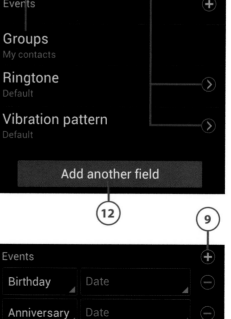

10. *Optional:* You can assign the person to one or more groups, based on member commonalities. The advantage of using existing groups (such as Co-workers) or defining new groups (such as Study Partners or Que Editorial) is that you can text or email all members of the group by addressing a message to the group rather than to each individual member. To assign the person to groups, tap the Groups field, tap the check box of each appropriate group, and tap Done. (To learn how to create and use groups, see "Working with Contact Groups," later in this chapter.)

11. *Optional:* To specify a distinctive ringtone or vibration pattern that will announce calls from this person, tap Ringtone or Vibration Pattern, select an option from the list that appears, and tap OK.

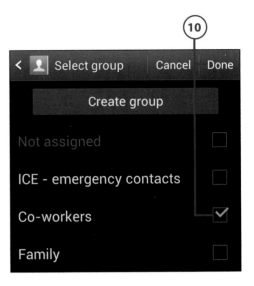

Specifying a Ringtone

Ringtones can be selected from those provided with the phone (Ringtones) or employ any audio file—such as a downloaded ringtone or a complete song—that you've stored on the phone. In the latter case, it's up to you to locate the file.

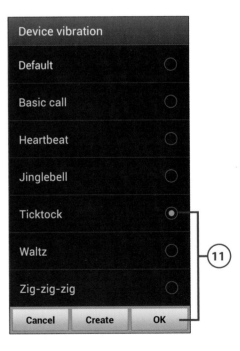

12. *Optional:* Tap the Add Another Field button to add a field to the record in which you can record an organization, instant messaging username, notes, nickname, website, or other information about the person.

13. When you've finished entering the initial information for this contact, tap the Save button at the top of the screen or tap Cancel to discard the record.

12

Add another field

Phonetic name

Organization

IM

Notes

Nickname

Website

Internet call

Relationship

13

< 👤 Create contact   Cancel   Save

Adding a Photo to a Contact Record

To easily and quickly identify a contact, you can add a photo to the person's record. You can use any photo that's stored on the phone, or—if you're creating the contact record while the person is standing in front of you—you can use the phone's camera to shoot the picture.

1. To associate a photo with the contact, tap the photo placeholder in the upper-left corner of the Create Contact or Edit Contact screen. (If the record already has a photo, you can tap it to replace it with a new photo.)

Robert Smith, M.D.

1

2. In the Contact Photo dialog box, tap Picture if the photo is stored on the phone or tap Take Picture to use the phone's camera to shoot the picture now.

3. If you tapped Picture in step 2, Gallery launches. Tap the folder that contains the photo, tap the photo's thumbnail, and go to step 5.

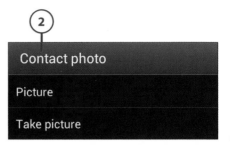

Picture (Gallery)

Take Picture (Camera)

4. If you tapped Take Picture in step 2, Camera launches. Tap the shutter button to take the person's picture. If you don't care for the shot, tap the Discard button and try again; otherwise, tap Save.

5. On the Crop Picture screen, move and resize the blue cropping rectangle to select the area of the photo that you want to use, and then tap Done. The cropped photo is added to the contact record.

6. If you're done creating or editing the record, tap the Save button at the top of the screen.

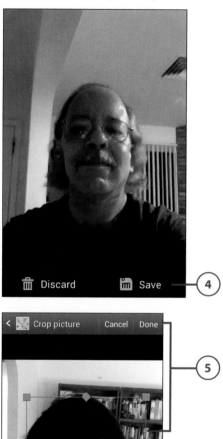

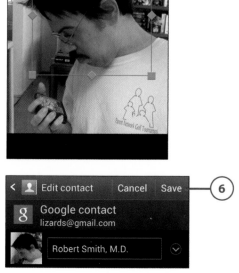

>>>Go Further

OTHER CONTACTS LAUNCH OPTIONS

You can also launch Contacts by doing either of the following:

- If you've replaced the Contacts icon at the bottom of the Home screen pages, go to the Home screen, tap Apps, select the Apps tab, and then tap the Contacts icon.

Apps screen

Apps tab ——

Contacts icon ——

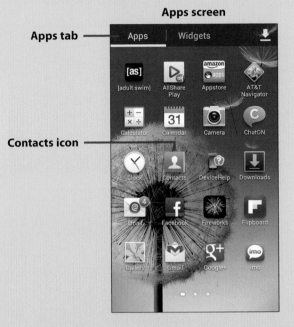

- Tap the Contacts tab in the Phone or Messaging app.

Phone screen

—— Contacts tab

Viewing Contacts

The bulk of what you do in Contacts involves finding and viewing individual contacts so you can call, email, or text them.

1. Launch Contacts by tapping its Home screen icon.

2. With the Contacts tab selected, contacts are displayed in an alphabetical scrolling list. By default, all contacts from all sources are listed. You can restrict contacts to a single source (such as LinkedIn contacts) and set other display options by following the instructions in "Setting Display Options" at the end of this chapter.

3. To find a particular contact, you can use any of the following techniques:

   • Flick up or down to scroll the list.

   • Tap an index letter on the right edge of the screen to go to that approximate spot in the alphabetical list.

   • Press and drag in the index letter list. As you drag, a large version of each index letter appears onscreen. Remove your finger when the correct letter is shown. For example, to find a person whose last name is Jones, release your finger when J appears.

   • To search for someone, tap the Find Contacts box and begin entering any element of the person's record, such as first or last name, street name, or email address. As you type, a list of likely matching contacts appears. When you see the correct record, tap the person's entry.

Search   **Contacts tab**

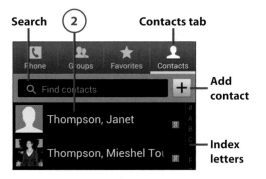

Add contact

Index letters

Clear search

Match list

4. When you find the desired contact, tap it to view the person's record. Depending on the information recorded for the contact, you can dial any listed number by tapping the phone icon, send a message to the person by tapping a mobile phone number's envelope icon, or address a new email to the person by tapping an email address' envelope icon.

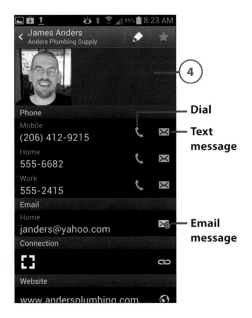

Dial

Text message

Email message

Editing Contact Records

Contact records sometimes require editing. You might have to add or change an email address or phone number, or you may want to add a better picture. Editing a contact employs the same techniques that you use to create contact records. In this section, you learn several ways to edit records, as well as delete them.

Editing Contacts

When changes to a record are necessary to bring it up-to-date, here's what you need to do:

1. In Contacts, tap to select the record that you want to edit.

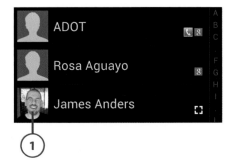

2. The complete record displays. Press the Menu key and tap Edit.

3. Using the techniques described in "Creating a Contact Record," make the necessary changes to the person's information. For example, you can do the following:

   - Tap in any text field to add, edit, or delete its contents.

   - To remove a field instance that's followed by a minus (–) sign, such as an email address or phone number, tap the minus sign.

   - To add a new instance to a field that's followed by a plus (+) sign, tap the plus sign and enter the new information.

   - To change a field label, such as those that precede a phone number, email address, or mailing address, tap the label.

   - To add, remove, or change the contact photo, tap the photo or its placeholder and then make a selection from the menu that appears. For more information, see "Adding a Photo to a Contact Record," earlier in this chapter.

4. Tap Save to save your edits or tap Cancel if you decide not to save the changes.

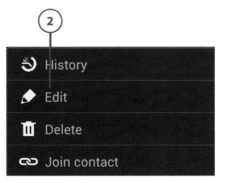

Picture placeholder ③

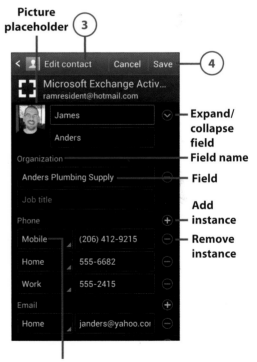

④

— **Expand/ collapse field**

— **Field name**

— **Field**

Add instance

— **Remove instance**

Field label

Setting Defaults for a Contact

Several contact fields can have multiple entries. For example, a record can have several phone numbers, email addresses, IM usernames, and mailing addresses. For some of these fields, you can optionally specify a *default entry*—that is, one that you want to treat as primary.

1. In the contacts list, tap the record for which you want to view, set, or change defaults.

2. The complete record displays. Press the menu key and tap Mark as Default.

3. On the Mark as Default screen, all items for which you can set a default are displayed. To set an entry as a default, tap its radio button. If necessary, scroll to see any additional items.

4. Tap the Done button to set the new defaults for the record.

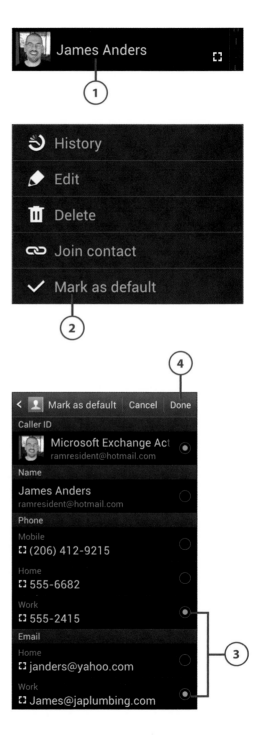

5. Whenever you view the record, default entries have a blue check mark.

Phone
Mobile
(206) 412-9215
Home
555-6682
Work
555-2415 ✓

Email
Home
janders@yahoo.com
Work
James@japlumbing.com ✓

⑤

Joining and Separating Contacts

Your contact records probably come from multiple sources. Some are created on the phone; others might originate in Google Contacts, LinkedIn, an Exchange Server account, or a social networking site. As a result, when you scroll through the entries in Contacts, you may find some duplicates. You can use the Join Contact command to merge the duplicates for a person into a single contact record.

1. Scroll through the contacts list and locate a pair of records for the same person.

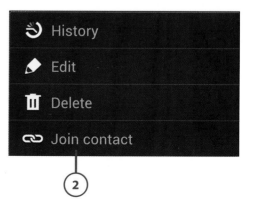

2. Tap one of the entries to open the record, press the Menu key, and tap Join Contact. (You can also press and hold the person's name in the Contacts list and choose Join Contact from the menu that appears.)

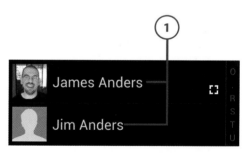

3. A Suggestions list appears. If it includes the person's other record, tap to select it. Otherwise, scroll down to look for the person's other record in the All Contacts section, and then tap to select it.

4. The two records are joined to create a single record. If you edit the record (display the record, press the Menu key, and tap Edit), you can see the sources of the joined records—in this example, Microsoft Exchange ActiveSync and Phone. If still more records exist for this person, you can join those as well by repeating steps 2 and 3.

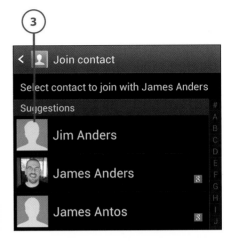

Separating Joined Contacts

If necessary, you can separate joined records, re-creating the original, individual records. Open the joined record, press the Menu key, tap Separate Contact, and tap the minus (–) sign beside one of the listed records.

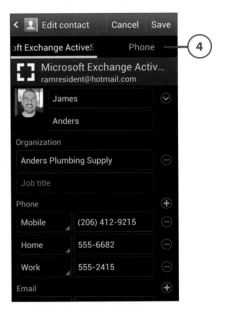

It's Not All Good

Check the Join Result

Following a join, scan the fields to see that all data looks correct and that nothing was omitted from the original records. If you aren't sure, separate the records, make note of the important data, and join them again.

Marking Contacts as Favorites

If you're like most people, your contact list contains people with whom you're in regular, frequent contact, as well as many people whom you're unlikely to ever contact again. To make it easier for you to quickly find people in the former group, you can mark their records as *favorites*. Doing so adds them to the contacts in your Favorites list.

1. On the Contacts or Groups tab, use one of the methods described in "Viewing Contacts" to locate the record that you want to mark as a favorite.

2. Do either of the following:

   • Press and hold the contact until a menu appears, and then tap Add to Favorites.

   • Tap the contact to open it for viewing, and then tap the star icon beside the person's name.

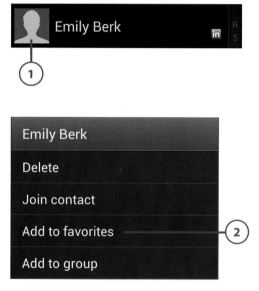

3. To remove a contact from Favorites, do either of the following:

- Press and hold the contact
  until a menu appears and
  then tap Remove from
  Favorites.

- Tap the contact to open it
  for viewing and then tap the
  star icon beside the name to
  remove the star.

- Select the Favorites tab, press
  the Menu key, and then tap
  Remove from Favorites. Tap
  the check box of each person
  that you want to remove
  from Favorites and then tap
  Delete. (Note that you can
  also remove people from the
  Frequently Contacted list by
  tapping their check boxes.)

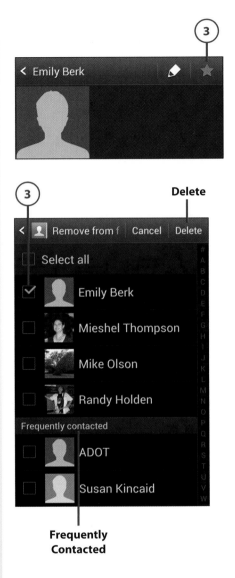

**Frequently
Contacted**

Deleting Contacts

People leave your personal and business life for many reasons. When
you're certain that you no longer
need their contact records, you can
delete them.

1. In Contacts, use one of the
methods described in "Viewing
Contacts" to locate the record that
you want to delete.

2. To delete a record while viewing the contacts list, press and
   hold the record, tap Delete in the
   menu that appears, and tap OK
   in the Delete confirmation dialog
   box.

3. To delete a record while viewing
   it, press the Menu key, tap Delete,
   and tap OK in the Delete confirmation dialog box.

4. To simultaneously delete multiple
   records, display the contacts
   list, press the Menu key, and tap
   Delete. On the Delete screen, tap
   the check box beside each record
   that you want to delete, tap Done,
   and tap OK in the Delete confirmation dialog box.

Working with Contact Groups

A *group* is a collection of contacts that have something in common, such as membership in a parents' group, editorial staff, bake sale committee, or high school friends. Because each group is a small subset of Contacts, you can use groups to quickly find every important person of some type (members of your department, for example). You can also use a group as the recipient for an email or text message, automatically sending it to all members. You can create groups and define their memberships from scratch, as well as use the built-in groups (Starred in Android, Family, and Friends, for example) and ones created for you by social media sites, such as LinkedIn and Facebook.

Creating a Group

1. In Contacts, select the Groups tab.

2. Press the Menu key and tap Create.

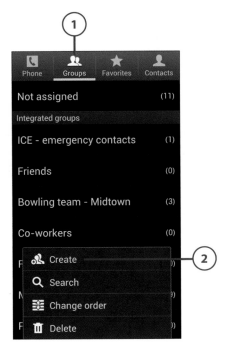

3. The Create Group screen appears.

4. *Optional:* If you've registered more than one Google account, you can specify the account of which this group will be a subset by tapping the Create Group In entry.

5. Enter a name for the group.

6. *Optional:* Specify a ringtone that will announce calls or text messages from group members.

7. *Optional:* Specify a vibration pattern that will announce calls or text messages from group members.

8. *Optional:* Tap Add Member to set the initial group membership. Select members by tapping their names and then tap Done. (Note that you can add members at any time.)

9. Tap the Save button to save the group name, settings, and membership. The group name is added to the Integrated Groups list. Whenever you want to view the group's membership, tap its name in the list.

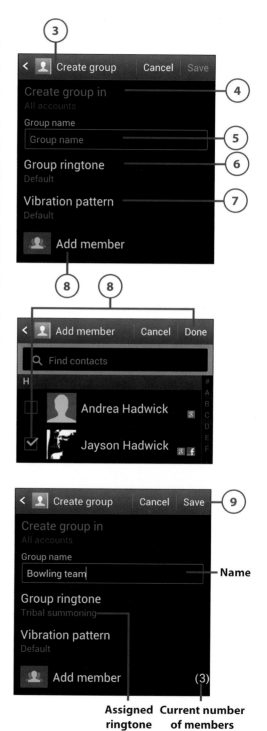

Changing a Group's Definition

1. With the Groups tab selected, press and hold the group name until a menu appears. Tap Edit Group.

2. The Edit Group screen appears. Referring to the steps in the previous task list, make any desired changes (including adding more members) and tap Save.

Group name

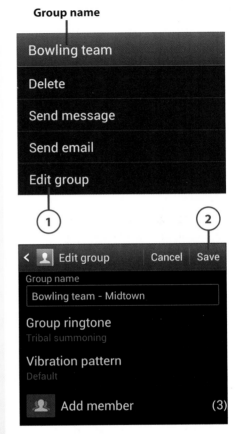

Adding or Removing a Person from Group Membership

1. With the Contacts tab selected, tap a person's name to open his or her record.

2. In the record, tap the Groups entry to expand it.

3. On the Select Group screen, add or remove check marks to assign or remove the person from the listed groups. Tap Done to save the changes. (Note that a person can be a member of multiple groups.)

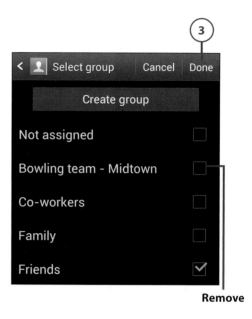

Remove

Quickly Removing Members

In addition to adding new members to the group, you can easily remove one or multiple members. With the group roster displayed, press the Menu key and tap Remove Member. On the Remove Member screen, select the members that you want to remove from the group and tap Done.

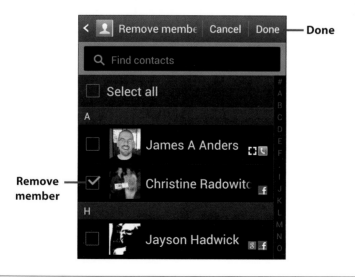

Emailing or Texting a Group

1. In Email or Messaging, click the Compose icon.

2. Tap the Contacts icon.

3. On the Select Contact screen, tap the Groups tab and then tap the group that you want to email or message.

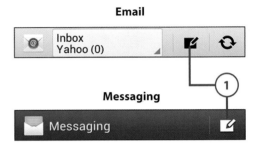

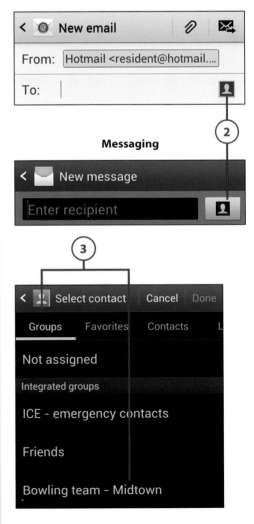

4. Tap the names of the group members that you want to email or message, or tap Select All to include the entire group as recipients.

Multiple Choice

If a selected individual has multiple email addresses or mobile phone numbers, a dialog box appears in which you must select the correct address or number.

5. Tap Done to transfer the selected members' email addresses or mobile numbers to Email or Messaging, respectively. Complete your email or compose your message as you normally do.

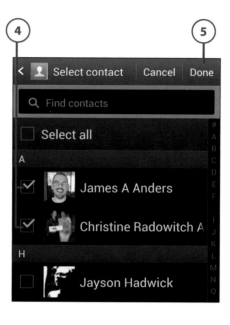

Email or Text Message from Contacts

You can also initiate a group email or text message from within Contacts. Tap the Groups tab, tap a group name, press the Menu key, and tap either Send Email or Send Message. Select the members, and tap Done.

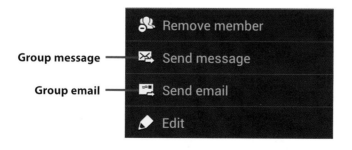

Group message —— Send message

Group email —— Send email

Reordering the Groups

1. With the Groups tab selected, press the Menu key and tap Change Order.

2. To change the position of a group on the Change Order screen, drag the group up or down by the dot pattern on its right edge. Release the group when it's in the desired position. Repeat for other groups whose positions you want to change.

3. Tap Done to save the new group list order.

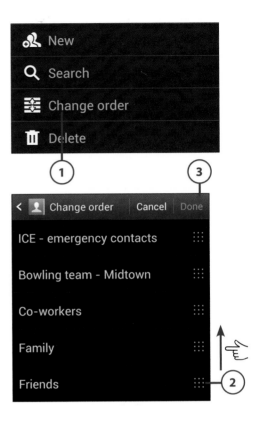

Deleting a Group

1. With the Groups tab selected, press the Menu key and tap Delete.

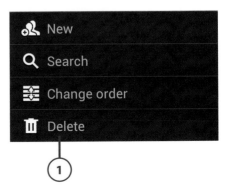

2. On the Delete screen, select the groups you want to delete by tapping check boxes and then tap the Delete button.

3. In the Delete dialog box, indicate whether you want to delete only the selected group(s)—leaving the associated contact records intact —or the group(s) *and* member contact records. (If you change your mind, press the Back key to dismiss this dialog box.)

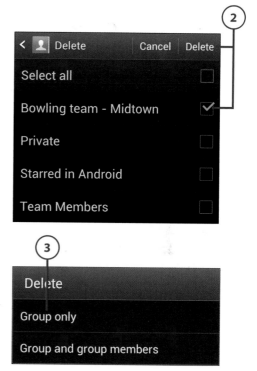

Backing Up/Restoring and Exporting/Importing Contact Records

To provide security against phone-related disasters or in preparation for switching to a new phone, you can back up your Contacts data to a memory card, built-in memory, or a SIM card, or you can merge the data with your Google or Samsung account.

You can also use export/import procedures to manually move copies of contact records from your computer-based email clients and address book utilities into Contacts.

Backing Up Contact Data

You have multiple options for backing up your Contacts data. First, you can merge your records with Google Contacts. The contacts on your phone will be treated as though they're all Google Contacts and will be available to you at gmail.com or mail.gmail.com. If something happens to your phone or you get a new one, your contacts will be restored from Google Contacts on your first sync.

Second, using a similar procedure, you can merge your phone's contacts with the Samsung account that you created during the phone's setup. However, only those contacts created with Phone as the source are merged; Google contacts are left unchanged.

It's Not All Good

To Merge or Not to Merge

Think carefully before performing a Merge with Google or—to a lesser degree—Merge with Samsung Account, especially if your contact records have many different sources and you want to keep those sources intact. Unlike the other backup and export procedures described in this section, the Merge commands modify the records by changing their creation source. Thus, use Merge with Google only if you're committing to using Google/Gmail as the repository of *all* your contact data.

Third, you can copy all or selected contacts' names, email addresses, and phone numbers to the phone's SIM card. Note that this procedure differs among service providers. As examples, the steps for copying to SIM are presented for AT&T and T-Mobile.

Finally, there are two options for backing up your Contacts data to the phone's built-in memory or to a memory card. In the latter case, if something happens to your phone or you get a new one, you can import your Contacts data from the memory card.

Merging with Google Contacts

1. With the Contacts list displayed, press the Menu key and tap Merge with Google.

2. Tap OK in the Merge with Google confirmation dialog box.

3. When you display the full contact list, you see that all records are now marked as Google contacts.

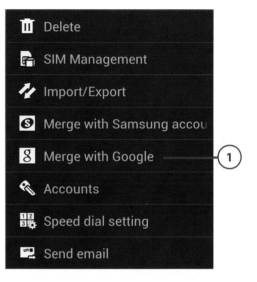

Merging with Your Samsung Account

1. With the Contacts list displayed, press the Menu key and tap Merge with Samsung Account.
2. Tap OK in the Merge with Samsung Account dialog box.

Copying Contacts to the SIM Card (AT&T)

1. Select the Contacts tab, press the Menu key, and tap SIM Management.

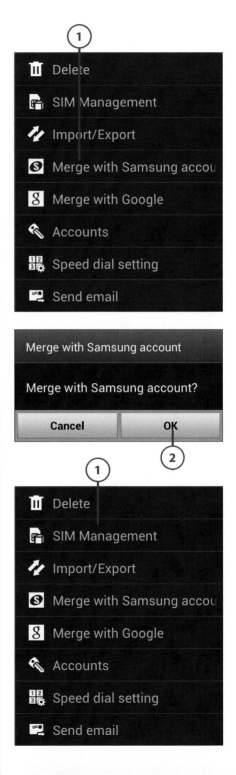

2. In the SIM Management dialog box, tap Copy Contacts to SIM.

3. On the Copy Contacts to SIM screen, select the contact records that you want to copy and then tap Done.

Selecting All or Most Contacts

If you want to copy most of your contacts but you need to leave a few out, scroll to the top of the list and tap Select All. Then tap the check boxes of only those records that you want to *omit*.

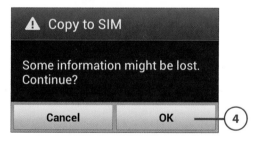

4. Tap OK in the Copy to SIM confirmation dialog box.

5. The selected records are copied to the SIM card. Tap OK to dismiss the confirmation dialog box.

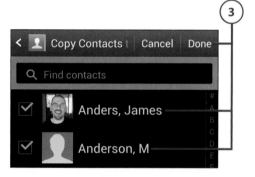

Copying Contacts to the SIM Card (T-Mobile)

1. Select the Contacts tab, press the Menu key, and tap Import/Export.

2. In the Import/Export Contacts dialog box, tap Export to SIM Card.

3. On the Export to SIM Card screen, select the contacts that you want to export and then tap Done.

4. Tap OK in the Copy to SIM dialog box. The selected records are copied to the SIM card.

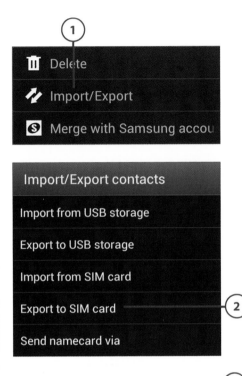

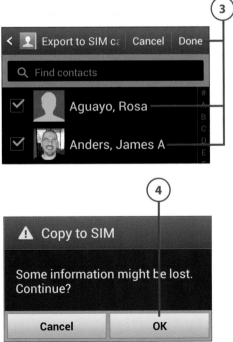

Backing Up to a Memory Card

1. Tap the Contacts tab, press the Menu key, and tap Import/Export. (Note that you *must* have a memory card installed in the phone to export your Contacts data.)

2. In the Import/Export Contacts dialog box, tap Export to SD Card.

3. Tap OK in the Confirm Export dialog box. The data is exported to the displayed vCard filename and memory card location. (The extSdCard in the file pathname indicates that your add-in memory card will be used.)

Multiple Backups

As time passes, you can export *multiple* backups of your Contacts database. Each new backup increments the filename by 1 over the highest-numbered backup on the memory card. For example, if there's already a 00002.vcf, the new backup will be 00003.vcf.

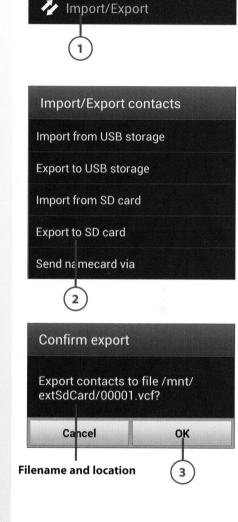

Filename and location

Exporting to USB (Built-in Memory)

1. Tap the Contacts tab, press the Menu key, and tap Import/Export.

2. In the Import/Export Contacts dialog box, tap Export to USB storage.

3. Tap OK in the Confirm Export dialog box. The data is exported to the displayed vCard filename and internal memory location.

🗑 Delete

📇 SIM Management

⚡ Import/Export

①

②

Import/Export contacts

Import from USB storage

Export to USB storage

Import from SD card

Export to SD card

Send namecard via

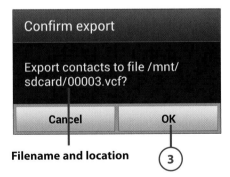

Confirm export

Export contacts to file /mnt/sdcard/00003.vcf?

| Cancel | OK |

Filename and location ③

It's Not All Good

Back Up *Everything!*

Before you begin experimenting with contact importing/exporting or sync-ing, it's extremely important to have current backups of *all* your contact data sources on your computer, the web, and company servers, as well as to back up the Contacts data on your phone. On a Mac, for example, that might mean backing up Microsoft Outlook or Entourage contacts, as well as your Address Book, Google Contacts, and Contacts. If something goes wrong (such as end-ing up with duplicates of every contact), you can delete all contacts in the affected applications and then restore the original data from the backups.

Restoring Backups

If something happens to your Contacts database or you switch to a new phone, you can restore the data from one or more backups.

Restoring Contacts from the SIM Card (AT&T)

1. On the Contacts tab, press the Menu key and tap SIM Management.

2. In the SIM Management dialog box, tap Copy Contacts from SIM.

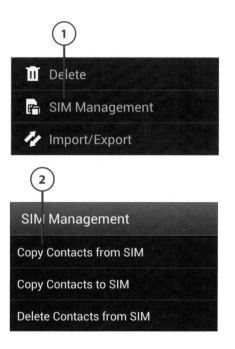

3. When the contacts are imported from the SIM, they must be associated with an account. Select an account from the Create Contact Under Account dialog box.

4. On the Copy Contacts from SIM screen, select the contact records that you want to restore and tap Done.

5. A dialog box shows the number of restored records. Tap OK to dismiss it.

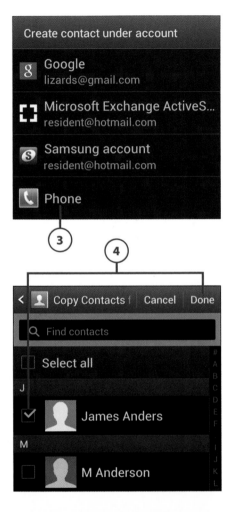

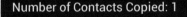

Restoring Contacts from the SIM Card (T-Mobile)

1. On the Contacts tab, press the Menu key and tap Import/Export.

2. In the Import/Export Contacts dialog box, tap Import from SIM Card.

3. When the contacts are imported from the SIM, they must be associated with an account. Select an account from the Save Contact To dialog box.

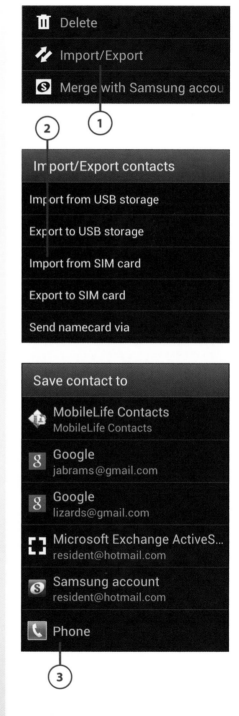

4. On the Import from SIM Card screen, select the contact records that you want to restore and tap Done.

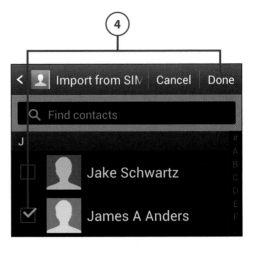

Restoring a Memory Card Backup

1. Install the memory card in the phone to which you want to restore your Contacts database. Launch the Contacts app.

2. On the Contacts tab, press the Menu key and tap Import/Export.

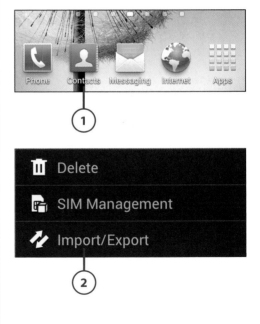

3. In the Import/Export Contacts dialog box, tap Import from SD Card.

4. When the contacts are imported, you must associate them with an account. Select an account from the Save Contact to dialog box.

Beware of Duplicates

When restoring a backup from a memory card, the procedure doesn't check for duplicate records. Thus, it's safest to restore to a device that contains no contact records or only new, unique records that you've created on the phone. Remember, too, that if you have any contacts that you previously created or synched with Google Contacts, those contacts will automatically be restored on your first sync. In other words, restoring from the SD card might be unnecessary.

Restoring a USB (Built-in Memory) Backup

1. On the Contacts tab, press the Menu key and tap Import/Export.

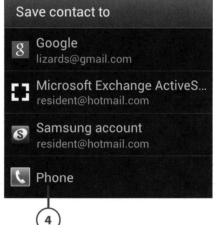

2. In the Import/Export Contacts dialog box, tap Import from USB Storage.

3. When the contacts are imported, they must be associated with an account. Select an account from the Save Contact To dialog box.

4. In the Select vCard File dialog box, indicate whether you intend to import a single, multiple, or all vCard files and then tap OK.

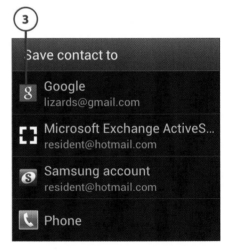

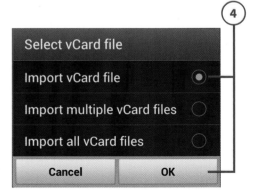

5. If you chose anything other than Import All vCard Files in step 4, a second Select vCard File dialog box appears. Select the file or files that you want to import and then tap OK. The specified data file or files are imported into the Contacts database.

Import vCard File dialog

Select vCard file

00001.vcf
(2012-08-26 15:57:51)

00002.vcf
(2012-08-26 21:47:51)

Cancel   OK

Import Multiple vCard Files dialog

Select vCard file

00001.vcf
(2012-08-26 15:57:51)

00002.vcf
(2012-08-26 21:47:51)

Cancel   OK

5

It's Not All Good

Problems with Restores

Although the steps required to restore most types of backups are straight-forward, the results might *not* be what you expect. In my experience, getting a clean restore that doesn't require hours of deleting duplicates and joining records from multiple sources is something of a rarity. Perhaps your best bet is to use Google Contacts as the repository of *all* contact records and just allow it to restore the Contacts database on the first sync.

Importing Contact Data from Other Sources into Google Contacts

Although Google Contacts (Gmail's address book) is the *de facto* source for Android contact data, it's *not* the place where many of us have chosen to store our contacts. You may already have years of contacts stored in email clients and address book utilities on your computer. In this section, you learn how to perform a one-time export from Address Book (Mac) and Microsoft Outlook 2010 (Windows) and import the data into Google Contacts, where it will be available for synching with and populating Contacts on your phone. You can also sync Outlook 2011 (Mac) and Address Book (Mac) directly with Google Contacts, as explained in Chapter 5, "Synchronizing Data."

Exporting Data from Address Book (Mac)

1. Launch Address Book. Specify the contacts to export by doing one of the following:

    - To export the entire database, select All Contacts in the Group column.

    - To export only selected contacts, select a specific group in the Group column or Command-click the name of each person that you want to export (in the Name column).

2. Choose File, Export, Export Group vCard.

3. In the Save As panel that appears, enter a filename and select a location for the exported data file. Click the Save button.

Picking a Save Location

When you save the exported data, make a note of the filename and the folder in which it's located. Google Contacts will need that information when you import the data. In general, it's best to save the export file somewhere you can easily find it, such as the Desktop.

Exporting Data from Outlook 2010 (Windows)

1. Launch Outlook 2010, select the File tab on the Ribbon, and click Options.).

2. In the Outlook Options dialog box, select the Advanced category and click the Export button.

3. In the Import and Export Wizard, select Export to a file. Click Next to continue.

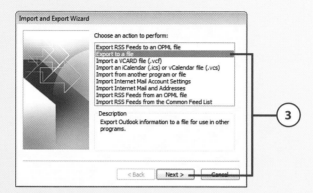

4. Select Comma Separated Values (Windows) and click Next.

5. Select the Contacts folder and click Next.

6. Click the Browse button.

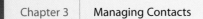

7. In the Browse dialog box, specify the name and folder to use for the exported data file, and then click OK. You return to the Export to File dialog box. Click Next to continue.

Folder

Filename

Output file type   **OK**

8. Click Finish to export the contact data to the specified file.

9. Close the Outlook Options dialog box by clicking OK or Cancel.

Importing the Exported Data into Google Contacts

1. In your browser, go to mail.google.com or gmail.com and log into your account. Open the Gmail menu and click Contacts.

Just in Case…

As a safety measure, you might want to back up the Google Contacts data by choosing More, Export. If the import described in this task list doesn't go as planned, you can restore your original Google Contacts data by choosing the More, Import command or by choosing More, Restore Contacts. The former command restores from your backup file, whereas the latter restores from one of several Google-provided backups.

---

2. To replace all current data in Google Contacts with the new data, you must delete all the records. From the first Contacts menu, choose All to select all visible records. Then from the More menu, choose Delete Contacts.

Selective Deletions

If Google Contacts contains records that do not exist in the imported data, you may want to delete all records *except* those.

3. If still more records exist, repeat step 2. Continue until all records have been deleted.

4. Choose More, Import.

5. To select the data file to import, click the Choose File button in the Import Contacts dialog box.

6. In the file dialog box that appears, select the exported data file and click the Choose button.

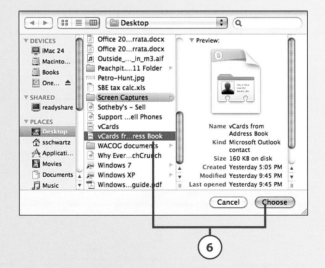

7. In the Import Contacts dialog box, click the Import button. The exported data appears in Google Contacts.

Odds and Ends

Contacts has a couple of other commands that you may occasionally find useful.

The Send Email and Send Message Commands

While viewing contact records, you can select recipients for a new email or text message. Press the Menu key, and then tap Send Email or Send Message. Select the Contacts or Groups tab, select recipients, and then tap Done to address the new email or text message.

Selected contact   Done

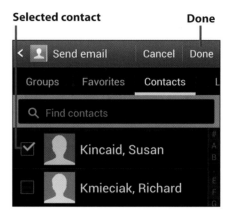

Setting Display Options

With the Contacts tab selected, you can set a variety of useful options that determine which records are shown and the order in which they appear.

1. Press the Menu key and tap Settings. The Settings screen appears.

2. Tap the Only Contacts with Phones check box to hide contact records that don't include a phone number. (To restore the full contacts list, tap it again to remove the check mark.)

3. You can sort contacts alphabetically by first name or last name. To change the current sort order, tap List By and then tap an option in the List By dialog box.

4. Regardless of the sort order specified in step 3, you can display each contact as first name first (Bob Smith) or last name first (Smith, Bob). Tap Display Contacts By and then tap an option in the Display Contacts By dialog box.

5. When you are finished making changes, press the Back key.

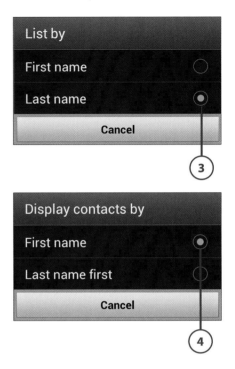

Specifying Contacts to Display

There's also an option to view only those contacts associated with a particular account. For instance, you can elect to view only your Facebook friends, LinkedIn colleagues, or people in your Google+ circles. With the Contacts tab selected, press the Menu key, tap Contacts to Display, and tap the account that you want to view.

All Contacts

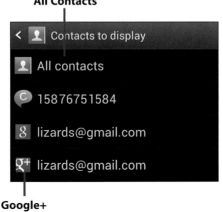

Google+

SAMSUNG
Today
Calendars
Aug
September 2012
Oct
W Sun Mon Tue Wed Thu Fri Sat
Labor Day
Money t...
Patriot D...
Drew an...
Bolts
Finish ...
Make deposit
Groceries
Bookkee...
Money t...
Make deposit
4:00PM (Start)-
Groceries
4:15PM – 5:15PM

In this chapter, you learn to use Calendar to create, view, and edit events and tasks. Topics include the following:

→ Adding Calendar accounts to display events and tasks from your Gmail, Exchange Server, and other account calendars

→ Creating events and tasks, viewing the calendar, and managing events and tasks

→ Responding to reminders for upcoming events and tasks

→ Setting Calendar preferences

Using the Calendar

Similar in design to a full-featured calendar application (such as the one in Microsoft Outlook), the Calendar app enables you to record upcoming events, meetings, and tasks and then receive reminders for them. If you already maintain calendars in Google, Facebook, Hotmail, or a corporate Exchange Server account, you can synchronize your Calendar app data with that of your other calendars.

Adding Calendar Accounts

If you've used a Google/Gmail account on your phone to access any Google service, Calendar has two calendars that it can immediately associate with new events and tasks: your Google/Gmail Calendar and My Calendar, a phone-specific calendar created by the Calendar app. In addition to these sources, Calendar can use data from and sync with Samsung, Facebook, and Microsoft Exchange Server calendars. Thus, before you experiment extensively with Calendar, decide which external calendar sources you want to use and keep in sync with Calendar (adding other accounts as necessary). You can find instructions for automatically and manually synchronizing your calendar data in Chapter 5, "Synchronizing Data."

1. To add a Facebook, Microsoft Exchange Server, Samsung, or Gmail calendar account (only these account types support calendar syncing with your phone), go to the Home screen, press the Menu key, and tap Settings.

2. On the Settings screen, tap Accounts and Sync.

3. On the Accounts and Sync screen, tap the Add Account button at the bottom of the screen.

4. On the Add Account screen, tap one of the following account types: Facebook (for syncing), Microsoft Exchange ActiveSync, Google, or Samsung Account.

Multiple Accounts of the Same Type

Account types that are marked with a green dot have already been added. You can have multiple Exchange and Google accounts, but only one instance of Samsung and Facebook accounts.

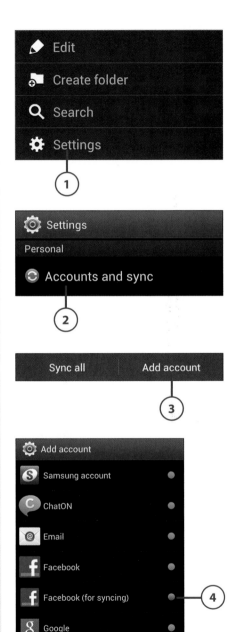

5. Follow the instructions to add the account. At a minimum, you'll need to supply your username and password. If offered as an option, ensure that Sync Calendar is enabled.

6. You can add other accounts by repeating steps 3–5. When you're done, press the Home key to return to the Home screen.

f Set up your Facebook account

facebook

Log in to use your Facebook account with SamsungMobile.

Get Facebook for Android and browse faster.

Resident@hotmail.com

•••••••••

Log In

5

Working in Calendar

Within Calendar, you can create events and tasks; set a view: Year, Month, Week, Day, Agenda, or Task; and edit or delete events and tasks.

Creating Events and Tasks

In addition to events and tasks that are pulled from your Gmail, Facebook, Exchange Server, and Samsung accounts, you can also create new items within the Calendar app. These new items can be synced with your accounts automatically, manually, or not at all. For information on syncing calendars, see Chapter 5, "Synchronizing Data."

Every Calendar item is either an *event* (a scheduled item for a specific date, with or without a start time) or a *task* (an unscheduled item with or without a due date). An event can be an all-day occurrence, such as a vacation day or birthday.

Creating an Event

1. Launch the Calendar app by tapping its Home screen shortcut or by tapping Apps, followed by Calendar.

2. *Optional:* On the calendar, select the date or time when you want to schedule the event. (Preselecting the start date or time saves you the trouble of specifying this information when you create the event.) To change the Calendar view so you can pick a start date or time, tap the view icon and select the Month, Week, or Day tab.

Be General or Specific

The more specific your selection (start date or date/time), the more information is prefilled for the event. On the other hand, regardless of the currently selected date or start time, you can set a *different* date or time when you create the event.

3. Tap the plus (+) icon.

View icon

More Plus Icon Options

The plus icon is sometimes at the bottom of Month view, too. You can also create a new event or task by tapping the plus icon in a Calendar widget.

Create event or task

Selected date

4. The scheduling screen appears. Ensure that the Add Event tab is selected.

5. To associate the event with a different calendar, tap Calendar and select an account to use. (My Calendar is the phone-specific calendar.)

Using Multiple Calendars

The calendar you specify for each new item is important. When you sync calendars, it's the one that will record the event. If you choose your Google/Gmail calendar, for example, the event will also be available to you from Google's site using any web browser. On the other hand, if you choose My Calendar, the event will be available only on your Galaxy S III. To use other account calendars with Calendar, see "Adding Calendar Accounts," at the beginning of this chapter.

6. Enter a title for the event.

7. Do one of the following:

- If this is an all-day event or one with no specific schedule other than the day on which it occurs, tap the All Day check box. The From and To times are removed, as well as the time zone. Go to step 8.

- If the From (starting) date or time is incorrect, tap the date or time item and correct it. Tap the arrow icons to increment or decrement a component (such as the day number or hour) by one unit. Alternatively, you can select the item you want to change and type the new value. Tap Set to accept the corrected date or time. Repeat this process for the To (ending) date and time.

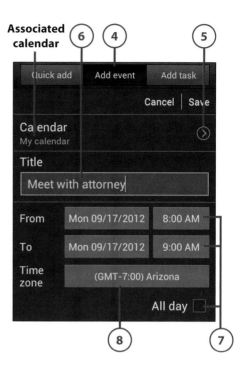

Associated calendar

Increase

Decrease

8. *Optional:* Tap the Time Zone entry to specify a different time zone to use for scheduling this event.

9. If the event will repeat at regular intervals (such as a weekly staff meeting on Monday at 1:00 p.m., a monthly mortgage payment, or an anniversary), tap Repeat and select a repetition interval. Then set a duration or end date (2 years, a specific date, or a certain number of repetitions) and tap OK.

10. *Optional:* Enter a location for the event by typing in the Location box or by tapping the Location icon, performing a search, and tapping Done.

11. *Optional:* In the Description text box, enter a detailed description of or notes related to the event.

12. A *reminder* (alarm) is set for each event in accordance with the Default Reminder Time setting. To change the reminder time, tap the first box and select a new interval from the scrolling list. (See "Setting Calendar Preferences" to change the Default Reminder Time setting.)

Multiple or No Reminders

If desired, you can set multiple reminders for an event. Tap the plus (+) icon to add a reminder. To remove a reminder, tap the minus (–) icon to its right.

13. You can attach existing or new S memos or photos to the event by tapping the plus (+) icon to the right of Memos or Pictures.

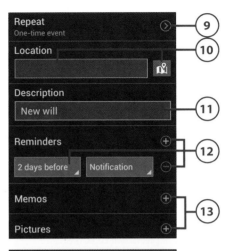

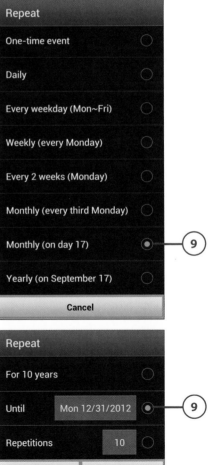

14. Tap the Save button to add the event to the calendar or Cancel to discard it.

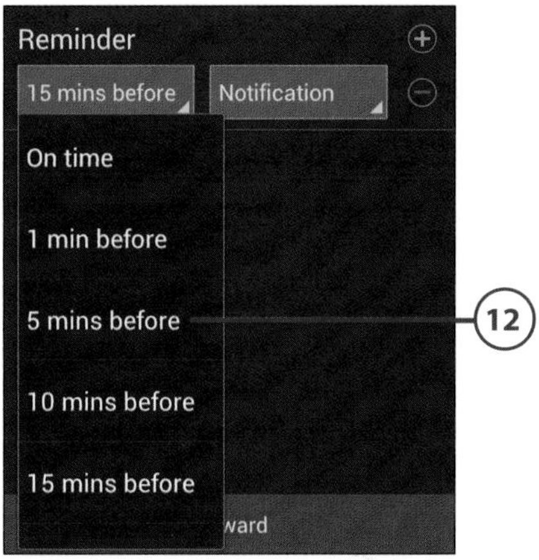

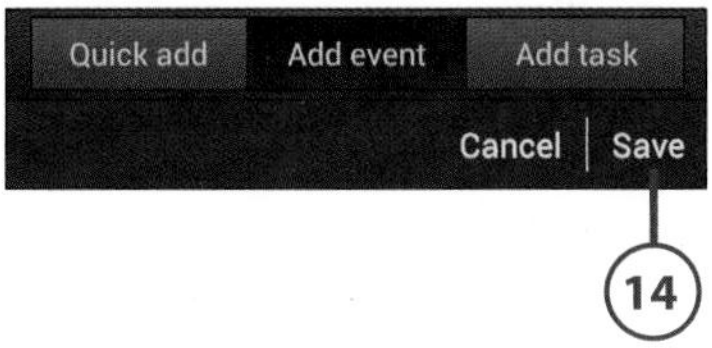

The Minimalist Approach

Unless you're a stickler for detail, it's quickest to enter only the essential information for each event or task: Title, From date/ time or All Day, and Reminder.

Calendar offers a variant of this approach called Quick Add. Tap the Quick Add button at the top of a new event/task screen, tap the microphone key on the keyboard, and dictate the details of the item, such as "Call jewelry store tomorrow." My success rate with this item-creation method, however, is currently only about 25 percent.

Reminder

15 mins before | Notification

On time

1 min before

5 mins before ⎯⎯⎯ ⑫

10 mins before

15 mins before

⎯ward

Quick add | Add event | Add task

Cancel | Save

⑭

Creating a Task

1. Launch the Calendar app by tapping its Home screen shortcut or by tapping Apps, followed by Calendar.

2. *Optional:* On the calendar, select the due date for the task's completion. (Preselecting the date saves you the trouble of specifying it when you create the task.) To change the Calendar view so you can select a due date, tap the view icon and select the Month, Week, or Day tab.

3. Tap the plus (+) icon.

4. The scheduling screen appears. Ensure that the Add Task tab is selected.

5. To associate the task with a different account, tap Task and select an account to use. (My Task is the phone-specific account.)

6. Enter a title for the task.

7. Do one of the following:

   • If there's a particular date on or by which the task must be completed, tap the Due Date button, specify the date in the Set Date dialog box, and tap the Set button.

   • If the task doesn't have a due date, tap the No Due Date check box.

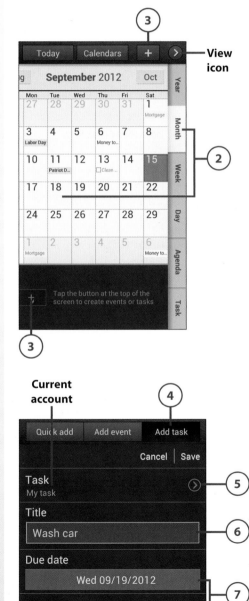

8. *Optional:* You can set a *reminder* (alarm) for each task. To change the Reminder date, tap the arrow icon. In the Reminder dialog box, select either On Due Date or Customize (to specify a different date). The selected date and the current time are set as the reminder. To change the time, tap its entry, specify the time in the Set Time dialog box, and tap the Set button.

9. *Optional:* Specify a completion priority (high, medium, or low) by tapping the arrow icon.

10. *Optional:* In the Description text box, enter a detailed description of or notes related to the task.

11. You can attach existing or new S memos or photos to the task by tapping the plus (+) icon to the right of Memos or Pictures.

12. Tap the Save button to add the task to the calendar or Cancel to discard it.

Reminder Tue 09/18/2012	8:15AM ⊘	8
Priority Medium	⊘	9
Group Default	⊘	
Description Need a new bucket and detergent		10
Memos	⊕	11
Pictures	⊕	

Reminder

Off ○

On due date ○

Customize ◉ — 8

Cancel

Viewing the Calendar

You can examine scheduled events and tasks in six *views:* Year, Month, Week, Day, Agenda, and Task. You interact differently with Calendar in each view.

1. When you launch Calendar, the last displayed view appears. To change views, tap the view icon followed by a view tab. The tab for the current view is beige.

2. *Year view.* You can't view events or tasks in Year view. Its purpose is to enable you to easily select a month for viewing—in this or another year. Scroll to previous or future years by tapping the arrow icons or by swiping the screen horizontally. When the desired month and year are displayed, tap the month to view it in Month view.

Other Year View Options

To immediately return to the current year, tap the Today button. Today's date is highlighted in gold.

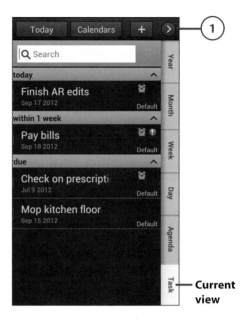

Current view

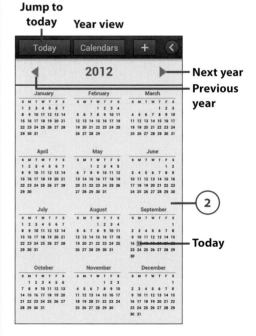

Jump to today

Year view

Next year

Previous year

2

Today

3. *Month view.* In Month view, event/task text is color-coded to match the calendar account with which the item is associated. For example, bright blue text is used to show My Calendar items and dark blue for Google Calendar items. Select a date to display events and tasks for that date at the bottom of the screen. To move forward or back one month, tap a month name or flick vertically.

4. *Week view.* In Week view, items are colored-coded to match the calendar with which they're associated. Tap an item to view its details, edit, or delete it. Scroll to the previous or next week by tapping an arrow icon or flicking horizontally. To view the items and schedule for a date, double-tap the date heading.

Jump to today **Month view**

Next month — Oct

Previous month

③

Selected date

Items for Sept. 15th

Jump to today **Week view** **Next week**

Previous week

Selected date

④

5. *Day view.* Use Day view to see scheduled items and their scheduled duration for a selected date. Items are colored-coded to match the calendar with which they're associated. Tap an item to view its details, edit, or delete it. Press and hold a time slot to create a new item with that start time. You can scroll the time slots by flicking vertically, and change days by tapping the arrow icons or swiping horizontally.

6. *Agenda view and Task view.* Select these views to see a chronological list of events or tasks, respectively. Items are color-coded to match the calendar with which they're associated. Tap an item to view its details, edit, or delete it. Scroll through the list by flicking vertically. In agenda view, you can display additional older or future events by tapping Tap to View Events at the top or bottom of the list. You can search for events or tasks by entering search text in the box.

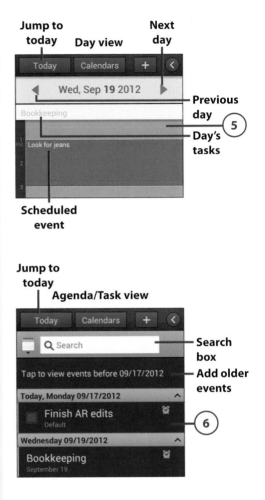

Searching in Other Views

To display the search box in Year, Month, Week, or Day view, press the Menu key and tap Search.

7. To go to a specific date, press the Menu key and tap Go To. In the Set Date dialog box, specify the target date, and tap the Set button.

8. You can display events and tasks from one or multiple calendar accounts. To select accounts to show, tap the Calendars button at the top of the current view, select the calendar and task accounts to display, and tap Done.

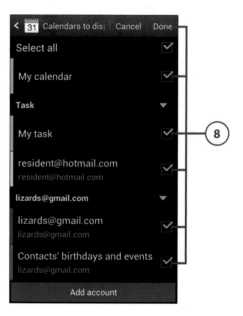

CONSIDER CALENDAR WIDGETS

You can do much of your Calendar viewing on the Home screen using one of several widgets. The widgets draw their data from Calendar and enable you to view upcoming events and tasks, as well as create new ones. You might consider adding one or more of these Calendar widgets to your Home screen:

Calendar widgets

- *Calendar.* This resizable widget shows scheduled events and tasks for the next 24 hours. Tap an item to view, edit, or delete it in Calendar. Tap the main date to view that day in Calendar.

- *Calendar (Month).* This full-screen Calendar widget is preinstalled on your phone. It shows the same information as Calendar in Month view. Select a date with scheduled items and tap it to see the next or most recent event for that date; select and tap any empty date to create a new event on that date in Calendar; or select a date and tap the plus (+) icon to create an event or task for that date.

- *Calendar (Mini Today).* This widget displays a day's events and tasks in a scrolling list. Tap any item to view, edit, or delete it in Calendar; tap an arrow icon to move one day forward or backward; tap a task's check box to toggle its completion status; and tap the plus (+) icon to create a new event or task.

- *Calendar (Tasks)*. This is a tasks-only widget. Tap a task to view, edit, or delete it in Calendar; tap a task's check box to toggle its completion status; and tap the plus (+) icon to create a new task.

For help with adding, moving, and removing widgets, see "Adding Widgets" and "Repositioning and Removing Home Screen Items" in Chapter 17.

Managing Events and Tasks

After creating an event or task, you can delete or modify any aspect of it, such as the title, start date, start time, description, or reminder interval.

1. Open the Calendar app and, in any view, double-tap the item that you want to delete or edit. The item opens in detail view.

2. Press the Menu key and do one of the following:

   - To delete the item, tap Delete and then tap OK in the confirmation dialog box. (If multiple items are shown for a date, you can delete all or only selected ones by tapping item check boxes.)

   - To modify the item, tap Edit. Make any desired changes and tap the Save button.

< 31 Detail view

Bookkeeping ———————— 1
Wednesday, September 19

| My calendar

Reminder   ⊕

| 1 hour before | Notification | ⊖
                                        2

◆ Edit ————————— **Modify**

▤ Copy

🗑 Delete ———————— **Delete**

< Share via

▤ Link memos

▨ Link images

Editing a Repeating Event

When you edit a repeating event, a dialog box appears that enables you to change only this occurrence, all occurrences, or all occurrences forward. A dialog box with similar options appears when deleting a repeating event.

Editing a Repeating Event

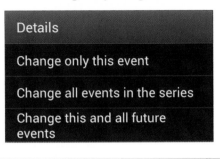

An Event Editing Shortcut

When examining an event in detail view, you can tap the item text to enter edit mode.

Responding to Reminders

When an event or task reminder is triggered, you are notified by an alert screen or a number appears in the status bar. In addition, a distinctive ringtone may play. The notification method is determined by Event Notification settings, as explained in "Setting Calendar Preferences," later in this chapter. You can respond to a reminder by *snoozing* (requesting that it repeat later), dismissing, or ignoring it.

Simple Alarms

If you just need an alarm to remind you that it's time to take daily meds or wake up in the morning, you don't need to schedule a Calendar event; you can create alarms in the Clock app.

1. If the Alerts and Notifications setting is Status Bar Notification, an icon showing the number of waiting reminders appears in the status bar. Pull down the Notifications panel and tap the reminder that you want to handle.

2. If the Alerts and Notifications setting is Alert (or you tapped the reminder in the Notifications panel in step 1), an icon showing the number of reminders appears in the status bar and the Calendar Notifications screen appears. There may be one or multiple waiting reminders at a time.

3. Specify the reminders to which you want to respond by doing one of the following:

   • If there's only one waiting reminder, skip to step 4.

   • To respond the same way to all displayed remind-ers, ensure that they're all checked. (Tap Select All to simultaneously check or uncheck all reminders.)

   • To respond the same way to multiple reminders but not all, ensure that only the reminders to which you want to respond are checked.

Status bar

1   Groceries

①

Notifications panel

Notifications   Clear

1   Pay bills

②

31   Calendar notifications

Select all   ✓

■   Make deposit   ✓
    September 18, 4:00pm – September

■   Groceries   ✓
    4:15pm – 5:15pm, September 18

③

Set snooze duration

Snooze   Dismiss

④

4. Do one of the following:

- To repeat the selected reminder(s) after the current snooze duration (such as 5 minutes), tap the Snooze button.

- To snooze the selected reminder(s) for a custom duration, tap the Set Snooze Duration button, select the duration and tap OK, and then tap the Snooze button.

- To cancel the selected reminder(s), tap the Dismiss button.

- To ignore the reminders for now, press the Back key. You can return to them when it's convenient by opening the Notifications panel, as explained in step 1.

Dismissing a Reminder

Dismissing an event or task's reminder doesn't delete the item from Calendar; it merely eliminates the reminder. To *delete* the event or task, you must perform the procedure described in "Managing Events and Tasks," earlier in this chapter.

5. *Optional*: To respond to other reminders, repeat steps 3 and 4.

Responding to a Lock Screen Reminder

If the setting for Notifications While Screen Is Off is enabled, full-screen notifications will appear when the screen is dark. To respond, press and hold the Dismiss or Snooze icon until its surrounding circle expands and then drag to the right or left, respectively. If you elect to snooze, the reminder is snoozed for the default duration.

Setting Calendar Preferences

You can set options on the Settings screen to customize the way that Calendar works.

1. Launch the Calendar app. (On the Home screen, tap the Calendar shortcut, or tap the Apps icon and then the Calendar icon.)

2. Press the Menu key and tap Settings to view the Settings screen.

3. *Week View.* This setting changes the Week view display mode to analog or timeline.

4. *First Day of Week.* Specify whether calendar weeks should start on Saturday, Sunday, Monday, or match local customs.

5. *Hide Declined Events.* When enabled, event invitations that you've declined aren't shown in Calendar.

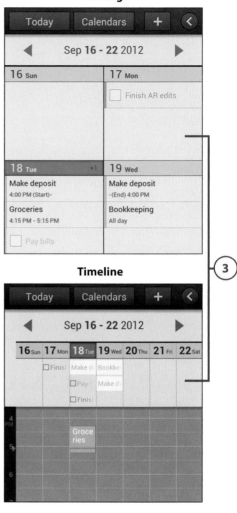

6. *Lock Time Zone.* When Lock Time Zone is disabled (unchecked), all event times reflect the phone's current location. When enabled (checked), event times always reflect the time zone specified in Select Time Zone (see step 7).

A Lock Time Zone Recommendation

This is the most confusing aspect of Calendar. In general, the easiest way to use Lock Time Zone is to leave it disabled. When you're home in California, for example, all event times reflect Pacific time. If you travel to New York, the events display Eastern times. Finally, when you return home, events automatically change to show Pacific times again.

7. *Select Time Zone.* To force all event times to reflect a particular time zone (when you're traveling or if you want events to always reflect the home office's time zone, for example), enable Lock Time Zone (see step 6) and tap Select Time Zone to choose a time zone.

8. *Show Week Number.* When enabled, Week view also displays the week number (1–52).

9. *Calendars.* Tap Calendars to select the account calendars to incorporate into Calendar, as well as dictate whether birthdays found in Contacts records are shown as events.

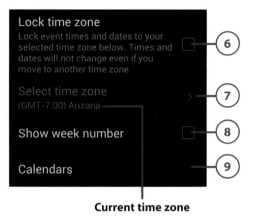

Current time zone

10. *Event Notification settings.* These settings determine the manner(s) in which reminders for upcoming events and tasks are presented.

⑩

Event notification

Set alerts & notifications ⊗
Status bar notification

Select ringtone ⊗

Default reminder time ⊗
15 minutes

Notifications while screen is ☑
Display notifications on full screen
while screen is turned off

Sync settings

Sync events/tasks

⑪

- Tap Set Alerts and Notifications to specify whether a reminder will display as a status bar icon (Status Bar Notification), as a full screen pop-up (Alert), or not at all (Off).

- Tap Select Ringtone to associate a ringtone with reminder alerts. (Select Silent if you prefer to disable this option.)

- Tap Default Reminder Time to set the default reminder interval that's proposed for new events. Note that you can still specify a different reminder time for each added event.

- Enable the Notifications While Screen Is Off setting to display a full-screen alert if a reminder is triggered when the phone's screen is dark.

11. *Sync Events/Tasks.* Tap Sync Events/ Tasks to review current sync settings, add a calendar account to the sync list, or perform a manual sync. For information on syncing calendar data, see Chapter 5, "Synchronizing Data."

Another Manual Sync Option

To quickly perform a manual Calendar sync based on current settings, press the Menu key and tap Sync.

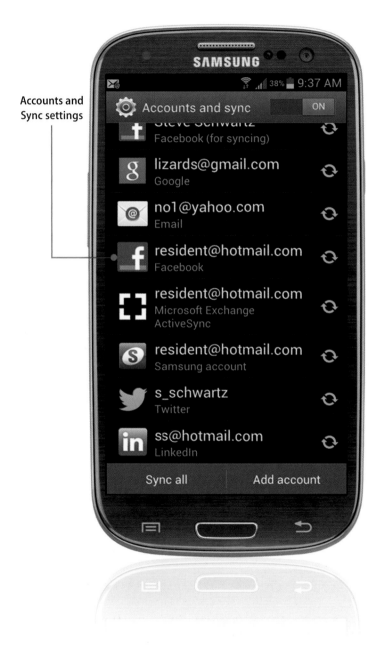

Accounts and
Sync settings

In this chapter, you learn how to synchronize calendar events, contacts, and other data on your phone with data stored elsewhere, such as in your web, computer, and Exchange Server accounts. Topics include the following:

→ Developing a synchronization strategy

→ Configuring the phone for automatic syncs

→ Performing manual syncs

Synchronizing Data

When you got your phone, you probably already had important data such as contact records and calendar events stored somewhere else: in one or several computer applications, on websites, or in an Exchange Server account. Instead of keeping that information separate from the data in your phone's apps, you might want to keep all your data sources synchronized. That is, no matter where you edit or create new data, you can synchronize the other data sources automatically or manually to match.

Developing a Sync Strategy

If you want to keep your phone's important data (such as Calendar events and Contacts records) synchronized with data stored on your PC or Mac, on a Microsoft Exchange Server, or in web-based applications, there are currently only two seamless solutions. By *seamless*, I mean that you can accomplish this automatically (or manually with a simple tap) over a 3G, 4G, or wireless connection. You don't have to hook up a USB cable or launch a separate application on your Mac or PC to perform a sync.

Although adding software and jumping through hoops are unnecessary, the seamless solutions *do* require that you accept either a Google/Gmail, Samsung, or Exchange Server account as the repository for your contact and calendar data.

Microsoft Exchange Server

If you work for a company or institution that employs Exchange Server to manage email, contacts, calendar, and other business data, your situation is the easiest. If you've added your Exchange email account to the phone, you have instant access on the phone to much of your important data—regardless of whether you create it on the phone or on one of several computers that you use. Each time you edit a contact or create a new calendar event, the server is responsible for synchronizing that data with every computer, phone, and tablet on which your Exchange account is registered.

Unfortunately, most users *don't* have an Exchange Server account. Internet service providers (ISPs) don't provide them nor do popular web-based services such as Hotmail and Yahoo! Note, however, that some Exchange hosting services will provide you with an account for a monthly fee. If you need constant access to your contact and calendar data, you might want to check out these services.

Google/Gmail

Because the Galaxy S III is an Android-based phone, Android is Google software, and you've probably added a Google/Gmail account to the phone, you can use this account to keep your calendar and contact data in sync. Several approaches facilitate this, but all except the first require concessions:

- If you already use Google and Gmail to manage your contacts and calendar events, you're all set.

- If you're willing to *switch* to Google/Gmail for managing your contacts and calendar events, you probably can export your data from the applications you currently use and import the data into Google Calendar and Gmail Contacts.

- Even if you aren't willing to switch to these Google web apps, you can perform the export/import just described as a one-time procedure. As long as you're willing to manually maintain the Contacts list on your phone and record all new Calendar events on the phone, you can disable the sync process. Everything important to you will already be on your phone, so there's no reason to sync.

- Finally, if you can live with the notion that chunks of your data will be out of sync much of the time and correct only on your computer, you can use Google/Gmail as an *occasional* data receptacle. Periodically delete the Gmail Contacts data on the web, import your computer's contact data into Gmail Contacts, and then perform a single sync to transfer the up-to-date contact roster to your phone. (For help with importing Microsoft Outlook and Apple Address Book contacts into Gmail Contacts, see Chapter 3, "Managing Contacts.")

Using a Samsung Account

The Samsung account that you created during the phone's initial setup (see "Creating a Samsung Account" in Chapter 1, "Galaxy S III Essentials") enables you to use certain apps such as ChatON. You also can optionally use it—like a Gmail/Google account—to sync your calendar and contact data. For instructions, see "Enabling Autosync" and "Performing Manual Syncs," later in this chapter.

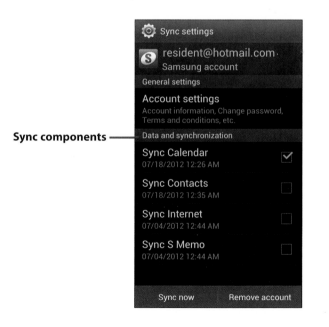

Sync components

SYNCING ADDRESS BOOK (MAC) OR OUTLOOK 2011 (MAC) CONTACTS WITH GOOGLE CONTACTS

If you're a Mac user and you use its Address Book application to record your contacts, you can sync it with Google Contacts. And if you use the Contacts component of Microsoft Outlook 2011 for Mac, you can sync it with Address Book—which, in turn, syncs with Google Contacts.

Microsoft Outlook → Address Book → Google Contacts

1. **Sync the Address Book with Google Contacts.** Launch Address Book on your Mac and choose Address Book > Preferences. Click the Accounts tab, check Synchronize with Google, and click the Configure button. Enter your Google/Gmail account username and password, and then click OK. (If you don't use Outlook, skip to step 3.)

2. **Sync Outlook 2011 Contacts with the Address Book.** Launch
   Outlook 2011 on your Mac, choose Outlook > Preferences, and click the
   Sync Services icon. Ensure that Contacts has a check mark.

3. To perform the initial sync with Google Contacts (whether you're an
   Address Book or an Outlook 2011 user), choose Sync Now from the Sync
   menu on the right side of the Mac's menu bar. To perform additional
   syncs after making changes to Outlook or Address Book contacts, repeat
   this step.

Sync menu ———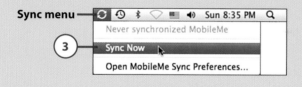

Alternative Software

If you prefer to enter important data on your computer using programs such
as Microsoft Outlook (PC or Mac), Address Book (Mac), or iCal (Mac), another
option is to search Android Market for an app solution that enables you to
continue using those programs. An Android app and a companion application installed on your computer generally manage the sync process.

The Missing Sync for Android

Test with Care

In reading about the Android/computer solutions, you might see a warning from the software company or in user comments concerning potential data loss. Before experimenting with any of these solutions, be sure to back up your application data.

The Sneakernet (Manual) Approach

Before the wide acceptance of networking, if a co-worker needed a copy of a Word or Excel document, you would use *Sneakernet*. That is, you would copy the file to a floppy disk, walk down the hall, and hand it to whoever needed it. *Moral:* Sometimes a manual approach is good enough.

This also applies to synchronizing data between your phone and computer. If you don't live in Google/Gmail and don't have access to an Exchange Server account, you might decide to ignore synchronizing. Create new events and contact records on the device you use most, create them on whatever device happens to be handy, or standardize on using your phone or a computer application for adding all the new data. If you decide that a particular record or event is crucial and needs to be in *both* places, re-create the data on the second device when you have time.

Enabling Autosync

When *autosync* is enabled, data from all accounts is automatically synched in the background on a repeating schedule. Most accounts enable you to set an autosync schedule, as well as specify which data types to sync and which ones to ignore. You can leave autosync on at all times, periodically disable it, or ignore it and run manual syncs on selected accounts whenever your data has changed.

1. On the Home screen, press the Menu key and tap Settings.

2. On the Settings screen, tap Accounts and Sync.

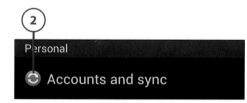

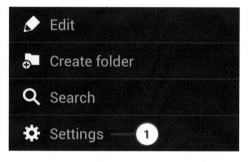

3. On the Accounts and Sync screen, all your accounts that can be synchronized are listed. If you want to enable autosync, ensure that the switch at the top of the screen is set to On.

Facebook Account Synchronization

If you've added your Facebook account to the phone, there are *two* sets of related autosync settings. Calendar and Gallery are synced in the Facebook (for syncing) entry; Contacts are synced in the Facebook entry.

4. Examine the sync settings for an account by tapping the account's name. Synchronization will be performed only for those data elements that are checked. Make any desired changes by tapping check boxes.

What About My Other Accounts?

Other accounts, such as POP3 and IMAP email accounts from your ISP, aren't listed. Only accounts that contain data that can be synched (such as events, contacts, tasks, and notes) are eligible to appear in the list.

5. You can specify a sync schedule for some accounts. Tap the appropriate option—Facebook uses Sync Interval Settings, for example—to view or change the sync schedule(s).

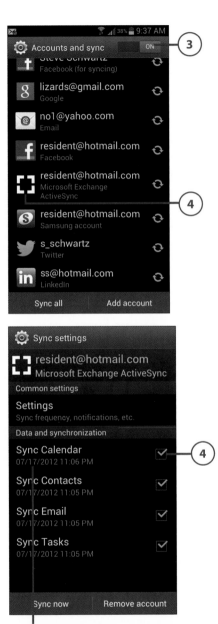

Most recent sync

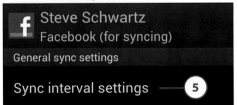

6. In the dialog box that appears, tap a new autosync interval or tap the Cancel button to retain the current interval. (Tap None if you don't want this data type to be included in autosyncs.) Repeat this step for each of the account's data types whose sync schedule you want to change.

7. When you're done examining and making changes to the account, press the Back key until the Accounts and Sync screen reappears. Repeat steps 4–6 for each additional account.

| None |
| 3 hours |
| 6 hours |
| 12 hours |
| Once a day |
| Cancel |

Enabling and Disabling Autosync

You can enable or disable autosync whenever you want. Return to the Accounts and Sync screen by performing steps 1 and 2, and then drag the slider at the top of the screen.

For example, you might disable autosync when you're away from your wireless network and then enable it when you return. This ensures that syncs are performed only when they won't count against your 3G or 4G data limits.

Performing Manual Syncs

You can perform manual syncs whenever you want—regardless of whether autosync is enabled.

1. On the Home screen, press the Menu key and tap Settings.

2. On the Settings screen, tap Accounts and Sync.

3. On the Accounts and Sync screen, choose one of the options in steps 4–6 to perform a manual sync.

4. To simultaneously sync all listed accounts (equivalent to performing a one-time autosync), tap the Sync All button at the bottom of the screen. This is the equivalent of performing an autosync, updating all accounts immediately.

5. To sync all checked components of a single account, tap the account name on the Accounts and Sync screen and tap the Sync Now button on the screen that appears.

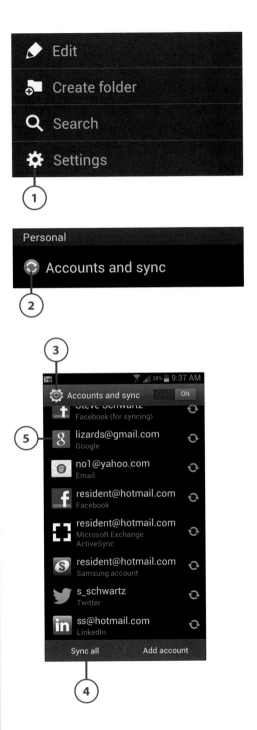

6. To selectively sync components of one account, tap the account name on the Accounts and Sync screen. On the screen that appears, double-tap the component that you want to sync. (It's necessary to double-tap in order to retain the component's original sync setting.)

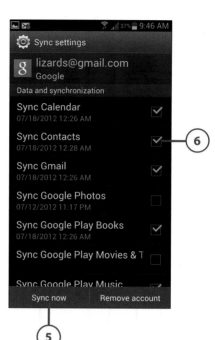

In this chapter, you learn to use the phone to place and receive calls. Topics include the following:

→ Dialing calls manually and from contact records
→ Using the call logs to return calls, redial numbers, and reply to messages
→ Dialing from embedded numbers in email and messages
→ Placing an emergency call
→ Speed-dialing
→ Blocking your caller ID
→ Making a three-way call
→ Receiving incoming calls
→ Using call waiting and call forwarding
→ Using in-call options, such as the keypad, speakerphone, and Bluetooth headset
→ Checking your voicemail
→ Enabling silent and airplane modes
→ Configuring call settings

Placing and Receiving Calls

With all the functionality your smartphone provides, it's easy to forget that you can also use it to make and receive calls. But smartphone power often comes at a price. To optimize your use of the phone *as* a phone, it's important that you learn the various calling procedures and the different options for performing each one.

Placing Calls

The Galaxy S III provides many convenient ways for you to make calls. You can manually enter numbers, dial a number from a contact record, use the call log to return missed calls and redial numbers, call embedded numbers in text or email messages, create and use speed dial entries, and make three-way and emergency calls.

With or Without the 1

When dialing a number, you need to add the dialing prefix/country code only when you're calling a country that uses a *different* code. As a result, most numbers that you dial manually, as well as ones stored in Contacts, can either omit or include the dialing prefix.

Manual Dialing

You can use the Keypad section of the Phone app to manually dial phone numbers. The procedure differs slightly if the number you're dialing is also associated with an existing Contacts record.

Dialing Someone without a Contacts Record

1. Tap the Phone icon at the bottom of the Home screen.

Launching Phone from the Lock Screen

If you're on the lock screen, you can go directly to phone by dragging the Phone icon at the bottom of the screen upward.

2. If the keypad isn't displayed, tap the Keypad tab. Then tap the digits in the phone number. (To make an international call, press and hold 0. A plus symbol appears as the first character in the number. Enter the country code, followed by the phone number.)

Mistakes Happen

If you make a mistake, you can press the Delete key to delete the last digit entered. To remove the entire number and start over, press and hold Delete. You can also use normal editing techniques to position the text insertion mark within the number and make necessary changes, such as inserting the area code.

Portrait or Landscape Mode

You can also dial calls while holding the phone in landscape mode.

3. *Optional*: To create a new contact record for this number or add the number to an existing contact record, tap Add to Contacts and select an option from the menu that appears.

4. Tap the green phone icon to dial the call. When you're finished talking, tap the red End Call icon to disconnect.

Keypad tab

Voicemail   4   Delete

Dialing Someone with a Contacts Record

1. Tap the Phone icon at the bottom of the Home screen.

2. Tap the Keypad tab if it isn't automatically selected. Then tap any of the phone number's digits. You can start at the beginning or with any consecutive string of digits that you remember. As you enter the digits, potential matches from Contacts and from numbers you've previously dialed are displayed.

3. Do one of the following:

   • To select the main suggestion, tap the person or company's name.

   • To view additional matches, tap the numbered down arrow and select someone from the Search Results list.

   • Continue entering digits until the correct match is suggested, and then tap the person or company's name.

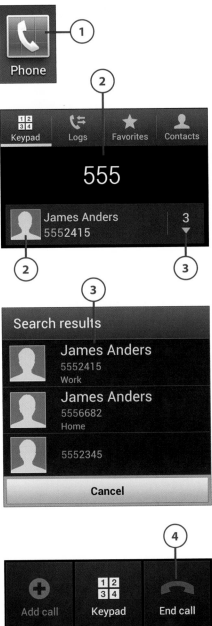

Dialing by Name

If you can't remember any part of a person's number but are sure he or she has a Contacts record, you can use the keypad to spell the person's name.

4. Tap the green phone icon to dial the call. When you're finished talking, tap the red End Call icon to disconnect.

Dialing from a Contact Record

Many of your outgoing calls will be to people and companies that have a record in Contacts.

1. Open Contacts by tapping its icon at the bottom of the Home screen, tapping the Phone icon on the Home screen and then selecting the Contacts tab, or accessing Contacts from another app, such as Messaging.

Contacts tab

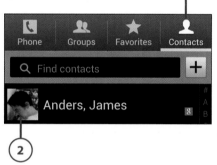

2. If it isn't already selected, tap the Contacts tab at the top of the screen. Find the desired record by scrolling or searching, and then tap the entry to view the full record.

3. Tap a listed phone number or its green telephone icon to dial that number.

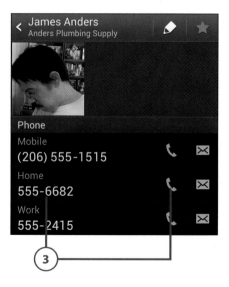

4. When you're finished talking, tap the red End Call icon to disconnect.

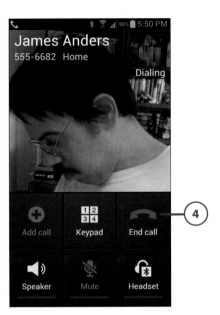

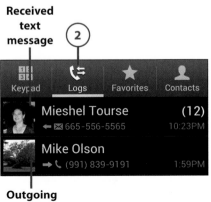

Dialing and Texting from the Call Log

Every incoming and outgoing call and message is automatically recorded in the Logs section of Phone. By viewing the logs, you can quickly determine which calls and messages need to be returned, as well as initiate a call or the creation of the new message.

Returning and Redialing Calls

By selecting a particular log in Logs, you can see whom you've called and who has called you. You can also see people with whom you've exchanged messages. You can then dial or message any log entry.

1. On the Home screen, launch Phone by tapping its icon.

2. Tap the Logs tab at the top of the screen.

Viewing the Logs from Contacts

You can also reach Logs from within the Contacts app. At the top of the screen, tap the Phone tab and then tap the Logs tab that appears.

Received text message

Outgoing call

3. *Optional:* Normally, the Logs section lists all outgoing and incoming voice calls and messages. To select a different log (such as missed calls or people to whom you've sent you a message), press the Menu key, tap the View By icon, and select an option from the View By menu.

4. Within each log entry, icons provide information about the call or message exchange. A phone or envelope icon denotes a call or text message, respectively. The icon beneath the person or company's name indicates the type of call or message.

5. To call a person without leaving the current screen, swipe his or her entry to the right. The number is automatically dialed.

6. To text a person, swipe his or her entry to the left. A new message window in Messaging appears.

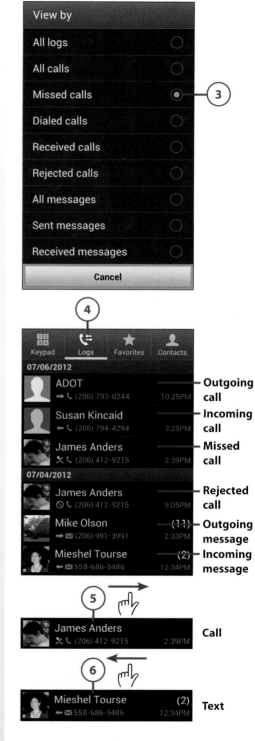

View by

All logs

All calls

Missed calls   (3)

Dialed calls

Received calls

Rejected calls

All messages

Sent messages

Received messages

Cancel

4

Keypad   Logs   Favorites   Contacts

07/06/2012

ADOT   **Outgoing**
➡ 📞 (206) 793-0244   10:25PM   **call**

Susan Kincaid   **Incoming**
⬅ 📞 (206) 794-4294   3:28PM   **call**

James Anders   **Missed**
✖ 📞 (206) 412-9215   2:39PM   **call**

07/04/2012

James Anders   **Rejected**
🚫 📞 (206) 412-9215   9:05PM   **call**

Mike Olson   (11)   **Outgoing**
➡ ✉ (206) 991-3991   2:33PM   **message**

Mieshel Tourse   (2)   **Incoming**
⬅ ✉ 558-686-5486   12:34PM   **message**

5

James Anders   **Call**
✖ 📞 (206) 412-9215   2:39PM

6

Mieshel Tourse   (2)   **Text**
⬅ ✉ 558-686-5486   12:34PM

Tap Versus Swipe

If swiping isn't your thing or you want more control over what happens, tap the log entry. On the screen that appears, you can call him or her by tapping the phone icon. To send a text or multimedia message to the person, tap the message icon.

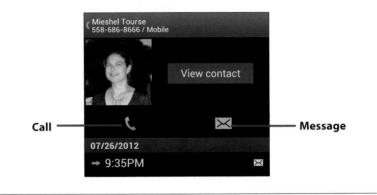

Other Log Options

Using the logs to return calls and messages is often more convenient than dialing manually or searching for the person's contact record. Here are some other actions you can take in Logs:

- Press and hold an entry to display a menu of commands specific to that person or company. (Note the Delete command, enabling you to delete this single entry, as well as the Add to Reject List command. Future calls from any number in the Reject List are automatically sent to voicemail.)

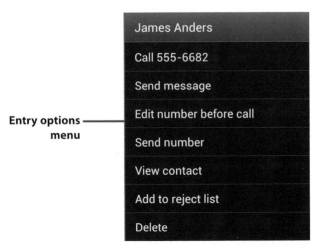

- You can clean up the logs by deleting old, duplicate, and unwanted entries. Press the Menu key, tap the View By icon, and select the log that you want to manage. Press the Menu key again and tap Delete. Select the individual messages that you want to remove (or tap Select All), tap the Delete button, and tap OK in the Delete confirmation dialog box.

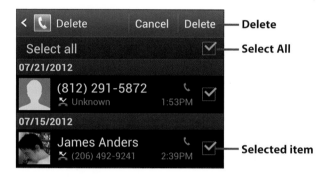

Dialing a Number in a Text or Email Message

A phone number in an email or text message acts as a *link* that, when tapped, dials the number.

Text Message Links

1. In Messaging, display the received or sent message that contains the phone number and then tap the number.

2. In the dialog box that appears, tap Call.

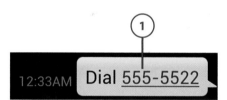

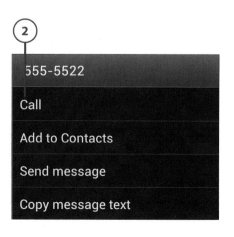

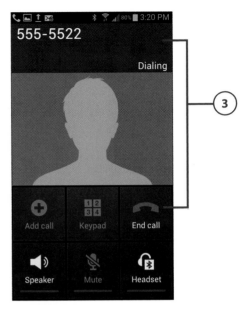

3. Phone launches and dials the number. When you're finished talking, tap the red End Call icon to disconnect.

Email Message Links

1. In Email, display the received or sent email message that contains the phone number and then tap the number.

2. The number appears in the Keypad section of Phone. If necessary, you can edit it (adding or removing the area code, for example) using normal editing techniques.

3. Tap the green phone icon to dial the number.

4. When you're finished talking, tap the red End Call icon to disconnect.

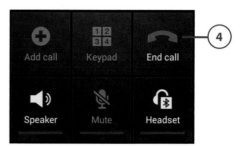

QUICK DIALING TECHNIQUES

For people and companies with a record in Contacts, you can also call them using a voice command, such as "Call Janice Gunderson." For information about using voice apps, see Chapter 17, "Customizing Your Phone."

You can quickly call anyone with a Contacts record whose name appears in the Logs or Favorites list of Phone/Contacts or with whom you've recently exchanged messages in Messaging. Locate the person or company in the Contacts, Logs, Favorites, or Messaging list and swipe the item to the right. The Phone screen appears, and the person or company's number is automatically dialed.

Emergency Calling

The Galaxy S III supports *e911* (Enhanced 911), enabling it to connect to a nearby emergency dispatch center regardless of where in the U.S. or Canada you happen to be. (The equivalent emergency number is different in other countries. In the United Kingdom, for example, it's 999.) When you place a 911 call, your position can usually be determined by the phone's GPS or by triangulating your position using nearby cell sites.

Calling 911

1. Do one of the following:

   - On the Home screen, tap the Phone app's icon.

   - If the lock screen is displayed and the phone is protected, you can go directly to the Phone screen by tapping the Emergency Call text at the bottom of the screen.

2. Using the keypad, enter **911** and tap the green phone icon to dial the number.

3. After completing the call, Emergency Callback Mode (denoted by a large red plus symbol) is automatically enabled, allowing you to redial 911 by simply tapping a button. On the Emergency Callback Mode screen, you can do any of the following:

   - Tap the Call 911 button to redial 911.

   - Slide the green Home icon to the right to return to the Home screen and use other apps while remaining in emergency calling mode.

   - Slide the red X icon to the left to exit emergency calling mode.

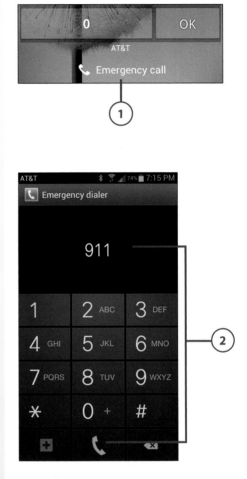

About the Emergency Call Text

Although tapping Emergency Call enables you to quickly make an emergency call without having to first unlock the screen and launch the Phone app, it has an important restriction. *Only calls to 911 and emergency responders (such as the police and fire department) are allowed; all others are blocked.* You cannot call your parents or spouse, for example. To emphasize this, the band at the top of the screen reads "Emergency Dialer." If you need to call someone other than an emergency responder, you need to unlock the screen by supplying your pattern, PIN, or password; launch the Phone app; and then dial normally.

Emergency Calling Tips

Keep the following in mind when seeking emergency assistance:

- Even if you've disabled the phone's location/GPS functions for all other uses, these features remain available for 911 use.

- Not all emergency dispatch centers support e911. Instead of assuming they've determined your location based on GPS or triangulation, be prepared to give your location.

- Some emergency dispatch centers use an automated voice menu that prompts you to enter numbers. According to Sprint, for example, "If you encounter a pre-recorded message instead of a live operator, wait for the appropriate prompt and say 'EMERGENCY' instead of pressing 1. Not all wireless phones transmit number tones during a 911 call."

Other Outgoing Call Options

The Galaxy S III also supports some additional outgoing call options: speed dialing, blocking your caller ID information, three-way calling, and inserting pause and wait commands.

Speed Dialing

To make it simple to dial your most important numbers, you can assign a *speed dial number* to anyone with a record in Contacts. The digits 2–100 are available as speed dial numbers; 1 is reserved for voicemail.

Accessing the Speed Dial Setting Screen

1. Launch Phone or Contacts by tapping an icon at the bottom of the Home screen.

2. To display the Speed Dial Setting screen, do either of the following:

   • With the Keypad tab in Phone selected, press the Menu key and tap Speed Dial Setting.

   • With the Contacts tab selected, press the Menu key and tap Speed Dial Setting.

What Next?

When you reach the Speed Dial Setting screen, jump to one of the following sections that describes the task you want to perform.

Assigning a Speed Dial Number

1. On the Speed Dial Setting screen, press a currently unassigned number—that is, one that says Not Assigned.

2. In Contacts, select the person or company in the contacts list with which to associate this speed dial number.

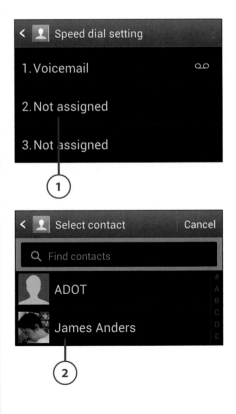

3. If the contact record contains only one phone number, the number is automatically used. If the person or company's contact record contains more than one phone number, select the number that you want to use.

4. The contact's phone number is assigned to the speed dial number.

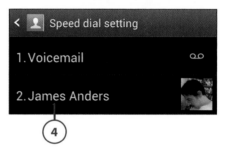

Replacing an In-Use Speed Dial Number

1. On the Speed Dial Setting screen, press and hold the number that you want to reassign.

2. In the dialog box that appears, tap Replace.

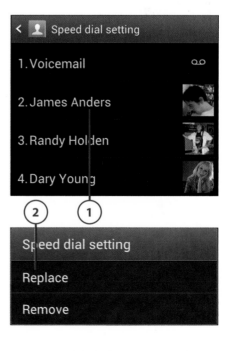

3. Select a person or company in the contacts list.

4. If the contact record contains only one phone number, the number is automatically used. If the person or company's contact record contains more than one phone number, select the number that you want to use.

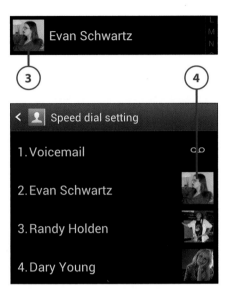

Removing a Speed Dial Number

1. On the Speed Dial Setting screen, press and hold the number that you want to remove.

2. In the dialog box that appears, tap Remove. The contact previously associated with that speed dial number is instantly removed.

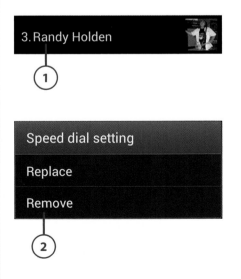

Rearranging Speed Dial Numbers

1. With the Speed Dial Setting screen displayed, press the Menu key and tap Change Order.

2. Select the contact thumbnail to which you want to assign a new speed dial number.

3. Tap the destination slot—it can be empty or currently occupied. If empty, the contact is assigned the new speed dial number. If currently occupied, the contacts swaps slots.

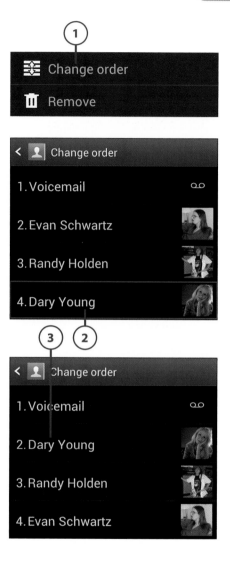

Dialing a Speed Dial Number

1. Launch Phone by tapping its icon at the bottom of the Home screen.

2. With the Keypad tab selected, enter the speed dial number. Press and hold the final digit.

3. The phone dials the person or company associated with the speed dial number. When you're finished talking, tap the red End Call icon to disconnect.

Keypad tab

Dialing from the Speed Dial Screen

If you can't remember a particular speed dial number, you can initiate a call or message from the Speed Dial Setting screen. Scroll to find the person or company's entry, tap it, and then tap Call or Message in the dialog box that appears.

Send message — Message   Call — Dial

Temporarily Blocking Your Caller ID

If you want to prevent your caller ID information from displaying on a call, precede the number with *67, such as *674861111 for a local call or *672105078912 for a long-distance call. The recipient's phone should display Private Caller rather than your name, city, or number. Note that *67 is the correct prefix in the United States and Canada only; other countries have a different prefix.

Number —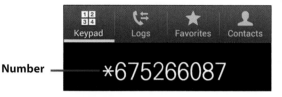

If you want to prevent your caller ID information from displaying on *every* call, contact your service provider for assistance.

Three-Way Calling

By making a three-way call, you can talk to two people at the same time. If you don't have an unlimited minutes plan, check with your service provider to determine how three-way calls are billed.

Dial

1. Launch Phone, enter the first phone number or select it from Contacts, and tap the green phone icon to dial the number.

2. When the first person answers, tell him or her to wait while you call the second person. Tap the Add Call icon and dial the second number. The first person is automatically placed on hold.

3. When the second person answers, tap the Merge icon.

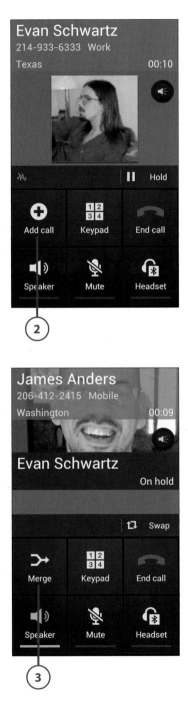

4. The display shows that you're all connected to a conference call. When the call is completed, tap End Call. All persons who are still connected will be disconnected.

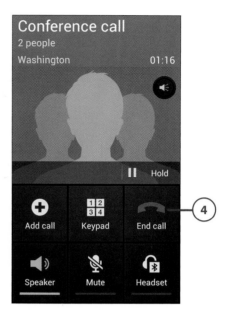

Pause and Wait Commands

If you're fed up with listening and responding to convoluted automated answering systems used by banks, insurance companies, telephone companies, and cable systems, you might consider programming their Contacts record to automatically tap the correct keypad digits in response to their menus. For instance, `2148527777,,1,2,6310,,43` might take you to your Internet provider's technical support group.

In addition to digits, each phone number can contain commas (,) and semicolons (;). Each comma represents a 2-second pause (you can string together multiple pauses), and each semicolon instructs the phone to wait until you enter any number or press a key. Creating a number that responds correctly to the voice prompts requires trial and error. For example, if you don't wait long enough (using pauses) before the next number is entered, the process fails.

As you're entering or editing a phone number, press the Menu key to insert a pause or wait. The best numbers in which to use pauses and waits are the simple ones, such as those for which the initial prompt is for an extension.

On the other hand, complex, multilayered menus take much longer to program and your efforts will "break" if the answering system's menu structure changes.

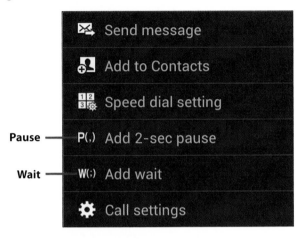

WI-FI CALLING (T-MOBILE)

T-Mobile Galaxy S III users can optionally make calls over a Wi-Fi network rather than using normal cellular service. This can be exceptionally useful when you live or work in a place that has a weak cell signal and, hence, poor call quality. Note that Wi-Fi calling doesn't cost extra, but it does use plan minutes. And if you want to make out-of-country calls, you must have an international plan.

To enable Wi-Fi calling, launch Settings, tap More Settings in the Wireless and Network section, and tap Wi-Fi Calling. To set calling preferences, tap Wi-Fi Calling Settings and make a selection in the Set Connection Preference dialog box.

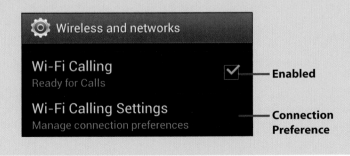

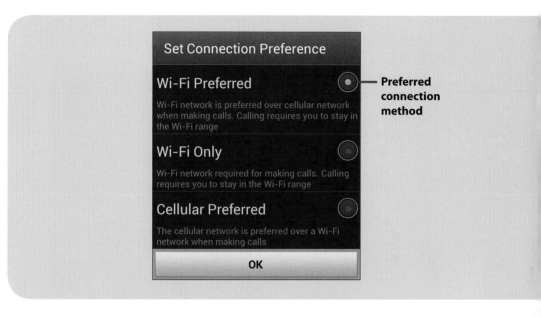

Set Connection Preference

Wi-Fi Preferred

Wi-Fi network is preferred over cellular network when making calls. Calling requires you to stay in the Wi-Fi range

Wi-Fi Only

Wi-Fi network required for making calls. Calling requires you to stay in the Wi-Fi range

Cellular Preferred

The cellular network is preferred over a Wi-Fi network when making calls

OK

Preferred connection method

Receiving Calls

The other half of the phone call equation is that of receiving and responding to incoming calls. For instructions on setting general and personal ringtones to announce incoming calls, see "Ringtones" in Chapter 17.

Responding to an Incoming Call

1. When a call comes in, the caller is identified by name and number (if he or she has a Contacts record), by number (if there's no matching Contacts record), or by Private Caller (if he or she has blocked his or her caller ID).

James Anders — 1
226-411-9255 Mobile
Washington   Incoming call

5:14 PM

To answer drag outside circle

Accept call

Reject call

Reject call with message

Send text message

2. You can respond in any of the following ways:

   - *Accept call.* Drag the green phone icon to the right.

   - *Reject call.* Drag the red phone icon to the left, sending the caller to voicemail.

   - *Ignore call.* Do nothing; let the phone ring. After a number of rings, the caller is transferred to voicemail.

   - *Reject with explanation.* Drag Reject Call with Message upward and select a text message to transmit to the caller. (Note that if the caller doesn't have a messaging plan or is calling from a landline, the text message might not be delivered.)

3. When the call concludes, tap the End Call icon.

Send a custom message

✉ Reject call with message

Create new message   +

I'm driving   Send

I'm at the cinema   Send

I'm in class   Send

I'm in a meeting   Send

Sorry, I'm busy. Call back later   Send

②

③

Add call   Keypad   End call

Speaker   Mute   Headset

Call Waiting

Call waiting enables you to answer an incoming call when you're already on a call.

1. Answer the incoming call by sliding the green phone icon to the right.

2. In the Accept Call After dialog box, tap Putting *caller* On Hold.

3. The initial call is automatically placed on hold while you speak to the new caller. To switch between callers, tap the Swap icon. The active call is always shown in green at the top of the screen.

4. To end the active call, tap the End Call icon. The other call automatically becomes active.

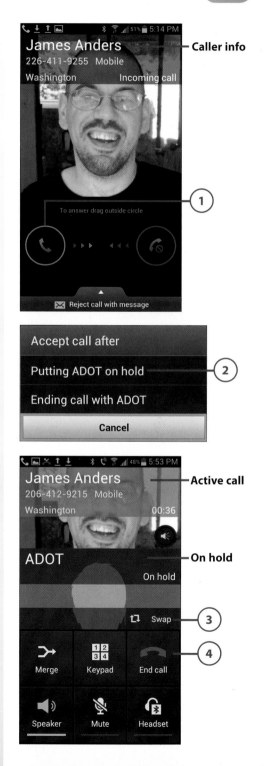

Caller info

Active call

On hold

Call Forwarding

You can have all calls that your cell phone would normally receive automatically forwarded to another number. Forwarding works even when the Galaxy S III is turned off. To restore normal calling, deactivate call forwarding when you're finished. (Check with your service provider or review your plan to determine the cost of using call forwarding.)

1. Tap the Phone icon on the Home screen.

2. Press the Menu key and tap Call Settings.

3. On the Call Settings screen, tap Call Forwarding.

4. On the Call Forwarding screen, tap Voice Call.

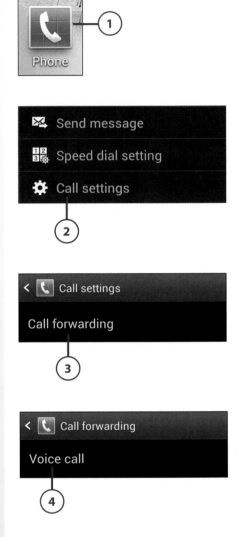

5. On Voice Call screen, select a forwarding option:

- *Always forward*. Forward all calls until this option is disabled. When Always Forward is enabled, other forwarding options are all disabled.

- *Forward when busy*. Forward only when you're already on a call.

- *Forward when unanswered*. When you ignore a call, it is forwarded rather than sent to voicemail.

- *Forward when unreachable*. Forward calls only when it's determined that you're out of your provider's service area or the phone is turned off.

6. In the dialog box that appears, enter, edit, or review the phone number to which calls will be forwarded. You can manually enter the number or select it from a Contacts record. Tap the Enable, Update, Disable, or Cancel button.

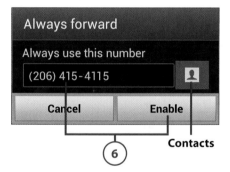

Ending Call Forwarding

To disable call forwarding, perform steps 1–4. On the Voice Call screen, tap Always Forward, and then tap the Disable button in the dialog box that appears.

In-Call Options

While on a call, you can access common in-call options by tapping icons at the bottom of the screen. (The first icon—variously labeled Add Call, Merge, or Swap—was discussed in previous sections.) Additional options are available via hardware controls and the Notifications panel.

Icon Options

During any call, you can tap the following icons:

- *Extra Volume*. You can boost in-call volume above the normal maximum by tapping the Extra Volume icon. When enabled, the icon is green. Tap it a second time to disable the volume boost.

- *Noise Reduction*. When activated, the noise reduction feature can improve call quality by reducing ambient noise. To toggle the state of this feature, press the Menu key and tap Noise Reduction On (or Off). Note that this feature is disabled when using the speakerphone.

- *Hold/Unhold*. Place the current call on hold. Tap the icon again to reactivate the call.

- *Keypad*. If you need to enter information (to respond to a voice prompt system or enter an extension, for example), tap the Keypad icon to display the normal dialing keypad. The Keypad icon's label changes to Hide. To dismiss the keypad, tap the Hide icon or press the Back key.

In-call option icons

Extra Volume icon

Hold/Unhold

Noise reduction status

Keypad

Hide keypad

- *Speaker.* To toggle the phone between normal and speaker-phone modes, tap the Speaker icon. When the speakerphone is active, a green bar appears beneath the icon.

- *Mute.* To temporarily turn off the phone's microphone so that the other party can't hear you, tap the Mute icon. When muting is active, a green bar appears beneath the icon.

- *Headset.* To use a Bluetooth head-set on the current call, tap the Headset icon. When Bluetooth is active, a green bar appears beneath the icon. To return to a normal, non-Bluetooth call, tap the icon again.

- *End Call.* Tap End Call to "hang up," disconnecting from the other party.

Speakerphone enabled

Other In-Call Options

Two other important options are available during calls that aren't rep-resented by onscreen icons.

- *Volume adjustment.* To change the volume, press the volume control on the left side of the phone. An onscreen volume indicator appears. Press the top half of the hardware volume control to raise the volume; press the lower half to lower the volume. You can also adjust the volume by dragging the onscreen slider.

Volume indicator

- *Notifications panel options.* Optionally, you can drag down the Notifications panel to access the Mute, Speaker, and End options.

Phone Call Multitasking

If desired, you can run apps while on a call. Return to the Home screen by pressing the Home key and then launch the apps. The status bar turns neon green to indicate that a call is in progress. When you're ready to end the call, launch Phone again or use the call controls in the Notifications panel.

Notifications panel

In-call controls

Using Voicemail

Using your service provider's voicemail, friends, family, and colleagues can leave messages for you when you're unavailable or the phone is turned off. See Chapter 1, "Galaxy S III Essentials," for instructions on setting up voicemail.

You can check your voicemail in two or more ways. First, you can tap a received New Voicemail entry in the Notifications panel. Second, you can launch the Phone app, and then press and hold 1 (the speed dial number assigned to voicemail) or tap the Voicemail icon on the keypad. Finally, your service provider may include or offer a separate voicemail app with which you can listen to and manage your voicemail.

When voicemail messages are waiting, a notification icon appears in the status bar. Note that if you set up voicemail to require a password (see "Setting Up Voicemail" in Chapter 1), you'll be asked to supply it each time you contact Voicemail. When prompted, tap each digit in the password and end by tapping the pound sign (#).

1. Connect to your carrier's voice-mail service by doing either of the following:

   - Drag down the Notifications panel and tap the New Voicemail entry. The carrier's voicemail is automatically dialed.

   - Launch the Phone app and open the Keypad by tapping its tab. Press and hold 1 (the speed dial number assigned to voicemail) or tap the voicemail icon. The Phone app dials the carrier's voice-mail.

2. You connect to your carrier's voicemail system. Because the menus require you to enter numbers to choose options, tap the Keypad icon to reveal the keypad—if it's currently hidden. Listen to the menu options and tap numbers to indicate your choices.

Voicemail indicator

Keypad tab

Voicemail icon

3. When you're done using voice-mail, tap the End Call icon.

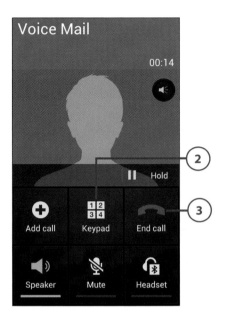

Changing Voicemail Settings

You can change your voicemail settings (such as your greeting, password, and notification methods) whenever you want. Connect with voicemail and follow the prompts.

Enabling Silent and Airplane Mode

Your phone has two special modes that you'll occasionally find useful: silent mode and airplane mode. Enable silent mode when your phone *must* remain quiet, such as when you're in a meeting or a place of worship. Enable airplane mode during flights to quickly make your phone compliant with government and airline regulations.

Silent Mode

In silent mode, all sounds except media playback and alarms are disabled. Incoming calls can optionally be signaled by vibration.

1. To enable Silent mode, do one of the following:

   • Press and hold the power button until the Device Options menu appears, and then tap Silent Mode. Incoming calls will be signaled by vibration.

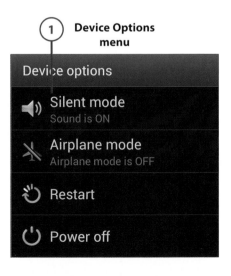

- On the Home screen, press and hold the volume down button until the onscreen volume control shows that you're in vibration or mute mode.

- Open the Notifications panel. Repeatedly tap the Sound icon to toggle between its three states: Sound, Vibrate, and Mute.

- Open Settings, tap Sound, and then tap Silent Mode. Select the desired option in the Silent Mode dialog box.

2. When silent mode is active, a Vibrate or Mute indicator displays in the status bar.

3. To restore normal sound, reverse any of the actions in step 1.

Volume control

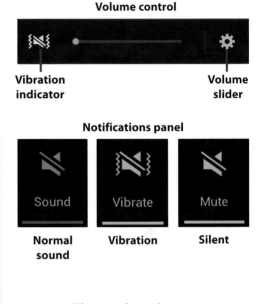

Vibration indicator   **Volume slider**

Notifications panel

Sound   Vibrate   Mute

Normal sound   **Vibration**   **Silent**

Silent mode setting

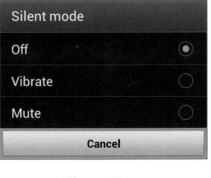

Silent mode

Off

Vibrate

Mute

Cancel

Vibrate   Mute

Airplane Mode

When flying, you can quickly set your phone to airplane mode, disabling its capability to place or receive calls and to send or receive data. Other functions operate normally.

1. To enable Airplane mode, do one of the following:

   - Open the Notifications panel, scroll to the right, and tap the Airplane Mode icon.

   - Press and hold the power button until the Device Options menu appears. Tap Airplane Mode.

   - On the Home screen, press the Menu key and tap Settings, tap More Settings in the Wireless and Network section, and tap the Airplane Mode check box.

2. Confirm by tapping OK in the Airplane mode dialog box. The Airplane mode indicator appears in the status bar, and 3G/4G, Wi-Fi, and Bluetooth are automatically disabled.

3. To restore normal call and data functionality, reverse any of the actions described in step 1.

Configuring Call Settings

You can set preferences for many phone operations in Call Settings. Although the default settings will suffice for most calling situations, here are a few settings that you might want to examine.

1. Launch Phone, press the Menu key, and tap Call Settings.

2. The Call Settings screen appears. Here are some of the more common, useful settings:

   - *Call Rejection.* Tap Call Rejection to enable/disable Auto Reject Mode for blocked callers, as well as add or remove numbers from the Auto Reject List.

   - *Set Reject Messages.* Add or delete text messages that you can send when manually rejecting an incoming call by dragging Reject Call with Message upward.

   - *Call Alert.* Specify whether the phone vibrates when the recipient answers and the call ends, whether tones denote each call connection and end, and whether status tones are used.

   - *Call Answering/Ending.* Optionally answer calls by pressing the Home key and end calls by pressing the Power button.

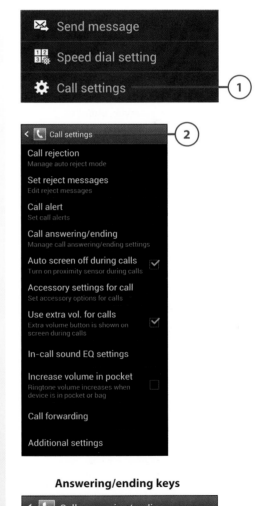

- *Auto Screen Off During Calls.* When enabled, the display is automatically turned off during calls to reduce battery consumption.

- *Accessory Settings for Calls.* When a connected Bluetooth headset is detected by the phone, the phone can be configured to automatically answer incoming calls.

- *Use Extra Volume for Calls.* When enabled, the Extra Volume button is displayed during calls. Tap the button to boost the volume for the current call.

- *In-Call Sound EQ Settings.* Adjust in-call audio to match the requirements of your headset.

- *Increase Volume in Pocket.* When enabled, the ringtone volume is boosted when the proximity sensor detects that the phone is in a pocket or bag.

- *Call Forwarding.* See "Call Forwarding," earlier in this chapter.

- *Additional Settings.* Of the Additional Settings, two that you might want to enable are Auto Redial and Noise Reduction.

- *Voicemail* and *Internet Call Settings.* Items in these two sections won't affect most users, but you should review them.

Extra Volume icon

Headset audio equalization

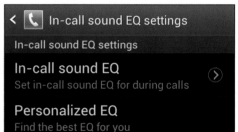

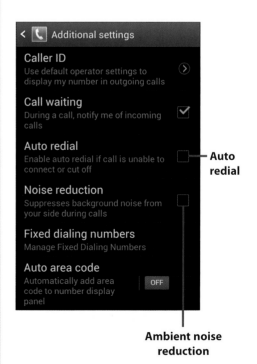

Auto redial

Ambient noise reduction

3. When you're done viewing and changing settings, press the Back key to return to the main Phone screen.

Received messages (yellow)

Sent messages (blue)

Multimedia message

Send

Create message

Add attachment

WIRELESS
Services at the
Northbrook Public Library

NORTHBROOK PUBLIC
LIBRARY

Usin

How to Connect
Northbrook's SSID is nbklibrary. It is a visible wireless network, broadcasting to any listening wireless network card. Your computer will ask if you wish to connect to the network. Once the connection is complete, open your browser. You must agree to the library's Acceptable Use Policy to access the Internet. Reception is best on the second and third floors.

VPN Access
Northbrook's wireless network does not support VPN (Virtual Private Network) access.

Cables
Internet cables for in-library use are available at the Periodicals Desk. You must leave an ID (library card, driver's license, state ID) and sign a form. A map of cabl outlets is available at both the Periodicals Desk and th Reference Desk.

Wi-Fi Printing Step-by-
http://printspots.com/northbrook/we

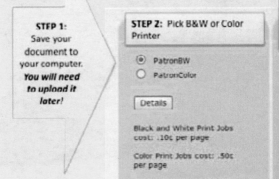

STEP 1:
Save your document to your computer.
You will need to upload it later!

STEP 2: Pick B&W or Color Printer

- ◉ PatronBW
- ○ PatronColor

[Details]

Black and White Print Jobs cost: .10¢ per page

Color Print Jobs cost: .50¢ per page

8.5x11, 8.5x14 or 11x17, single sided printing

In this chapter, you learn how to send and receive text and multimedia messages. Topics include the following:

→ Creating text and multimedia messages
→ Managing multiple conversations and their messages
→ Setting messaging preferences

Text and Multimedia Messaging

Phone calls can be time consuming and, depending on the caller's timing, intrusive. To get a quick message to a friend or colleague, you can *text* that person by sending a text or multimedia message. A message exchange between you and another person is called a *conversation* or *thread*. The messaging process is similar to what you're probably familiar with from Yahoo! Messenger, Microsoft Messenger, iChat, or Google Talk online chats. Either party can start a conversation. After the conversation is initiated, it can progress in a back-and-forth manner, with each person's contributions shown in colored balloons.

Two types of messages can be exchanged: *SMS* (Short Message Service) text messages and *MMS* (Multimedia Messaging Service) messages to which you've attached a photo, video or audio clip, or similar item. Although text messages are normally exchanged between mobile phones, your service may also allow you to text to an email account or landline.

Texting is strikingly similar to emailing. You specify recipients, compose the message text, and—optionally—add attachments. The main differences are that texting generally occurs between mobile phones, the messages must be short (think Twitter short), and a subject is optional rather than the norm.

Creating Messages

You can use the Messaging app to create both text (SMS) and multimedia (MMS) messages. When creating a message, what distinguishes a text message from a multimedia message is that the latter contains an attachment, such as a photo or video clip.

Composing a Text Message (SMS)

A *text message* can contain only text and is limited to 160 characters. If a message is longer, it is transmitted as multiple messages but recombined on the recipient's screen.

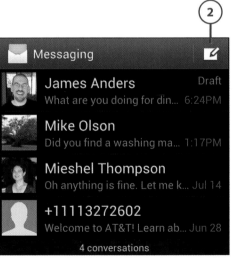

1. Tap the Messaging icon at the bottom of the Home screen. (If you've removed the Messaging shortcut, tap Apps and then tap Messaging.)

2. A screen showing all stored/ongoing conversations appears. Tap the Compose Message icon.

3. A message can have one or multiple recipients. To choose recipients from your stored contacts, tap the Contacts icon. (If you know that the recipient doesn't have a Contacts record, type the person's mobile phone number in the Enter Recipient box and skip to step 7.)

Adding Recipients by Typing

Another method of adding recipients is to type part of the person's contact record (such as a name, number, or email address) in the Enter Recipient box and then select the desired entry from the match list.

Finding Recipients in Contacts

To find someone in Contacts, you can scroll through the list by flicking up or down, go directly to an alphabetical section of the list by tapping its index letter, or drag down or up in the index letters and release your finger when the first letter of the person's name is displayed.

You can also filter the list to show only certain people. To view people with whom you've recently spoken or messaged, tap the Logs tab. Tap the Favorites tab to restrict the list to contacts you've marked as *favorites*. To search for a person, type part of the name, email address, or phone number in the Search box; press the Back key to view the results; and tap the person's check box.

4. Select a recipient from the list by tapping the person's check box.

5. If the selected contact has only one phone number or you've set a default number for him or her, that phone number is automatically used. Otherwise, a screen appears that lists the person's numbers and email addresses. Tap the number to which you want to send the message. The contact list reappears and the person's name is checked as a recipient.

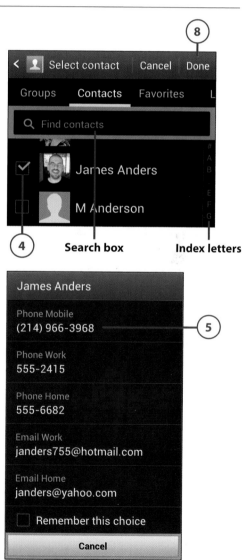

Search box   **Index letters**

Limited or Default Contact Info

If the selected record has only one piece of usable contact information (a single phone number or an email address) or you've set a default number for the person, Messaging assumes that's where you want to send the message. In that case, no selection screen appears and the record is automatically checked. Before sending the message, you may want to open the Contacts application and ensure that the person's record contains a mobile phone number.

6. To add other recipients, select them from the contact list as you did in steps 4 and 5.

7. *Optional:* To remove a recipient, tap the Enter Recipient box to show all current recipients. Tap the recipient that you want to remove and then tap Delete. Similarly, you can modify the person's phone number or email address by tapping Edit.

8. When you're done, tap Done to create the recipient list. The message screen reappears.

9. *Optional:* You can create a subject for the conversation by pressing the Menu key, tapping Add Subject, and then typing or dictating the conversation subject in the Enter Subject box.

10. Enter your message in the large text box. You can type the message or tap the microphone key to dictate your message. (If the microphone isn't shown on the key, press and hold the key and *then* select the microphone.) As you type or dictate, the number of remaining characters is shown above the Send button.

Adding Smileys

If you like to use smileys (also called *emoticons*) in your messages, press the Menu key, tap Insert Smiley, and select the smiley that you want to insert. The smiley appears at the text insertion mark. (You can also select smileys from the keyboard. Tap the **123 Sym** key and repeatedly tap the key above it until **3/3** is displayed on the key.)

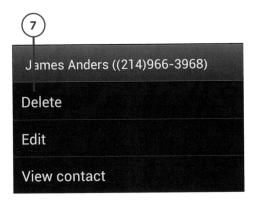

11. *Optional:* To insert a location, contact record, memo, or calendar item into the message, press the Menu key, tap Add Text, and select an option.

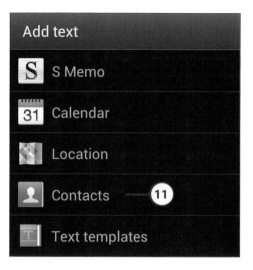

More Special Text Options

If a message contains a web address or phone number (displayed as underlined text), you can tap the text and choose Open URL or Call to visit the page using the phone's browser or dial the phone number, respectively.

12. To transmit the message, tap the Send button.

Saving a Message As a Draft

If you aren't ready to send the message, you can save it as a draft by pressing the Back key. To later open the message, tap it in the conversation list. You can then edit, send, or delete it.

Texting to Email or a Landline

If a recipient doesn't have a mobile phone, some carriers allow you to send text messages to an email address or a landline phone. Create the message as you normally would, but specify an email address or landline number in the Enter Recipient box. As appropriate, the text message is emailed, or the service calls the landline and a computer voice reads the text when the phone is answered.

MORE WAYS TO START A CONVERSATION

Choosing a contact record is only one of the ways to start a texting conversation. Others include these:

- Immediately after completing a call, you can begin a conversation with the person by tapping the envelope icon on the screen that appears.

- To text someone to whom you've recently spoken, open the call log by tapping Phone on the Home screen and then tapping the Logs tab. Find the person in the log and then swipe the entry to the left. You can also use this swipe technique in Contacts and Favorites.

- Open Contacts, select the person's record, and then tap the envelope tab to the right of the mobile phone number.

- You can also send a message to a *group* that you've defined (see "Working with Contact Groups" in Chapter 3, "Managing Contacts"). Launch Contacts, tap the Groups tab, press and hold the group name, and tap Send Message. Select the particular group members that you want to message and tap Done.

Composing a Multimedia Message (MMS)

A *multimedia message* is any message that has one or more attachments—regardless of the attachment type(s).

1. Perform steps 1 through 10 of the previous "Composing a Text Message (SMS)" task.

2. At any time during the message-creation process, tap the paper clip button.

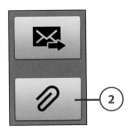

3. In the Attach dialog box, tap the item type that you want to attach to the message. If you're attaching a file that's already on your phone, continue with step 4. If you want to create a *new* file to attach or insert a map location, skip to step 5.

4. Open the enclosing folder and tap the thumbnail of a stored picture, S memo, or video clip to attach it to the message. To add an audio clip, contact record, or calendar item, select it and tap the Done button. Go to step 6.

It's Too Big!

Existing video clips and audio recordings such as songs are often too large to transmit as part of an MMS message. Messaging rejects such items as attachments. Photos, on the other hand, are automatically compressed by Messaging to meet MMS size limits.

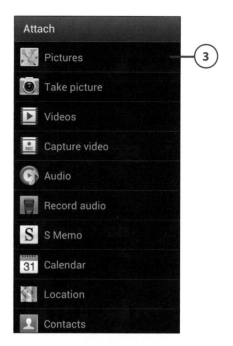

5. Take a new picture or capture a video, and tap Save to add it to the message or tap Discard to try again. Recorded audio is saved and added to the message when you tap the Stop button.

6. A thumbnail representing the media is inserted into the message or the item is shown as a file attachment. As you add items, the total size of the message and attachments is updated.

7. If you want to view/play, remove, or replace a multimedia item, press its thumbnail and then select the appropriate option. (If you remove *all* attachments from a message, it reverts to a text message.)

Another Removal Option

You can also remove a multimedia item by selecting it and tapping the Delete key.

8. When the message is complete, tap Send.

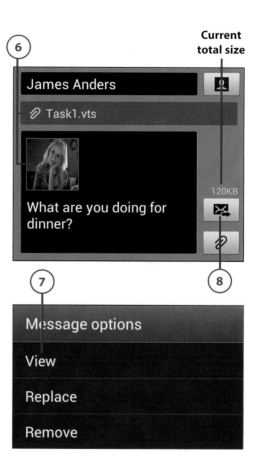

Current total size

James Anders

⌀ Task1.vts

What are you doing for dinner?

120KB

Message options

View

Replace

Remove

It's Not All Good

Managing Conversations

There's more to participating in conversations than just creating new messages. The following tasks explain how to respond to new message notifications; continue, review, and delete conversations; and search for messages.

Responding to a New Message Notification

If you're in Messaging and a message for the current conversation arrives, it simply appears onscreen as a new balloon. If you're doing something else with the phone, the phone is resting quietly on your desk, or you're viewing a different conversation, a new message notification appears.

Depending on your Messaging settings (see "Configuring Messaging Settings," later in this chapter) and what you're doing with the phone, you may be notified of a new message in one of several ways.

- The message text appears briefly in the status bar and is replaced by an envelope icon. The Messaging icon on the Home screen shows the number of new messages and a ringtone may sound.

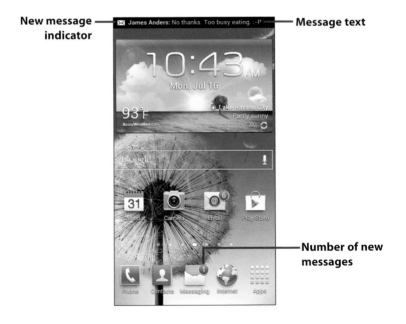

New message indicator — James Anders: No thanks. Too busy eating. :-P — Message text

Number of new messages

Lock Screen Notification

If your screen is dark when a message arrives, press the Power button to display your Lock screen. To view the message in Messaging, slide the new message indicator to the left. You can also launch Messaging from this screen—whether a new message is waiting or not—by swiping the Messaging icon upward.

New message ⎯⎯⎯⎯⎯⎯⎯

New message

Launch Messaging

- You can also view the new message by opening the Notifications panel and tapping the new message notification.

New message ⎯⎯⎯⎯

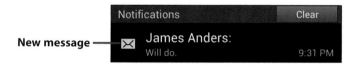

- Finally, you can launch Messaging (if it isn't currently running) and open the conversation that contains the new message.

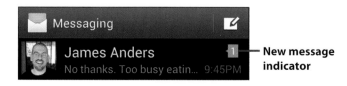

New message indicator

Continuing a Conversation

The default length for a conversation on your phone is 200 text or 20 multimedia messages—whichever occurs first. As long as the length limit hasn't been exceeded, a conversation can be continued immediately or whenever either participant desires—days, weeks, or even months after it was begun.

1. If Messaging isn't already running, launch it by tapping the Messaging icon on the Home screen.

2. Select the conversation that you want to continue by tapping it. The conversation appears.

3. Tap in the Enter Message box at the bottom of the screen.

4. Create a text or multimedia message as described in "Creating Messages," earlier in this chapter.

5. Tap the Send button to transmit the message. It is appended to the end of the conversation.

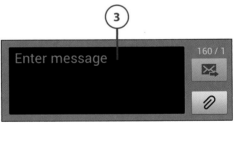

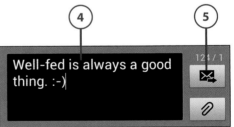

Reviewing a Conversation

As long as you haven't deleted a conversation, you can reread it whenever you like. This is especially useful when a conversation contains important information, such as the scheduled time of an upcoming meeting, a phone number, a URL, or driving directions. To review a conversation, select it on the Messaging screen (as described in the previous task) and scroll through the messages by flicking or dragging up and down.

An Uncluttered View

If you like, you can also display a conversation as one message per screen. Tap any message in the conversation and then flick to the left or right to move from message to message. Press the Back key or tap the Back arrow at the top of the screen when you want to restore the normal, vertically scrolling message list.

Back — < ✉ Mike Olson

8:59AM 08/02/2012

I managed to get spooky into the house while I was talking on the phone to susan. I threw a rock for him to fetch. He picked it up, dropped it In the doorway, and walked into the house. 🤖

Deleting Conversations

For the sake of privacy, saving storage space, or eliminating clutter in the conversation list on the Messaging screen, you can delete entire conversations (*threads*).

1. Tap the Messaging icon on the Home screen. (If you're currently in a conversation, press the Back key until the conversation list appears.)

2. Press the Menu key and tap Delete Threads.

Deleting a Single Conversation

To delete a *single* conversation, press and hold the conversation and tap Delete Thread in the dialog box that appears.

3. Select the conversations that you want to delete or tap Select all to select all conversations.

4. Tap the Delete button.

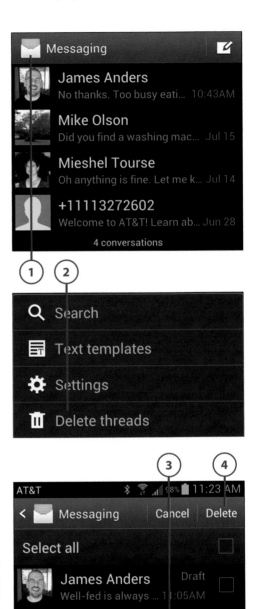

5. Confirm the conversation
deletion(s) by tapping OK.

Deleting Messages

In addition to deleting entire conversations, you can selectively delete
messages from a conversation.

1. In Messaging, open the conversation from which you want to
delete messages.

2. Press the Menu key and tap
Delete Messages.

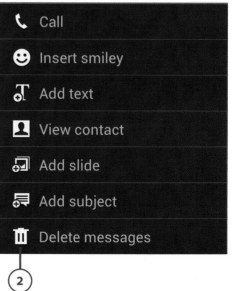

3. Scroll through the conversation and select each message that you want to delete.

4. Tap the Delete button.

5. Tap OK to confirm the deletions.

Deleting a Single Message

To delete a *single* message in a conversation, you can press and hold the message, and then tap Delete Message in the Message Options dialog box that appears.

Other Options for Individual Messages

In addition to deleting individual messages, you can copy a text message to the Clipboard (for pasting elsewhere), lock a message (to prevent it from being deleted), save the multimedia elements in an MMS message to an SD card, forward a message to others, or view a message's properties.

1. Within a conversation, press and hold a message for which you want to display options. The Message Options dialog box appears. SMS and MMS messages offer slightly different options—as explained in step 2.

SMS (text) message

Message options
Delete message
Copy message text
Lock message
Forward
Copy to SIM
View message details

MMS (multimedia) message

Message options
Delete message
Copy message text
Lock message
Save attachment
Forward
View message details

2. Tap a menu option to perform one of the following actions on the message:

- **Delete Message.** Delete the current message.

- **Copy Message Text.** Copy the entire message to the Clipboard, making it eligible for pasting into another message or app, such as an email message.

- **Lock Message.** Prevent an important message from being inadvertently deleted—even if you delete the conversation that contains the message. After a message has been locked, the Lock Message command is replaced by Unlock Message. You can optionally override the lock while attempting to delete the message or delete its conversation.

- **Forward.** Send the message to another recipient—passing along a picture, phone number, address, or driving directions, for example.

- **Copy to SIM (SMS messages only).** Copy the contents of the message to the carrier SIM card that was preinstalled or added by you. (A SIM identifies the phone as authorized to work on the carrier's network. Do not confuse it with an add-in memory card.)

- **Save Attachment (MMS messages only).** Save an attached item, such as a picture or video.

- **View Message Details.** Examine the message properties, such as who sent it and when, the date and time it was received, and its total size including attachments.

Searching for Messages

Within Messaging, you can search all conversations for a specific bit of text.

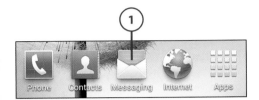

1. If Messaging isn't currently running, tap its icon on the Home screen.

2. On the Messaging main screen (the conversation list), press the Menu key and tap Search. A Search Messages text box appears at the top of the screen.

3. Enter the search text; matches appear as you type. Continue typing until the desired message is shown and then tap to select it.

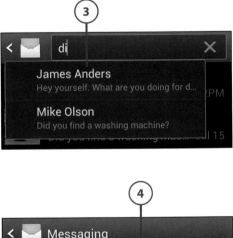

4. The selected message appears on a new screen.

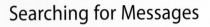

5. *Optional*: If desired, you can tap the message to view the entire conversation. The text of the found message is displayed in boldface.

Configuring Messaging Settings

You can customize the way Messaging works by changing its settings. All changes take effect immediately.

1. Tap the Messaging icon on the Home screen. If you're already in or viewing a conversation, press the Back key until the conversation list appears.

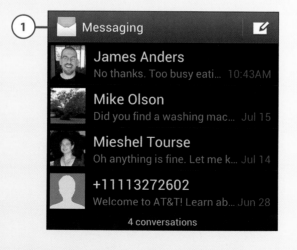

2. Press the Menu key and tap Settings. The Settings screen appears.

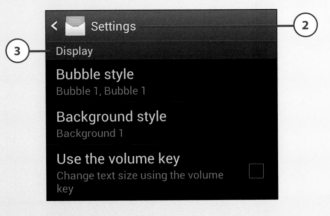

3. **Display Settings.** These settings determine the appearance of conversations.

- Bubble Style enables you to vary the shape and/or color of the message bubbles. The selected top bubble is used to display your messages and the bottom one is used for messages received from others. (Note that the top and bottom sets scroll horizontally—and independently—to show additional colors and styles.) Select a top and a bottom bubble style, and then tap Save.

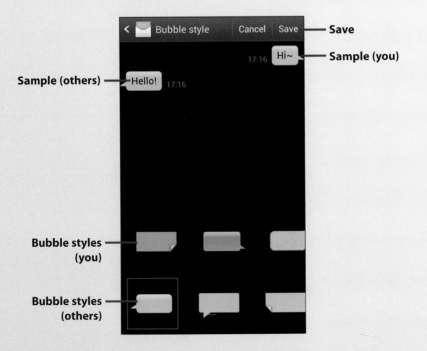

- Background Style enables you to specify a different color and/or style background on which to display the conversations. (Note that the style thumbnails scroll horizontally.) Select a style and then tap Save.

- When enabled, Use the Volume Key lets you use the hardware volume control on the left side of the phone to increase or decrease the size of message text.

4. **Storage Settings.** You can modify these to free up space on the phone and ensure that you aren't needlessly wasting space.

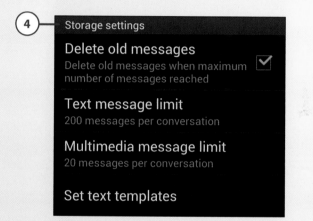

- Enable Delete Old Messages to automatically delete the oldest messages in any conversation that exceed either the text or multimedia message limits (see the next bullet). When disabled, the maximum numbers of text and multimedia messages per conversation are ignored.

- Tap Text Message Limit or Multimedia Message Limit to change the maximum number of messages of that type in a conversation.

- *A text template* is boilerplate text that you can use to quickly create messages or responses to incoming calls. Examples include "What's up?" and "Please call me when you get this message." Tap Set Text Templates to create a new template by clicking the plus (+) icon at the top of the screen, delete unwanted templates by clicking the trash can icon, or edit a text template by pressing and holding it and then choosing Edit. To insert template text into the current message, press the Menu key and tap Add Text, Text Templates, *template phrase*.

5. **Text Message (SMS) Settings.** Specify settings for the creation and handling of text messages. For most users, the default settings are correct. Before changing these settings, you may want to ask your carrier's advice.

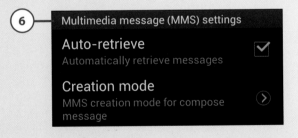

- Manage SIM Card Messages applies only to messages that you've saved to your SIM card with the Copy to SIM message option.

- Message Center displays the phone number of the message center that houses your messages while they're awaiting delivery. If it's necessary to change the number, tap this setting.

- Input Mode enables you to set the default format for text messages to GSM Alphabetic, Unicode, or Automatic.

6. **Multimedia Message (MMS) Settings.** These settings govern the creation and handling of multimedia messages.

- When Auto-retrieve is enabled, the entire content of each multimedia message is automatically retrieved—the message header, body, and attachments. Otherwise, only the message header is retrieved. (If you're on a limited data plan and have friends who constantly attach material to their messages or you find that Auto-retrieve uses up too much of your battery charge, you might want to disable this setting.)

- Setting a Creation Mode enables you to specify the type of multimedia (MMS) messages that you can create. The intent is to avoid creating messages for which your plan assesses special charges. Contact your carrier for the proper setting: Restricted, Warning, or Free.

7. **Push Message Settings.** When Push Messages is enabled (default setting) and new messages are received by the network, they are *pushed* to your phone. That is, you don't have to perform an action to receive the messages—they are simply transmitted to you.

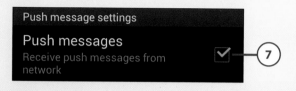

8. **Cell Broadcast (CB) Settings.** When CB Activation is enabled, your phone can receive messages that are designated for many users within a specified area; that is, broadcast messages. (Normal SMS and MMS messages are intended for one-to-one or one-to-few transmission.) You can modify Channel Configuration only when CB Activation is enabled.

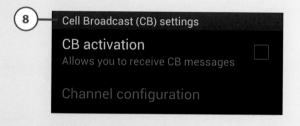

9. **Notification Settings.** These settings determine whether you receive notifications of newly received text and multimedia messages, as well as the manner in which the notifications are presented.

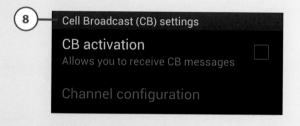

-   Enable Notifications to display notifications of new messages (in the status bar, Notifications panel, and lock screen). To assign an optional sound effect/ringtone to signify a received message, you must first enable Notifications.

-   Tap Select Ringtone to specify the ringtone that announces new messages. Select a ringtone and tap OK.

Ringtone Options

When you tap a ringtone on the Ringtone screen, its sound plays—enabling you to sample many ringtones before committing to one. If you'd rather *not* hear a ringtone when a message arrives, select Silent.

Want to Know More?

For more information about message notifications, see "Responding to a New Message Notification," earlier in this chapter.

10. When you've finished reviewing and changing settings, press the Back key. Changes take effect immediately.

>>>Go Further

MESSAGING CONSIDERATIONS

Here are a few practical and etiquette considerations for texting:

- *Know your service plan.* Although your Galaxy S III is capable of creating and receiving text and multimedia messages, your plan determines how you're charged—whether they're unlimited, limited to a certain number per month, or subject to a per-message charge. Received messages generally count, too—including unsolicited ones. Review your plan before you leap into texting.

- *Check with the recipient before texting.* Whether you *should* text someone depends on many factors, such as the recipient's phone (not all phones can display multimedia messages and many older phones can't handle text messages) and the recipient's data plan. Unless someone has texted you first, it's a good idea to ask before initiating a conversation.

- *You can refuse all incoming messages.* If your plan doesn't allow for texting or it's expensive and you have no interest in receiving messages, contact your plan provider to see if there's a way to block incoming messages. Incoming messages typically cost the same as those you initiate, so you may prefer to refuse them.

Bookmarks

Reload

Windows

In this chapter, you learn how to use the Internet app, the Galaxy S III's built-in web browser. Topics include the following:

→ Launching the browser
→ Visiting web pages
→ Setting options for viewing pages
→ Creating and organizing bookmarks
→ Configuring the browser

Browsing the Web

You're probably already familiar with the basics of using a web browser. Making the transition from browsing on a computer to doing so on your phone will be relatively easy. As with a desktop browser, you can enter page addresses by typing, click links, and bookmark your favorite sites to make it easy to visit them whenever you want.

Launching the Browser

You can launch Internet (the phone's browser app) in several ways. The three most common are as follows:

- On the Home screen, tap the Internet icon at the bottom of the screen. The browser opens to its home page.

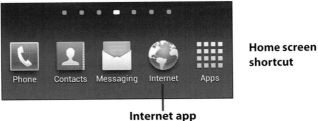

Home screen shortcut

Internet app

- Tap a link in an email message. Links can be blue underlined text, images, or other objects. If the item you tap is a link, it executes immediately and the linked page appears in the browser.

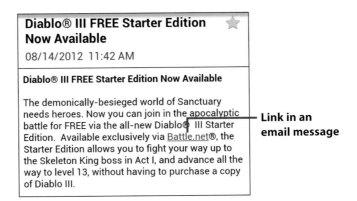

Link in an email message

- Tap a blue underlined web link in a text message. In the dialog box that appears, tap Open URL to open the page in the browser or press the Back key if you've changed your mind.

Link in a text message

Open in browser

Unexpected Web Redirections

Apps and certain documents can contain links that automatically redirect you to web pages, causing the browser to launch if it isn't currently running. For example, if you tap text, an icon, or a button in some apps when searching for instructions, a help file or manual might open in the browser.

Visiting Web Pages

You can go to a particular web page (called an *address* or *URL*) using the same methods that you use with Internet Explorer, Safari, and other popular desktop web browsers. The most common methods are typing the address; tapping a link on the current page; choosing a bookmarked, frequently visited, or recent site or page; and searching for a site or page with one of the popular search engines.

Typing the Address

1. From the Home screen, launch the browser by tapping the Internet icon. The browser opens to its home page.

2. Tap the Address field. The current address is selected.

3. Enter the new address and tap Go. (Because the current address is already selected, typing anything immediately replaces the address.) The web page loads.

Fast Address Selection

As you type, a list of potential addresses appears. If you see the one you want, you can tap it instead of completing the address.

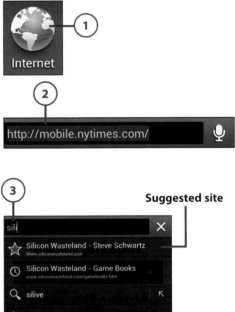

Suggested site

Delete

Go

Following a Link

In the browser, if you tap an object, graphic, or text that represents a link, the linked web page appears. If the item you tap is indeed a link, it's briefly high-lighted in gold before the link is followed.

Page link

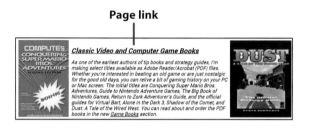

Not Every Link Leads to a Page

Other than special *mobile* versions of web pages (designed for viewing on cellphones), the pages displayed in Internet are identical to those you see in Internet Explorer, Safari, and other desktop browsers. That means that they also contain links designed to download PC and Mac applications, device drivers, and the like. Of course, such programs and drivers can't be used by your phone.

To remove these downloads, press the Menu key and tap Downloads. Tap the check box for each inappropriate download and then tap the Delete icon.

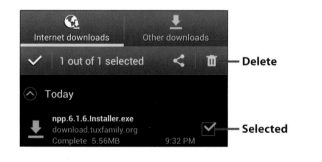

Visiting a Bookmarked, Recent, or Saved Page

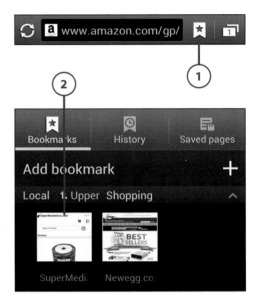

1. Scroll the page up until the Address field is visible and tap the star icon on the right.

2. To visit a *bookmarked* page (one whose address you stored), tap the Bookmarks tab and then tap the page's thumbnail or name. (For information about creating and managing bookmarks, see "Working with Bookmarks," later in this chapter.)

Display Options

Bookmarks can be viewed as a thumbnail grid or a scrolling list. Press the Menu key and then tap List View or Thumbnail View.

You can alter the order of the bookmark thumbnails or list items by pressing the Menu key and tapping Change Order. In Thumbnail View, press and hold any thumbnail and drag it to a new location. In List View, select a bookmark by pressing the dot grid to its right, drag it up or down in the list, and release when it's in the proper position. When you're satisfied with the changes, tap Done—or to ignore the changes, tap Cancel.

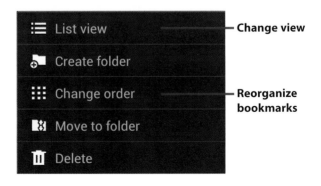

3. To go to a *saved* page (one that you saved for later reading—even when offline), tap the Saved Pages tab, locate the page in the scrolling list, and tap its thumbnail.

Saved Pages

Saving a Page

To add the current page to Saved Pages, press the Menu key and tap Save for Offline Reading. Use this command for any pages that you want to read later or that might not be readily available later, such as receipts for online purchases.

4. To revisit a page you've recently viewed, tap the History tab, locate the page in the scrolling list, and tap its name. To make it easier to find the page in the list, you can show or hide selected page-view periods (Today, Yesterday, Last Month, and so on) by tapping section heads.

Revisiting Favorite Pages

To return to a page that you regularly visit—regardless of whether you bookmarked it—expand the Most Visited section at the end of the History list and then tap the page's name.

Searching for a Site or Page

1. Tap the address box and enter your search phrase, such as "Bally," "exercise machines," or "trimming a parrot's beak." As you type, the search engine builds a list of potential sites and search topics. (The search links take you to your default search engine's site and perform the search; other entries go directly to the specified page.)

2. Do one of the following:

   • Tap a link in the suggestion list to load that page or site.

   • Tap a search entry in the suggestion list—that is, an entry preceded by a magnifying glass—to perform that search in the default search engine's site.

   • Tap the Go key to perform a search using the exact wording and spelling of your search phrase.

Link

Search phrase

Go

Viewing Pages

Similar to your computer browser, the Internet app provides several ways for you to view pages, such as viewing in portrait or landscape mode, scrolling the page, changing the magnification, reloading the page, and displaying multiple pages in separate windows.

Portrait Versus Landscape View

Depending on the direction that you rotate the phone, you can view any page in *portrait* (normal) or *landscape* (sideways) mode. You can change the phone's orientation whenever you want; the page adjusts automatically. (If the orientation doesn't change when you rotate the phone, launch Settings, tap Display, and enable Auto-Rotate Screen.)

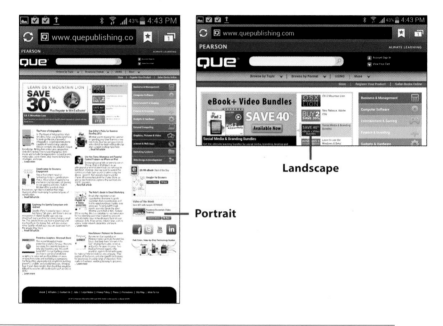

Landscape

Portrait

Scrolling the Page

Many pages won't fit entirely onscreen. To view parts that are presently off-screen, flick or drag up, down, right, or left, depending on the direction you want the page's material to scroll.

Magnification (Zoom)

You can increase the magnification of the current page to make it easier to read (*zoom in*) or reduce it to get a bird's-eye view of the entire page (*zoom out*).

- To *zoom in* (making everything on the page larger), put your thumb and forefinger on the page and spread them apart.

- To *zoom out* (making everything on the page smaller), put your thumb and forefinger on the page and pinch them together.

Zoomed in   **Zoomed out**

Zoom by Tapping and Tilting

You can quickly zoom in or out by double-tapping the screen. Repeat to reverse the zoom. And if you've enabled Tilt to Zoom (a Motion setting), you can place two fingertips on the screen and tilt it toward you to zoom in or away from you to zoom out.

Refreshing the Page

If the current page didn't load correctly or you think the content might have changed while you were viewing it, you can refresh the page. Tap the Reload icon to the left of the address box.

Reload

If a page is loading slowly, you can stop it from finishing. Tap the X icon to the left of the address box.

Stop loading

Working with Windows

The tabbed interface of current Mac and PC browsers allows you to keep several web pages open simultaneously and easily switch among them. The Internet app mimics this feature by enabling you to open multiple *windows*. Each window is the equivalent of a new browser and operates independently of other open windows.

- To create a new window, press the Menu key and tap New Window. You can also tap the Windows icon, followed by the plus (+) symbol on the screen that appears. A window opens, displaying the browser's home page.

- To navigate among or manage the open windows, tap the Windows icon. (You can also get to this screen by pinching when the page is already at its smallest size.) Swipe to the right and left to view the open windows or touch the navigation dots beneath the thumbnails. To view one of the windows, tap its thumbnail. To remove a window that you no longer need, tap its minus (–) icon.

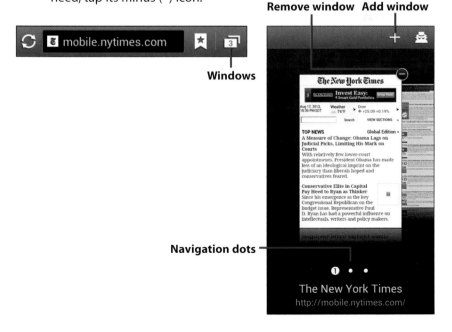

Other Ways to Create a New Window

You can create additional new windows on the window-management screen. On the Bookmarks or History tab, if you press a site's name, you can tap Open in New Window in the menu that appears.

Page Navigation

As you replace the current page with new ones by entering new addresses, tapping links, and selecting bookmarks, Internet provides Back and Forward commands to enable you to move through the stack of pages.

- To return to the previous page, press the Back key. You'll go back one page for each press.

- If you've gone back one or more pages, you can move forward through the stack by pressing the Menu key and tapping Forward.

Forward ———

Adjusting the Browser's Brightness and Colors

If Automatic Brightness isn't enabled (Settings, Display, Brightness), you can manually adjust the browser's brightness and colors.

1. Press the Menu key and tap Brightness and Colors.

2. If it's enabled, remove the check mark from the Automatic Brightness check box.

3. Drag the Brightness slider to the desired setting. The higher the setting, the faster the battery drains.

4. Set the background color level by tapping a radio button. At lower levels (Default or 1), the colors are more saturated but the battery drains quicker.

5. Tap OK.

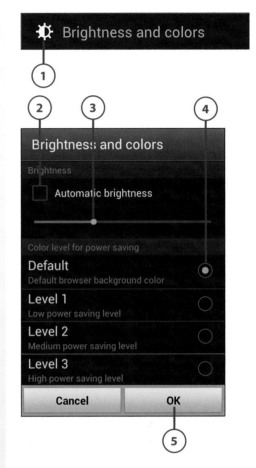

Incognito Browsing

The Internet app supports *incognito browsing* in which no entries are recorded in History, searches aren't recorded, and cookies aren't stored. Rather than make this a general browser setting, Internet enables it only for pages loaded into a designated incognito window.

1. Tap the Window icon at the top of any browser page.

2. At the top of the Windows screen, tap the Incognito icon.

3. A new incognito window appears; the address bar is preceded by an incognito icon. Web activities performed in this window are secure; activities performed in *other* Internet windows are recorded normally.

4. To restore normal browsing, tap the Window icon at the top of any browser page, scroll to the incognito page, and delete the page by tapping the minus (–) icon in its upper-right corner.

You've gone incognito. Pages you view in this window won't appear in your browser history or search history, and they won't leave other traces, like cookies, on your device after you close the incognito window. Any files you download or bookmarks you create will be preserved, however.

Going incognito doesn't affect the behavior of other people, servers, or software. Be wary of:

- Websites that collect or share information about you
- Internet service providers or employers that track the pages you visit
- Malicious software that tracks your keystrokes in exchange for free smileys
- Surveillance by secret agents
- People standing behind you

Yahoo!
http://m.yahoo.com/?tsrc=sam...

Working with Bookmarks

As explained earlier in this chapter, *bookmarks* are stored addresses of websites and pages that you regularly visit. The purpose of creating a bookmark is to enable you to view the site or page again by simply tapping an entry in the Bookmarks grid or list rather than having to reenter its address.

Creating a Bookmark from the Current Page

It's common to decide to bookmark a page as you're viewing it.

1. Scroll the page up until the Address field is visible and tap the star icon at the right.

2. Tap Add Bookmark.

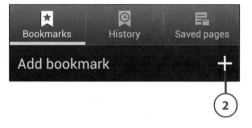

Another Path to the Dialog Box

You can also go to the Add Bookmark screen by pressing the Menu key and tapping Add Bookmark.

3. On the Add Bookmark screen, edit the bookmark name, address, and storage folder, if necessary.

Using Bookmark Folders

By default, new bookmarks are stored in the Home folder. If you've created additional folders (see "Organizing Bookmarks in Folders," later in this section), you can also specify the folder in which the bookmark is stored.

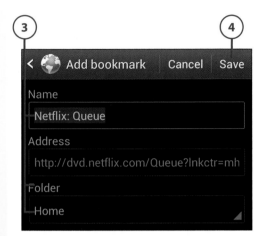

4. Tap Save to store the new bookmark.

Creating a Bookmark from the History List

If you've recently visited a page, the quickest way to add it as a new bookmark is to locate it in the Most Visited or History list.

1. Scroll the current page up until the Address field is visible and tap the star icon at the right.

2. Tap the History tab and locate the page that you want to bookmark.

3. Tap the star icon to the right of the entry, or press and hold the entry and tap Add Bookmark.

4. On the Add Bookmark screen, make the necessary corrections and tap Save.

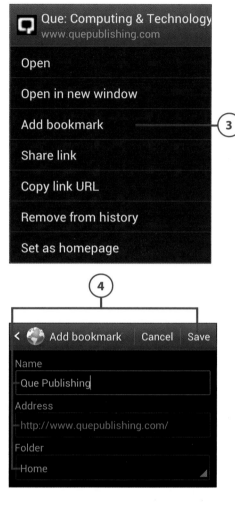

Editing Bookmarks

You can edit a bookmark's title, its address (setting it for a site's main page or another specific page), or the folder in which it's stored.

1. Scroll the current page up until the Address field is visible and tap the star icon to the right.

2. Tap the Bookmarks tab and locate the bookmark that you want to edit.

3. Press and hold the bookmark until the menu appears. Tap Edit Bookmark.

4. In the Edit Bookmark dialog box, make the desired changes to the name, URL, and/or folder and tap Save.

Editing the URL

Although you normally won't want to edit a page's URL if it requires a lot of typing, it's relatively simple to change a page-specific URL to one that goes to a site's main page. In the example shown in step 4, I changed the reference from a Newegg promotions page to the site's main page.

Organizing Bookmarks in Folders

After amassing more than a handful of bookmarks, you can optionally create additional folders in which to organize your bookmarks instead of storing them loose in the main folder (Home). When creating a new bookmark or editing an existing one, you can freely move it into the most appropriate folder.

Creating a Bookmark Folder

1. Scroll the current page up until the Address field is visible and tap the star icon to the right.

2. With the Bookmarks tab selected, press the Menu key and tap Create Folder.

3. On the Select Folder screen, tap to select the *parent* (containing) folder for the new folder.

4. On the Create Folder screen, enter a name for the new folder and tap Save. The new folder is added to the Bookmarks list.

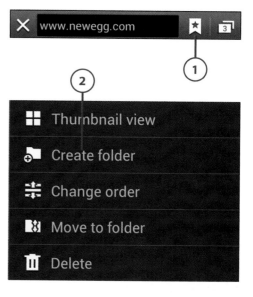

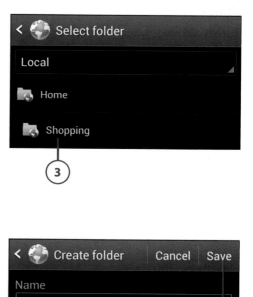

Moving Bookmarks into Folders

1. Scroll the current page up until the Address field is visible, and tap the star icon to the right.

2. With the Bookmarks tab selected, press the Menu key and tap Move to Folder.

3. As necessary, open folders to expose the bookmarks that you want to move. Select each bookmark to move by tapping its thumbnail (in Thumbnail View) or its check box (in List View), and then tap Done.

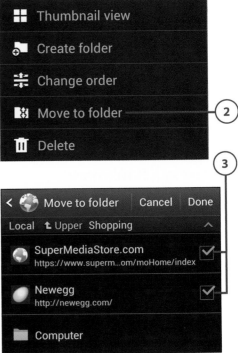

Selecting Bookmarks in Thumbnail View

When a bookmark is selected in Thumbnail View, a green—difficult to see—check mark is added to its thumbnail. Because of this, it may be easier for you to work in List View.

Selected bookmarks

4. On the Select Folder screen, tap the destination folder. All selected bookmarks move to the designated folder.

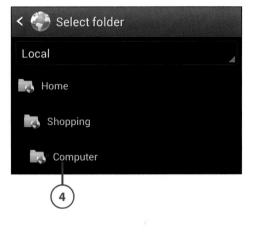

Deleting Bookmarks

You can delete bookmarks that you no longer use. (Preinstalled bookmarks *cannot* be deleted. Only the bookmarks that you created are eligible for deletion.)

1. Scroll the current page up until the Address field is visible, and tap the star icon to the right.

2. Tap the Bookmarks tab and locate the bookmark that you want to delete.

3. Press and hold the bookmark until the menu appears. Tap Delete Bookmark.

4. Confirm the bookmark's deletion by tapping OK.

Deleting Multiple Bookmarks

When deleting a single bookmark, using the method described in this task list is very efficient. If you want to clean house, though, the Internet app enables you to simultaneously delete as many bookmarks as you want.

With the Bookmarks list displayed, press the Menu key and tap Delete. Scroll through the bookmarks and tap the check box of each one that you want to delete. Tap the Delete button to complete the process.

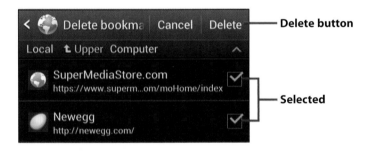

More Menu Commands

The menu contains additional useful commands. Here's an explanation of what the remaining ones do.

1. With any web page displayed, press the Menu key to reveal the scrolling menu. Other than Desktop View, Downloads, Brightness and Colors, and Settings, each command applies only to the current page.

2. *Forward.* If you've gone back one or more pages, you can tap Forward to move forward one page through the stack.

3. *New Window.* Create a new window (for the Android equivalent of tabbed browsing). For information about working with multiple windows, see "Working with Windows," earlier in the chapter.

4. *Add Bookmark.* Create a bookmark for the current page (see "Working with Bookmarks," earlier in this chapter).

5. *Add Shortcut to Home.* Place a shortcut icon for the current page on the phone's Home screen. When you tap the shortcut, the Internet app launches and displays the web page.

6. *Share Page.* Share the page with another person or device using a variety of methods.

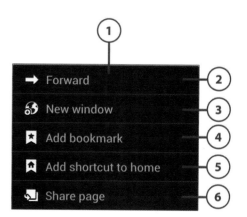

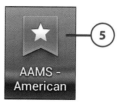

7. *Find on Page.* Search the current page for a text string. Each match (if any) is highlighted. To move between matches, press an arrow key. The page scrolls as necessary to display each match.

8. *Desktop view.* Display all pages as though they were being viewed on a desktop browser.

9. *Save for Offline Reading.* Adds the current page to Saved Pages, enabling you to read it at any time—including when you're offline. For more information, see "Visiting a Bookmarked, Recent, or Saved Page," earlier in the chapter.

10. *Brightness and Colors.* Adjust the screen brightness and color saturation (see "Adjusting the Browser's Brightness and Colors," earlier in the chapter).

11. *Downloads.* Display a list of downloaded files. Tap the day or date range heading to expand or collapse a section. To open a downloaded item, tap its name. To share or delete items, tap each one's check box, followed by the Share or Delete icon that appears at the top of the screen. To change the current sort order, tap the button at the bottom of the screen.

12. *Print.* Print the current web page on a compatible Samsung Wi-Fi printer.

13. *Settings.* View and modify Internet preferences (see "Configuring the Browser," in the next section).

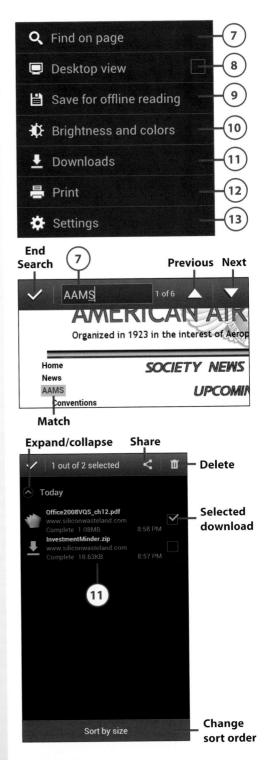

Configuring the Browser

As is the case with a Mac or PC browser, you can configure Internet to match your preferred way of working and perform common browser actions, such as clearing the cache and managing cookies.

1. With any web page displayed, press the Menu key and tap Settings to display the Settings menu.

2. The Settings screen appears, divided into six categories:

   - *General.* Set a home page; enable form auto-fill.

   - *Privacy and Security.* Clear the cache and history; accept and clear cookies; remember and clear form data, location access, passwords, and notifications.

   - *Accessibility.* Zoom control; text size and scaling; inverted screen rendering; contrast.

   - *Advanced.* Set default search engine; open new windows in foreground or background; enable/disable JavaScript and plug-ins; default storage location and zoom magnification; auto-fit pages to fit screen; block pop-ups; reset browser settings to defaults.

   - *Bandwidth Management.* Preload search results; disable web page image downloads.

   - *Labs.* Hide parts of the display.

   To view or modify settings, tap a category, make the necessary changes, and press the Back key repeatedly until the browser screen reappears.

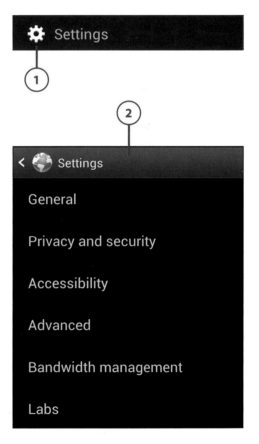

Select account or folder

Compose message

Refresh

Expand/ collapse group

Unread message

Read message

Flagged message

Inbox
Hotmail (9)

Today (3)   07/22/2012

Today's Shell Shocker De...
Newegg.com   11:30 PM
Ensure delivery by adding promo@e...

Steve, you have notificati...
Facebook   10:47 PM
= To login to Facebook, follow the li...

Weekly Offers: Save up to ...
goHastings.com   4:10 AM
40% OFF USED Books & CDs*, 30...

Yesterday (2)   07/21/2012

Weekend Deals! $179.99 ...
Newegg.com   07/21/2012
To view this email with images, clic...

Today's Shell Shocker De...
Newegg.com   07/21/2012
Ensure delivery by adding promo@e...

Friday (5)   07/20/2012

Dice JobAlert - writer: Me...
Dice JobAlert   07/20/2012

In this chapter, you add important email accounts to the phone so that you can send and receive email and attachments. Topics include the following:

→ Adding and configuring email accounts

→ Automatically and manually checking for new email

→ Reading mail and working with attachments

→ Composing new messages, replying to messages, and forwarding messages

→ Adding attachments and inserting material into messages

→ Managing email by deleting messages, moving messages to a different folder or account, starring and flagging important messages, and toggling a message's read status

Sending and Receiving Email

You can easily configure your phone to send and receive mail for your POP3, IMAP, and Exchange Server email accounts. In addition, the Email app supports many web-based accounts—as long as they also provide POP, IMAP, or Exchange support. If you aren't sure what types of email accounts you can set up, contact your *ISP* (Internet service provider), call your IT department, or review the Help information for your web-based accounts. (For information on creating and adding *Gmail accounts*, see Chapter 1, "Galaxy S III Essentials.")

Adding Email Accounts

You can add accounts to your phone in two ways. First, for many POP and IMAP accounts, you may be able to add accounts *automatically* by entering only your email address and the account password.

Second, if this method fails, if the wrong Internet standard protocol is selected for you (POP3 instead of IMAP, for example), or if you have an Exchange Server account, you can enter the necessary information *manually*. Note that you may need to know the names of the account's incoming and outgoing mail servers. If you're adding an Exchange Server account, contact your network administrator or IT department for the necessary information.

Automatically Adding an Account

1. On the center Home screen, tap the Email icon. (If the icon isn't present, you can tap Apps and then Email.)

2. On Email's main screen, press the Menu key and tap Settings.

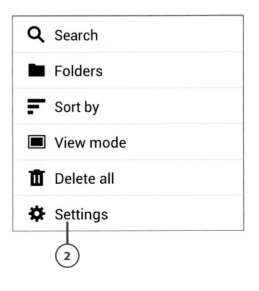

3. On the Settings screen, tap the plus (+) icon to add an account.

4. On the Set Up Email screen, enter your full email address and account password. If you have difficulty using the onscreen keyboard, tap the Show Password check box to ensure that you're entering the password correctly.

5. *Optional:* If you want the phone to treat this as your main, default account from which email is normally sent, tap the Send Email from This Account by Default check box.

6. Tap the Next button.

7. Email attempts to verify the account and determine the correct Internet standard protocol to use: POP3, IMAP, or Exchange.

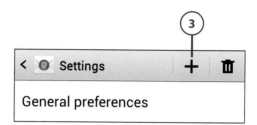

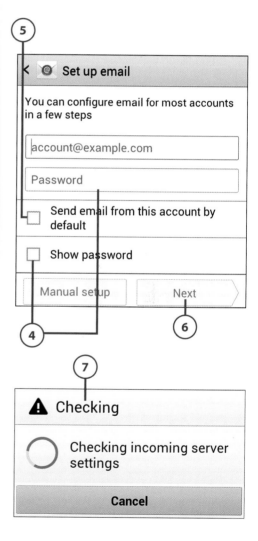

8. If successful, you're given an opportunity to name the account and specify the name that is displayed on outgoing mail from the account. Make any necessary changes and tap Done.

No Option to Set the Display Name

Certain account types, such as Hotmail, automatically take the display name from your current account information.

9. The account's Inbox appears, and email is downloaded to the account.

Try Manual Setup

If there's a problem, an error dialog appears. Tap the Edit Details button to return to the previous screen, check your username and password for errors, and try again. If automatic setup fails *repeatedly*, use the manual setup method described in the next section.

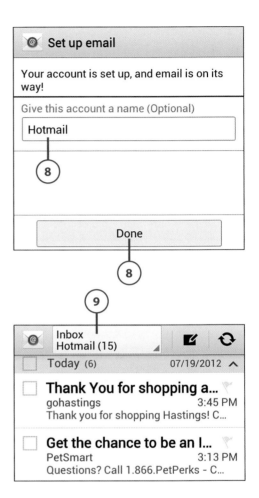

Edit Details button

Manually Adding an Account

1. Perform steps 1–5 of the previous task list ("Automatically Adding an Account") and tap the Manual Setup button.

Continuing from Automatic Setup

If you just performed an automatic setup and it failed with an error in step 7, you can also begin manual setup here.

---

2. On the Add Email Account screen, specify the Internet standard protocol for sending and receiving account email by tapping its button. If you aren't sure which protocols are supported, contact your ISP or IT department for the correct option(s).

3. Check the proposed settings on the Incoming Server Settings screen and make any necessary changes. Tap the Next button.

< @ **Incoming server settings**

User name

lizards —————— **Username**

Password

••••••••

IMAP server

imap.cable.com

Security type

None ◢

Port

143

IMAP path prefix

Optional

Next

3

Entering Your Username

Depending on the account provider, the username may be the part of the name that precedes the @ symbol or it may be the complete email address. If this step fails and an error dialog appears, tap the Edit Details button, enter the username the other way, and try it again.

Delete Mail from Server (POP3 Only)

If you're adding a POP3 account, scroll to the bottom of the screen and you'll see a Delete Email from Server option. Normally, POP3 email is deleted from the mail server immediately after it's delivered. If this account is also on other devices, such as your computer or tablet, leave this option set to Never to ensure that the messages are also delivered to the other devices. If this is your *only* device, choose When I Delete from Inbox.

This option isn't presented for IMAP accounts. Because IMAP is designed to synchronize across all your devices, if you delete an email message on *any* device, it's simultaneously deleted from *all* devices. Otherwise, the message remains on the server indefinitely.

Delete email —— Never
options (POP3)

When I delete from Inbox

4. The Outgoing Server Settings screen appears. Check the details, make any necessary changes, and tap Next.

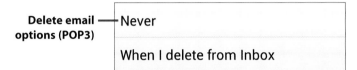

< @ **Outgoing server settings**

SMTP server

smtp.cable.com

Security type

None

Port

587

☑ Require sign-in

User name

lizards@cable.com

Password

••••••••

Next —— ④

5. On the Account Options screen, specify settings and tap Next.

6. Name the account and specify the name to display on outgoing mail from the account. Tap Done.

7. The account's Inbox appears, and email is downloaded to the account.

< ◎ Account options

Email check frequency

Every 15 minutes

☐ Send email from this account by default

☑ Notify me when email arrives

☑ Automatically download attachments when connected to Wi-Fi

Next

⑤

@ Set up email

Your account is set up, and email is on its way!

Give this account a name (Optional)

Cable (Lizards)

Your name (Displayed on outgoing messages)

Steve Schwartz

Done

⑥

⑦

@ Inbox
Cable (Lizards) ...

1 month ago (1) ⌃

☐ Welcome to Keep On Truc... ☆
E.R. Stephens, Founder ...   06/19/2012
Dear Steven We wish to welcome yo...

It's Not All Good

Tips for Adding Accounts

Adding an email account doesn't always go smoothly. In my recent attempts, for example, success was sporadic. Here are some actions to take when adding an account fails:

- *Try, try again.* When using automatic setup, if you're certain that the username and password are correct, wait awhile and try again. Because of the vagaries of the Internet and the fact that mail servers aren't available 100% of the time, you may simply have been unlucky on the initial attempt—or three.

- *Switch to manual.* When repeated automatic attempts fail, it's time to switch to manual. If you try manual setup immediately after an automatic failure, much of the correct information is already filled in. Leave it as is, but try the username as the full email address and as only the username—with *@domain* stripped off. Some mail servers have specific requirements for the username and will accept it only in one form. (In automatic mode, you *must* use the full email address—even if only the username portion is all that's normally accepted.)

- *Contact your ISP or IT department.* When all else fails, contact your ISP or network administrator, find out the *exact* settings needed, and—in manual mode—override the proffered settings with the ones you're given.

Configuring Email Accounts

With the exception of General Preferences, the settings for each email account can differ. After adding each email account, check its settings to ensure that the default choices are satisfactory. (To view or change the General Preferences, display any message list, press the Menu key, tap Settings, and then tap General Preferences.)

Editing Account Settings

You can change a variety of settings to ensure that your messages are retrieved on a reasonable schedule, display proper identifying information, and so on. Note that an Exchange ActiveSync account (such as a Hotmail or a corporate Exchange Server account) has some additional options that aren't available for POP or IMAP accounts.

1. Within Email, press the Menu key and tap Settings.

2. The Settings screen appears. Tap the account whose settings you want to review or change.

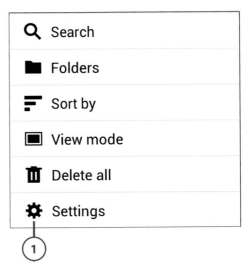

3. *Account Name*. To change the name used to label the account in Email's account list, tap Account Name, make the necessary changes, and tap OK.

4. *Your Name*. To change the name used to identify you to recipients of your email, tap Your Name, make the desired changes, and tap OK.

5. *Signature*. To automatically add a personal *signature* to each outgoing message, enable the Signature option by sliding it to On. To change the signature, tap Signature, edit the current signature, and then tap OK.

6. *Default Account*. If you have multiple email accounts on the phone, you must enable Default Account for one of them. When composing a new email message, the default account is automatically proposed as the sending account—although you're always free to choose a different account before sending. (When replying to or forwarding a message, the current account is proposed instead of the default account.) To designate this account as the default account for outgoing messages, tap the Default Account check box.

< errata@link.net

Common settings

Account name
errata   ⊘ — 3

Your name
Steve Schwartz   ⊘ — 4

Signature
From my Android phone on
T-Mobile. The first
nationwide 4G network.   ON — 5

Default account
Send email from this account by
default   ☐ — 6

Always Cc/Bcc myself
Include my email address in Cc/Bcc
line   ⊘

Forward with files   ☑

Recent messages
25   ⊘

Show images   ☐

5

Signature

Carefully crafted by Steve Schwartz

Cancel | OK

7. *Always Cc/Bcc Myself.* Specify whether outgoing messages automatically include this account in the *CC* (carbon copy) or *BCC* (blind carbon copy) recipient list. The purpose is to ensure that a backup copy of each outgoing message from this account is also delivered to the account's Inbox. If you choose Cc, the recipient will see your name as a recipient; if you choose Bcc, your name won't be visible as a recipient.

8. *Forward with Files.* Enable this option if you want to forward received email with any attachments that the original message contained; otherwise, only the message body is forwarded.

9. *Recent Messages.* Tap to set the number of recent messages to be shown at one time. You can specify from 25 to all (Total).

10. *Show Images.* Enable this option to automatically display all linked images that are present in messages.

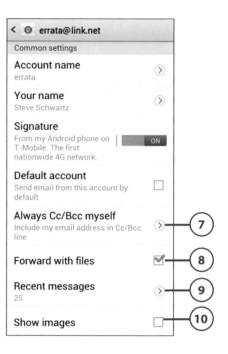

Newegg email with images hidden

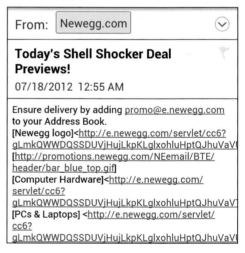

SHOW IMAGES JUDICIOUSLY

If you shop on the Internet, you probably receive sales fliers from sites such as Amazon, Newegg, and JC Penny. To make these messages smaller, they frequently contain *links to images on the web* rather than the actual images. To automatically see the images, you must enable Show Images.

Unfortunately, spammers also include linked images in their emails. If you display them in a spam message, the image is retrieved by Email—simultaneously verifying to the spammer that your email address is a real, active one. *Loads* of spam is liable to follow. The safest approach is to disable Show Images. To view linked images in a trusted, *safe* message, scroll to the end of the message, tap the Load More Details button, and then tap the Show Images button that appears directly under the message header. Another option for trusted messages—if the message provides it—is to click a link to view the message in your phone's browser (Internet).

Download and display linked images

Show images

Click to view this email in a browser ——— View in browser

11. *Email Check Frequency.* Specify how often the phone will automatically check for new, incoming email from this account.

Check Frequency Suggestions

Some web-based email accounts (such as Hotmail) must not be automatically checked more than once every 15 minutes. For accounts that seldom receive new mail, you might choose Once a Day or Never—periodically performing a manual *refresh* to check for new mail, as explained later in this chapter.

12. *Size to Retrieve Emails.* Specify the maximum size message that will automatically be delivered to the phone: 2, 50, or 100 KB. Larger messages—primarily those with attachments—must be manually retrieved by tapping the message header.

(11)

Data usage	
Email check frequency Every 15 minutes	⟩
Size to retrieve emails 50 KB	⟩

(12)

Email check frequency	
Never	○
Every 5 minutes	○
Every 10 minutes	○
Every 15 minutes	○
Every 30 minutes	○
Every hour	○
Every 4 hours	○
Once a day	◉ — **(11)**
Cancel	

13. *Email Notifications.* Enable this option if you want an email icon to appear in the status bar whenever new mail arrives.

14. *Select Ringtone.* Change the notification sound that plays when new mail arrives. In the Select Ringtone menu, tap ringtones to hear them. When you've made your selection, tap OK.

No Ringtone

Select Silent if you don't want an audible notification of new mail.

15. *Vibrate.* Tap this option to specify whether the phone also vibrates when it receives mail and when it occurs.

---

(13)

Notification settings

Email notifications
Notify in status bar when email arrives

Select ringtone ─(14)
Postman

Vibrate ─(15)
Never

---

(13)

✉@   ✳ 📶 ᵃ|| 100% 🔋 10:19 PM

Select ringtone

Harmonics   ○
Join Hangout   ○
Join Hangout   ○
Knock   ○
On time   ○
Opener   ○
Postman   ⦿
Pure bell   ○
Temple bell   ○ ─(14)
Tickety-tock   ○
Whistle   ○

| Cancel | OK |

Vibrate

Always   ○
Only in silent mode   ○
Never   ⦿─(15)

Cancel

16. In the Server Settings section, tap Incoming Settings or Outgoing Settings to modify the specifications for the incoming or outgoing mail server (described in "Adding Email Accounts," earlier in this chapter).

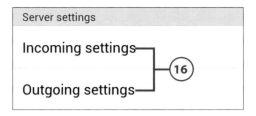

Deleting an Account

You can delete any email account that you no longer want on your phone. Deleting an account simultaneously removes the account's messages and other data from your phone. (Note that deleting an account merely removes it from the phone; it doesn't *cancel* the account.)

1. Within Email, press the Menu key and tap Settings.

2. The Settings screen appears and displays your list of email accounts. Tap the trash icon at the top of the screen.

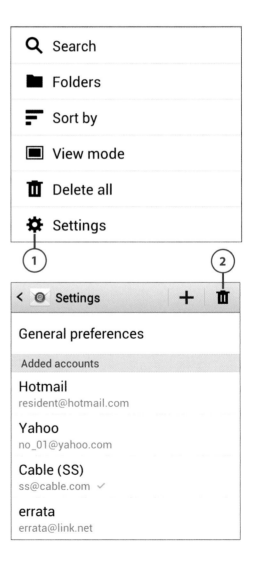

3. Tap the check box of each account that you want to remove from the phone, and then tap the Delete button.

4. Tap the Delete button in the Delete confirmation dialog box.

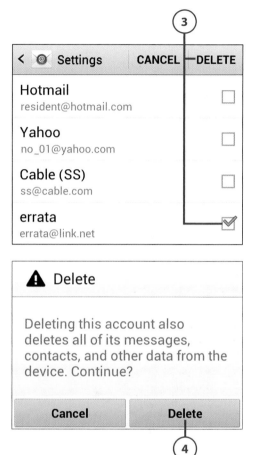

Retrieving Mail

Email can be delivered to your phone in two ways. First, a check for new mail is automatically performed for each account according to the schedule that you set—every 15 minutes or once per hour, for example. For information on setting a retrieval schedule for an account, see step 11 of "Editing Account Settings." Second, you can manually check for new mail whenever you like—regardless of an account's schedule—by tapping the Refresh icon.

1. Launch Email by tapping its Home screen icon or by tapping Apps, followed by Email.

2. When viewing a message list (such as Inbox for a particular account or Combined Inbox for all accounts), tap the Refresh icon. When the message list is for a single account, only that account is checked for new mail. When viewing Combined Inboxes, all accounts are checked.

Active account/ folder   Select a different account or folder

Reading Mail

When new mail arrives or you want to review older messages, you can read the email on your phone. Messages can be read in portrait mode or—by rotating the phone—in landscape mode.

1. Launch Email by tapping its Home screen icon or by tapping Apps and then Email.

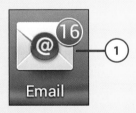

Other Ways to Launch Email

You can also open Email by responding to a received mail notification:

- Touch the status bar and open the Notifications panel by dragging downward. Tap the Email notification.

Email notification —

- If you've installed the Email 4 x 4 widget, tap a message header to open that message in Email.

Email widget

2. *Optional:* To view a specific account's Inbox, tap the folder/account indicator at the top of the screen and make a new selection. Select Combined View to simultaneously view all accounts' Inboxes, select a specific account to view only its Inbox, or select Show All Folders to view a different folder within the current account or selection.

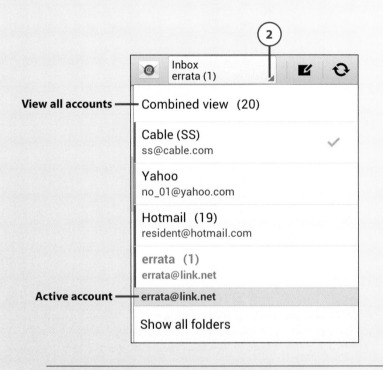

View all accounts ── Combined view

Active account ── errata@link.net

Interpreting the Accounts Information

If present, the number to the right of an account in the list indicates the number of unread messages it contains. By scanning the list, you can quickly determine which accounts have new messages.

3. In the current message list, tap the header of the message that you want to read. Headers in black boldface type are unread messages; headers on a gray background denote previously read messages.

4. The message appears. You can change the magnification by pinching your fingers together or spreading them apart. Drag to see parts of the message that are off-screen.

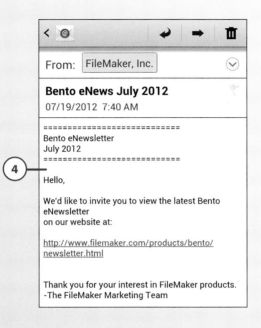

5. If you rotate the screen, you can view the message in landscape mode. (Note that the Auto-rotate Screen option in Display Settings must be enabled. See Chapter 17, "Customizing Your Phone," for information on viewing and changing settings.)

6. To read another message in the current list, do either of the following:

   • Press the Back key to return to the message list and tap the header of the next message that you want to read.

   • Swipe the screen to the left or right to view the next or previous consecutive message in the list, respectively.

Viewing and Saving Attachments

Some email messages contain *attachments* (accompanying files), such as photos and documents. If you want, you can download the attachments and—if you have compatible app(s)—view the files on your phone.

1. In the Email message list, files that contain attachments are denoted by a paper clip icon. Tap the message header to open the message.

2. Tap the Attachments tab to view the list of attached files.

3. To open an attachment for viewing, tap its filename. The file downloads to your phone and, if a compatible app is installed, the file's contents are displayed or played.

4. *Optional*: To save a copy of the file on your phone, click the disk icon to the right of the filename or click the Save All disk icon to download and save all attachments. The file or files are stored in the Download folder of the phone's built-in memory.

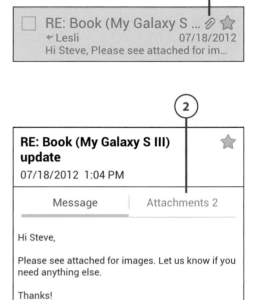

Revisiting a Downloaded Attachment

To later view a downloaded attachment, you can open the file by launching My Files, navigating to the Download folder, and then tapping the filename. If the attachment is an image file, you can also open it by launching Gallery, opening the Download folder, and tapping the file's thumbnail.

Folder location — (path)

Downloaded — attachment

STANDARD VERSUS CONVERSATION VIEW

To more easily find messages, you can configure the message list in either of two views: standard or conversation. In standard view, each message, reply, and forwarded message is shown with a separate message header and the messages are organized in groups, such as Date or Sender. You can collapse or expand the headers for any group by tapping the icon to the right of the group designator. In addition, you can sort standard view in several other ways, such as by sender or read/unread status. Press the Menu key and tap Sort By to set a new sort order.

In conversation view, messages are grouped by conversation, according to their Subject. For example, suppose that you and a co-worker exchange several messages with the subject Budget Proposal. In the Inbox, all received messages with the subject Budget Proposal and RE: Budget Proposal are grouped together under a single expandable message header. To change views, display the message list, press the Menu key, tap View Mode, and select Standard View or Conversation View.

Although helpful, conversation view falls short when compared to its implementation in Microsoft Outlook and other email clients. Although conversation view groups together messages *from* the same person (in the Inbox) or *to* the same person (in Sent), you can only see one side of a conversation. To view the entire conversation, you have to switch back and forth between the account's Inbox and Sent folders.

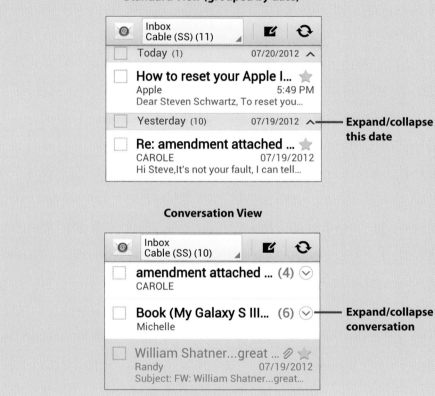

Composing and Sending Mail

Within Email, you can create new messages, as well as reply to or forward received messages.

Creating a New Email Message

1. In Email, display the message list for Combined View or a specific account, and then tap the Create Message icon.

2. A new message screen appears, addressed from the current account. (If you're viewing the Combined View message list, your default email account is proposed instead.)

3. *Optional:* To send the message from a different account, tap the account name in the From box. In the Select Email Address list, select the account from which the message will be sent.

4. *Optional:* The address section normally contains only a To box in which to enter message recipients. To add *Cc* (carbon copy) and *Bcc* (blind carbon copy) boxes, press the Menu key and tap Add Cc/Bcc.

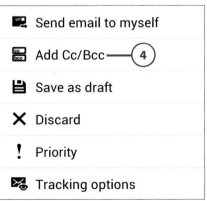

| | Inbox |
| @ | Hotmail (5) |

(2) (3) (1) (5)

| < @ | New email | | 📎 | ✉ |

From: Hotmail <resident@hotmail....

To: 👤

Subject:

↺ ↻ ⛰ T⁺ Tᴛ **B** *I*

Select email address

Yahoo
no_01@yahoo.com

Cable (SS)
ss@cable.com

Hotmail
resident@hotmail.com

errata —— (3)
errata@link.net

Cancel

✉ Send email to myself

Add Cc/Bcc —— (4)

💾 Save as draft

✖ Discard

❗ Priority

✉ Tracking options

5. Select the To, Cc, or Bcc box and add one or more recipients by doing the following:

- To select recipients from Contacts, tap the Contacts icon to the right of the To, Cc, or Bcc box. Select each person that you want to add and then tap Done. (If there are multiple email addresses for a person and you haven't specified a default address for him or her, a dialog box appears in which you can choose the appropriate address.)

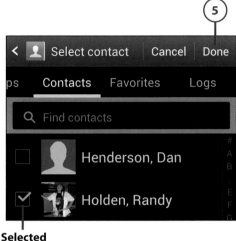

Selected recipient

Filter the Contacts

In addition to selecting people from the normal Contacts list, you can select people from any of the other lists (Groups, Favorites, or Logs) by tapping the appropriate tab at the top of the screen.

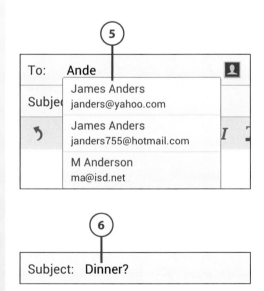

- Select the To, Cc, or Bcc box, and begin typing part of the recipient's name, email address, or other identifying information stored in the person or company's contact record. Select the recipient from the match list that appears.

6. Enter the message subject in the Subject box.

7. Type or use voice input to enter the message body.

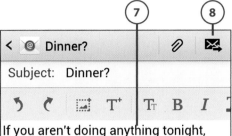

Be Gone Plain Text!

While composing the message, you can tap icons in the toolbar to format selected text, insert material, and assist in editing or making corrections. The icons' functions are similar to those found in a typical word-processing application. You can use Undo and Redo to correct errors and typos, insert boilerplate text and other material into the message body, and format currently selected text by changing its size, color, highlighting, or style. Read "Entering Text" and "Editing Text" in Chapter 2 for additional helpful information.

8. Tap the Send button to transmit the message.

Attachments and Inserts

An email message can optionally include embedded material or be accompanied by attached files. For instructions, see "Adding Attachments and Inserts," later in this section.

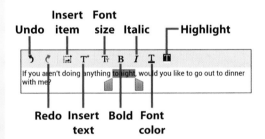

Replying to Mail

1. With the email message open for reading, tap the Reply icon.

Replying in the Message List

You can also create a reply while viewing the message list. Press and hold the header of the message to which you want to reply, and choose Reply in the pop-up menu that appears.

2. A message appears, formatted as a reply to the original sender. The text insertion mark is positioned for your reply. The original message text is displayed at the bottom of the window.

3. Enter your reply text in the top section of the message window.

4. If desired, you can edit the original message text or you can delete it by pressing the minus (–) icon.

5. Tap the Send icon to send the message.

From: ethel

A joke to cheer you
07/20/2012 6:57 PM

Does the name "Pavlov" ring a bell?

Message subject

Reply to message

A joke to cheer you

Delete

Reply

Forward

Mark as Unread

RE: A joke to cheer

From: Cable <ss@cable.com

To: Ethel

Subject: RE: A joke to cheer you

Very funny, Ethel. Thanks for thinking of me. :-)

Sent via the Samsung Galaxy S™III, an AT&T 4G LTE smartphone

Original message

Does the name "Pavlov" ring a bell?

Forwarding Mail

1. With the email message open for reading, tap the Forward icon.

Forwarding from the Message List

You can also forward a message while viewing the message list. Press and hold the header of the message that you want to forward, and choose Forward in the pop-up menu that appears.

2. A message formatted for forwarding appears. Specify recipients in the To, Cc, and/or Bcc boxes, as described in "Creating a New Email Message."

3. You can optionally add your own text to a forwarded message. Enter it in the top section of the message window. (You can trim or edit the original message text in the bottom section of the window, if desired.)

Original Message Attachments

Whether attachments received in the original message are also forwarded depends on the Forward with Files setting. If you notice that the original attachments aren't automatically added to forwarded messages, see step 8 in "Editing Account Settings."

4. Tap the Send icon to send the message.

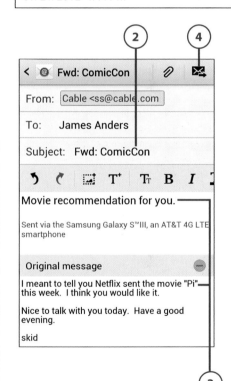

Adding Attachments and Inserts

Any message sent from Email—whether a new message, reply, or forward—can optionally include one or more file attachments, such as photos and Office documents. The recipient uses a compatible program or app to open and view the attachments. (The maximum size for a message and attachments created in Email is 50MB. Note, however, that the recipient's email account normally has a size limit for incoming messages and it may be smaller than this.)

In addition to sending file attachments with a message, you can insert any of the following directly into the body of a message: an image file from Gallery, selected text from a Contacts record, a location, or a Calendar event.

Adding Attachments

1. Create a new message, a reply, or a forward, as described earlier in this section.

2. At any point during the message-creation process, tap the Attach icon.

3. From the Attach menu, choose the type of item that you want to attach. (Choose My Files to select any file that's stored on your phone, or choose a specific item type.)

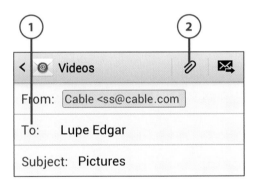

Create an Attachment on the Fly

You can choose Take Picture, Capture Video, or Record Audio to use the phone to create a photo, video, or audio recording to send as an attachment.

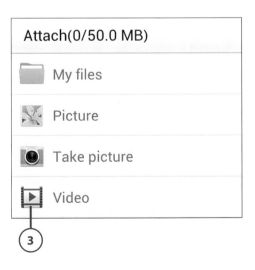

4. Select the particular file that you want to attach to the message, and respond to any dialog boxes or menus that appear. When sending a picture, for example, you can specify a resizing percentage.

5. To add other attachments, repeat steps 2–4. To remove an attachment, expand the attachments list and tap the red minus (–) sign to the right of the item.

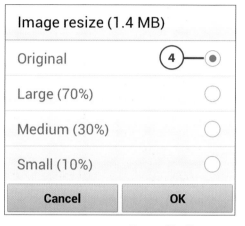

Expand/collapse attachment list

Adding Inserts

1. In the message you're composing, position the text insertion mark at the spot in the message body where you want to insert the item.

2. Tap the Insert icon in the toolbar above the message text.

3. Choose an item type from the Insert menu. Options include an image from the Gallery, an S Memo, Calendar events, selected elements of a Contacts record (such as an email address), and a physical location/address.

4. The image or text appears at the text insertion mark.

Resizing Inserted Images

You can change the size of an inserted photo by tapping it and then dragging one or more of the handles that appear around its edges. To resize proportionately, drag any corner handle.

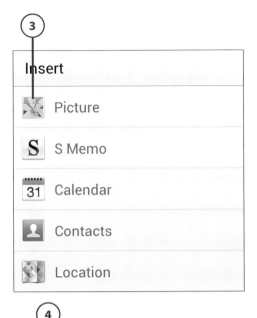

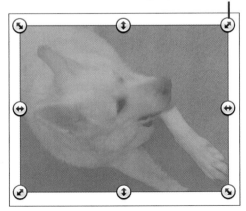

Resize proportionately

Managing the Mail

Although the Email app has fewer message-management options than a typical PC or Mac email client, you can manage message list clutter by deleting unwanted messages, moving messages to different folders, changing the status of messages from read to unread (and vice versa), and flagging important messages.

Deleting Messages

You can delete messages while you're viewing a message list or reading a particular message using these techniques:

- While reading a message, tap the Delete icon at the top of the screen. Note that such deletions currently happen immediately—without requiring a confirmation.

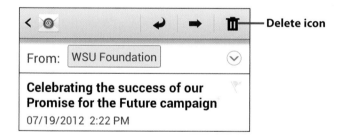

Delete icon

- While viewing the message list, press and hold the message that you want to delete, tap Delete in the dialog box that appears, and then tap the Delete button in the confirmation dialog box.

Message subject

Delete message

- You can simultaneously delete multiple messages while viewing a message list. Tap the check box that precedes each message that you want to delete, tap the Delete icon at the top of the screen, and then tap the Delete button in the confirmation dialog box.

Delete a Message Group or Conversation

In *standard view*, you can select an entire group of messages for deletion (such as all messages for a particular day or from a particular sender) by tapping the blue group header above the messages. In *conversation view*, you can select all messages in a conversation for deletion by tapping the conversation header.

Delete the selected messages by tapping the Delete icon and then tapping the Delete button in the confirmation dialog box that appears.

Select all messages in conversation

Number of messages in conversation

- While viewing a message list, you can simultaneously delete all messages in the current folder (an account's Inbox, for example). Press the Menu key, tap Delete All, and then tap the Delete button in the confirmation dialog box that appears.

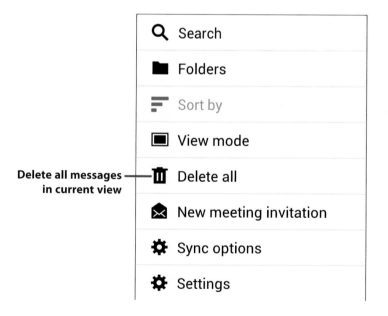

Delete all messages in current view

Moving Messages

You can move an email message to a different folder in the current account, as well as to a folder in another account. For example, you can move a message from the Trash back into the Inbox or a project-related message into a project folder. You can move messages while you're viewing a message list or reading the message.

While Reading a Message

1. Press the Menu key and tap Move.

2. In the Move To dialog box, select a destination folder in the current account or a different account.

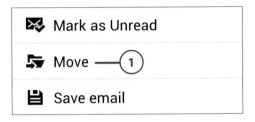

While Viewing a Message List

1. Select each message that you want to move to a particular destination folder. (Each selected message is preceded by a green check mark.)

2. Tap the Move icon above the message list.

3. In the Move To dialog box, select a destination folder in the current account or a different account (as described in step 2 of the preceding task).

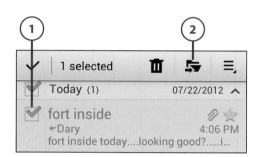

Creating Account Subfolders

Although custom account folders are typically created in your Mac/PC email application or, for web-based clients such as Hotmail, using your browser, you can also create them in Email. In an account's message list, press the Menu key and tap Folders. Then tap the plus (+) icon at the top of the screen, select a *parent folder* in which to create the new folder, name the folder, and tap OK.

Changing the Message Read Status

Sometimes it's useful to be able to change a previously read message's status to unread or a new message to read. For example, if you've fallen behind in reading incoming messages from an account, you can mark the unimportant ones as already read.

- While reading a message, you can mark it as unread by pressing the Menu key and tapping Mark as Unread in the pop-up menu that appears.

The message list immediately reappears and the message shows that it hasn't been read.

Toggle message status — Mark as Unread

Move

Save email

- While viewing the message list, you can toggle the read status of a single message by pressing and holding its header and tapping Mark as Read or Mark as Unread.

Re: Sydney

Delete

Reply

Forward

Toggle message status — Mark as Unread

- While viewing the message list, you can toggle the read status of multiple messages by tapping the check box of each message of the same kind (read or unread), tapping the menu icon at the top of the screen, and then choosing Mark as Read (or Mark as Unread).

✓ | 2 selected 🗑 ↪ ☰ — **Menu icon**

☐ Yesterday (4) | Mark as Unread — **Toggle status**

Selected message — ✓ connect att
Affinity Shadow | Add star
hear steve your slow ass phone we...

Selected message — ✓ P.S. ☆
↩ethel 07/21/2012
It's a good thing I wrote to you. I rea...

Marking Important Messages

If you'd like to mark certain messages as important, you can designate them as *favorites* (POP3 and IMAP accounts) or *flag* them (Exchange Server/ActiveSync accounts).

- *Favorite messages.* In a message list or while reading the message, tap the star icon to the right of the message subject. To remove the star from a previously marked favorite, tap the star icon again.

Marking Multiple Messages as Favorites

While viewing the message list, you can simultaneously mark *multiple* messages as favorites. Tap the check box in each message header that you want to mark as a favorite. Then tap the menu icon above the message list and choose Add Star. You can remove stars in the same fashion—select several starred headers and choose Remove Star from the menu icon.

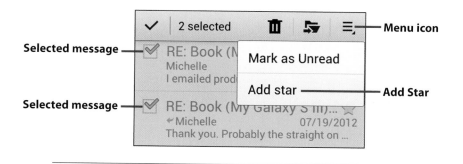

- *Flagged messages.* In a message list, tap the flag icon to the right of the message subject. Note that the flag works as a toggle. Tap it to cycle between flagged (red flag), completed (blue check mark), and cleared (blank).

Chat friend

See your battery usage trends

Tap to load previous

Me 2:39 PM
Feel like grabbing dinner tonight?

James Anders 2:40 PM
Can't... busy cleaning today... but thanks for asking

Me 2:41 PM
Cool..maybe tomorrow

Compose message

Your message

Send message

Predictive text area

Record audio clip

Insert emoticon

In this chapter, you learn how to keep current with your favorite social networking sites and use your phone to participate in text chats. Topics include the following:

→ Using Flipboard to keep up with news, entertainment, and social networking friends and colleagues

→ Using imo for text chats on a variety of major chat services

Social Networking and Socializing

In addition to making phone calls, playing games, and listening to your favorite tunes, you can use your Galaxy S III for social and business networking, as well as keep up with the news of the day. For example, you can use the included Flipboard app to read articles, watch videos, and follow feeds posted by your Facebook, Twitter, and LinkedIn friends. If you're looking for a more interactive experience, you can install the imo app and participate in text chats with friends on any of a dozen popular chat services.

Using Flipboard

If your main interest is keeping up with Facebook, Twitter, or LinkedIn friends, one of the simplest methods is to use the preinstalled Flipboard app. Flipboard lets you view status updates, read posted comments, and post your own status updates and comments. In addition, you can use Flipboard to view news and technology articles from a variety of respected news sources.

Dedicated Apps

Rather than use Flipboard for a full-blown—and potentially overwhelming—social networking *experience*, you may prefer to install dedicated apps for the social networking sites that you consider most important. The major sites, such as Facebook, Twitter, and LinkedIn, all have dedicated official Android apps that you can download from Google Play/Play Store.

Adding Social Networking Accounts

One of the first steps in using Flipboard is to link your *SNS* (social networking service) accounts that you want to track. If you aren't currently a member of a social network, visit its website and sign up first. Currently supported sites include Facebook, Twitter, LinkedIn, Google+, Google Reader, Instagram, Flickr, Tumblr, 500px, Sina Weibo, Renren, and YouTube.

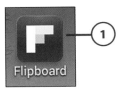

1. From the Home screen, launch Flipboard by tapping Apps and then Flipboard.

2. To link an account to Flipboard, tap the red magnifying glass icon on any Flipboard main page and tap Accounts on the screen that appears.

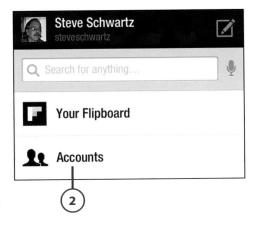

About the Main Pages

Flipboard's main pages serve as a visual table of contents. The number of pages expands and contracts as you add or remove content categories and subcategories. Within these pages, every content category and subcategory has its own thumbnail that takes you directly to its content.

3. On the Accounts screen, scroll down to the Add an Account section and tap the name of the account that you want to track with Flipboard. Only accounts that you haven't already linked are listed.

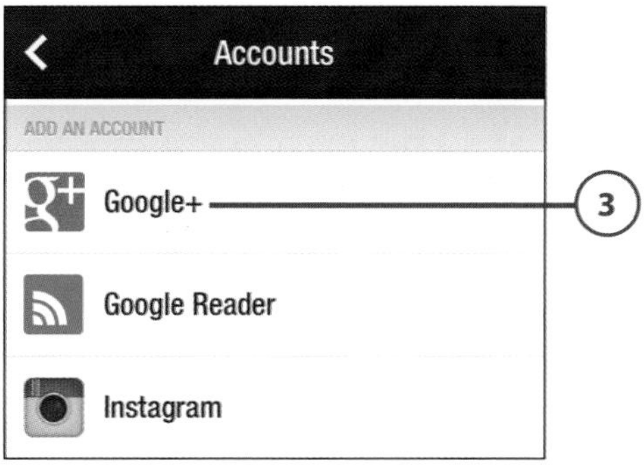

4. On the next screen, sign into your account by entering your username (or email address) and account password. Then tap the Sign In button.

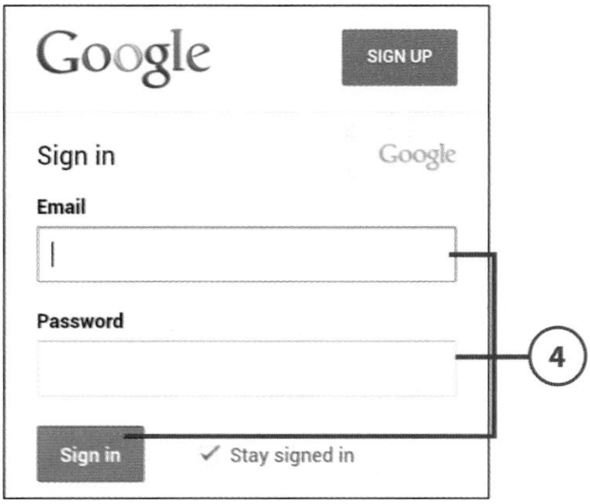

Lost Passwords

If you can't *remember* your account username, email address, or password, use your browser to visit the social networking site. There's usually a conspicuous link for requesting the forgotten info.

---

5. On the next setup screen, review the SNS's permissions statement and tap the Allow Access button. If you don't approve of the permission requirements, tap No Thanks.

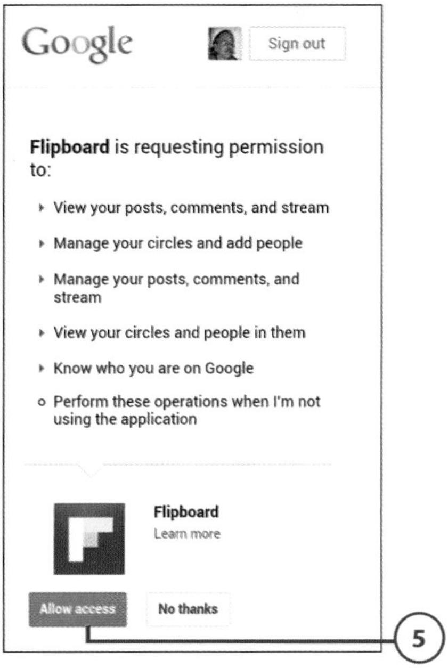

6. The site's current feed appears. When you're ready to return to the main Flipboard screen, tap the back icon or press the Back key.

Removing an SNS Account

Although you can't remove an SNS account from within Flipboard, there *is* a way to do it. From the Home screen, press the Menu key, tap Settings, tap Accounts and Sync, and select the account that you want to remove. Tap the Remove Account button and confirm the removal in the dialog box that appears.

Back

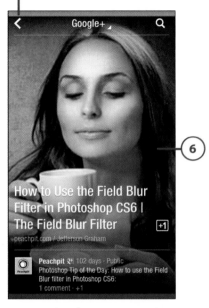

Remove SNS account

Adding Content Feeds

In addition to SNS feeds, you can add content (such as news, music, and movies) from a variety of sources.

1. From the Home screen, launch Flipboard by tapping Apps and then Flipboard.

2. Tap the red magnifying glass icon on any Flipboard main page.

3. In the scrolling list, tap a content area that you want to configure, such as News or Tech & Science.

4. To view a sample of a content source, tap its name. To add the source to your Flipboard feed, tap the plus (+) icon to the right of its name. Repeat this step for other content sources that you want to add. When you're done, tap the Back icon or press the Back key.

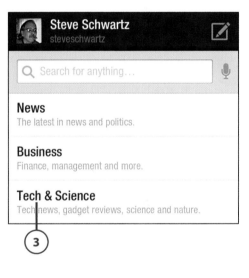

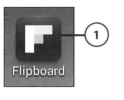

View current content

5. The selected content feeds are added and now available to you from Flipboard's main pages.

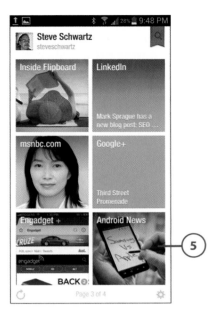

Viewing and Interacting with Content and Feeds

You can use Flipboard to view content and status updates, as well as post your own updates.

1. Launch Flipboard or, if it's already running, tap the back arrow in the upper-left corner of the screen or press the Back key until the main pages appear.

2. To locate the content that you want to view, navigate through the main pages by flicking up and down. When you see the desired category or subcategory, tap its thumbnail.

3. To navigate within a category or subcategory, flick up and down as you do in the main pages. When you see an item that you want to read or view, tap anywhere within its content to view the complete item.

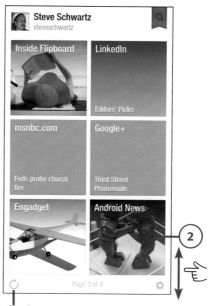

Refresh

4. When reading a lengthy article, flick up and down to scroll the material. When you're finished, tap the back icon or press the Back key to return to the content pages.

5. To interact with an item, you can tap icons on the page, such as Like, Retweet, Favorite, Share, or Comment. Different content sources and feeds have different icons and options.

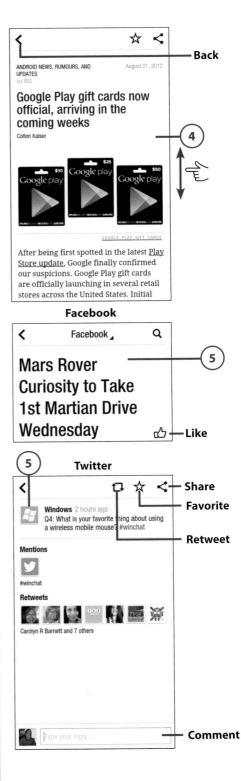

Back

Facebook

Like

Twitter

Share

Favorite

Retweet

Comment

6. To post a status update, tap the red ribbon icon on any main page, tap the Compose icon (in the upper-right corner), tap your name, select the account to which the update will post, compose the update, and tap Send.

Add a Photo

To attach a photo to a status update, press the Menu key and tap Take Photo or Choose from Library.

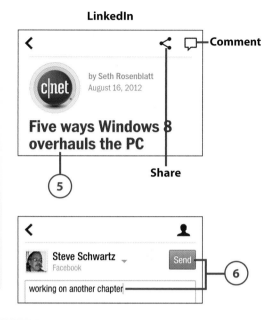

OTHER WAYS TO KEEP CURRENT WITH SOCIAL NETWORKING

Although the Flipboard feeds are in a convenient format, you may prefer another option for checking recent Facebook, Twitter, LinkedIn, or other SNS activity. First, you can use the Internet app to go directly to the SNS web site, just as you would with your computer. Second, each service offers a free, dedicated app that you can download from Google Play. Tap the Play Store icon and search for Facebook, Twitter, or LinkedIn.

Chatting with imo

Before texting (see Chapter 7, "Text and Multimedia Messaging") became popular, people relied on dedicated chat programs to conduct online conversations. Many of those same programs are now available as Android apps. Unlike texting, chat messages carry no per-message surcharge and there's no limit to the number of messages that can be exchanged in a billing cycle.

Although Google Talk is preinstalled on the Galaxy S III, you can use it to chat only with other Google/Gmail users. As an example of a general chat program with a wider audience, the rest of the chapter shows you how to use imo, a free download from Play Store/Google Play. (Downloading apps is explained in Chapter 11, "Installing and Using Applications.") You can use imo to chat with friends who have an account on any of a dozen popular chat services, such as Yahoo! Messenger, AIM/ICQ, MSN, and Facebook.

Another Chat Option: ChatON

ChatON, Samsung's dedicated chat service, is preinstalled on your Galaxy S III. (Owners of other Android phones can download ChatON from Play Store/Google Play.) Unlike imo, ChatON can only be used to chat with other ChatON users. ChatON has a clean, text message–style chat interface and includes many interesting features, such as group chats, animated emoticons, and support for file attachments. All you have to do is convince your friends that they need yet another dedicated chat service/app if they want to chat with you.

ChatON chat window ——

About imo Instant Messenger

The Android version of imo enables you to chat with buddies who use any of the following chat services: Microsoft Messenger, Skype, Yahoo! Messenger, Google Talk, Facebook, AIM/ICQ, Jabber, MySpace, Hyves, and VKontakte. Unlike most chat services, imo doesn't require you to first create a separate account. While chatting, you can optionally record and send short audio clips, too.

Setting Up imo: First Launch

After downloading and installing imo, you need to register the existing chat accounts that you want to use, determine which accounts you want to link together (for simultaneous sign-on), and review the Preferences settings.

1. On the Home screen, tap Apps and then tap imo.

2. Tap the icon of a service that you want to access using imo. You must already have an account with the selected service.

3. Enter your username and password for the selected service, and tap Sign In.

4. If the sign-in is successful, the chat account is added to the list on the Me tab and you're logged into the account.

5. To add other chat accounts, tap the Add Account button and repeat steps 2–4.

6. *Optional:* To change your current Availability (preventing others from requesting chats while you're setting up imo, for example), tap the text beside your picture placeholder on the Contacts tab and select an option from the menu that appears.

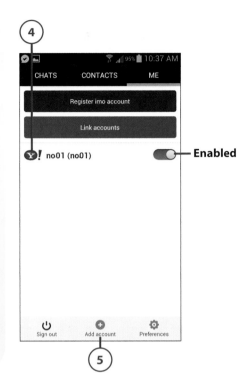

Setting Your Availability

imo remembers your most recent Availability setting the next time you launch the app. To sign in as Invisible, choose it before you log out.

7. *Optional:* To add a picture that identifies you during chats, tap the picture placeholder on the Contacts tab, select the stored picture that you want to use, crop the image as desired by moving and resizing the blue selection rectangle, and tap Done.

8. *Optional:* If you've registered two or more chat accounts in imo, you can *link* them by tapping the Link accounts button on the Me tab. When accounts are linked, signing in to one of them automatically signs you in to *all* of them.

Unlinking a Linked Account

Linking initially treats all accounts as a single linked group. You can selectively unlink certain accounts by tapping the account name on the Me tab and then tapping Unlink Account in the dialog box that appears. You can still manually sign in to the unlinked accounts whenever you like by dragging its slider. (Note that you can also *remove* a selected account from imo by tapping Delete.)

Steve (resident@hotmail.com)
Sign out
Unlink account ——Unlink account
Delete

9. To review Preferences for imo, tap the Preferences icon at the bottom of the Me tab. When you're done making changes, press the Back key. Preferences in the Privacy section that you might want to immediately review include these:

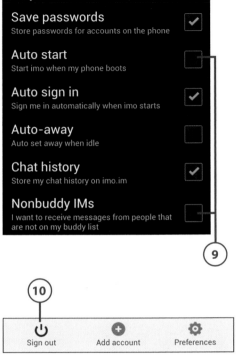

- *Auto Start*. When checked, imo automatically launches each time you turn on the phone. Because imo contributes to battery drain and you may not always want to be available for chats, you can remove the check mark and manually launch imo when needed.

- *Nonbuddy IMs*. Clear this check mark to prevent people who aren't in your Buddies or Friends lists from messaging you.

10. When you're done using imo, you can simultaneously sign out of all accounts and exit the program. On the Me tab, tap the Sign Out icon and then confirm by tapping Yes in the dialog box that appears. (You can also choose Sign Out from the Availability menu on the Contacts tab.)

Starting a Chat

Either you or a friend can initiate a chat, but you must both be logged into the same service, such as Yahoo! Messenger. It doesn't matter whether you're both using imo, whether you're directly connected to the chat service with its dedicated application, or whether you're using different types of devices (computer, phone, or tablet, for example).

1. Launch imo, tap the Me tab, and ensure that you're signed in to the desired service(s).

About Signing In and Out

If some or all of your chat accounts are linked, the act of signing in to any linked account automatically signs you in to *all* linked accounts. The Me screen always shows a green slider for each account to which you're signed in. To manually sign in to or out of an account, drag the account's slider to the correct position.

2. *Optional:* If desired, change your Availability by selecting the Contacts tab, tapping the current setting, and choosing an option from the Availability menu that appears.

3. On the Contacts tab, see if the person you want to chat with is available. Tap the person's entry to begin a chat session.

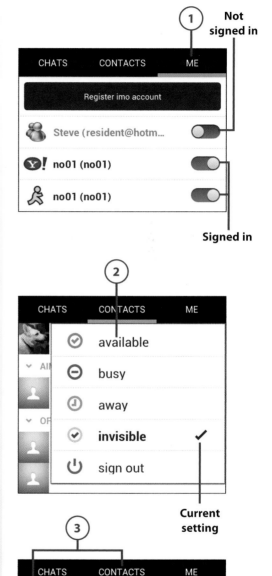

4. Enter the initial message and tap the Send button.

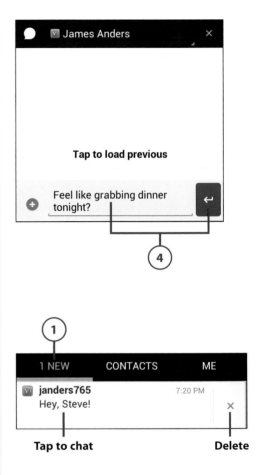

Tap to load previous

Feel like grabbing dinner tonight?

Responding to a New Message

When imo is running on your phone, you can respond to incoming messages.

1. The other person sees that you're online and available for chat, and then messages you—or he or she simply sends you a message, *hoping* that you're online. If imo is onscreen, a new message notification (1 New) appears on the Chat tab. Tap the notification, and then tap the message text to participate in a chat. Alternatively, you can tap the X to discard the message.

1 NEW   CONTACTS   ME

janders765   7:20 PM
Hey, Steve!

Tap to chat   Delete

New Message Notifications

Depending on your Notifications Preferences, the LED lights, an alert tone sounds, the phone vibrates, and/or an indicator appears in the status bar.

Status bar — janders765: hey, steve!
notification

2. If imo is running but is *not* currently onscreen, you can do either of the following:

- Open the Notifications panel and tap the message entry.

- Respond to the message on the lock screen by typing and sending a Quick Reply. (The advantage of doing this is that you can reply without leaving the lock screen.)

Received message

Send

>>>Go Further

IMO CHAT OPTIONS AND TIPS

There's more to imo than its convenient handling of chat session and buddies from multiple services. You may find the following options and tips helpful. For more information about imo and its capabilities, visit https://imo.im/features.

- If you don't feel like being interrupted, you *can* set your Availability to Away or Busy—but the best option is to select Invisible. In that mode, you can still receive incoming messages but no one can tell you're online.

- In addition to selecting an Availability setting, you can add a Status message that displays beside your icon in Buddy lists. For instance, you can explain *how* you're Busy. To add a Status message, tap the Contacts tab, tap the text box beside your availability, enter/edit the text, and tap Update. (When your Status changes, be sure to change or delete the message.)

Status text

- You can add a new buddy by tapping the Add Contact icon at the bottom of the Contacts tab. You'll need to know your friend's chat username and the chat service that he or she uses.

- Those cute smiley faces (*emoticons*) are available for you to insert into messages. Instead of typing the characters needed to create an emoticon (such as :-) to denote a smiling face), you can just pick the one you want to insert. When typing a message, press and hold the emoticon key when you want to insert a smiley. In the pop-up palette, tap the emoticon that you want to insert. (If the desired emotion is currently displayed on the key, you can insert it by simply tapping the key.)

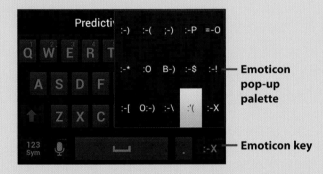

- Although you can't conduct a voice chat in imo, you *can* transmit short audio recordings (30 seconds or less). To start a recording, tap the plus (+) icon and choose Voice IM from the pop-up menu that appears. Tap the Hold and Speak button and record your audio clip.

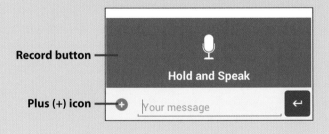

In this chapter, you learn the essentials of downloading, installing, running, and maintaining applications on your phone. Topics include the following:

→ Running an application
→ Downloading and installing applications from Google Play (Android Market)
→ Enabling application downloads from other sources
→ Downloading applications from the Amazon Appstore
→ Adding Home screen shortcuts to your favorite applications
→ Uninstalling unwanted applications
→ Installing application updates

Installing and Using Applications

Applications (or *apps*, as they're called when referring to smartphone software) are programs that run on your phone. They add new functionality to the phone, such as enabling you to stream video, manipulate databases, play video games, and do almost anything else you can imagine.

The Galaxy S III comes with a couple dozen apps preinstalled, ready for you to use. In addition, you can download and install other apps from Google Play, the Amazon Appstore, and developers' websites.

Running an App

In this section, you learn the fundamentals of running apps: launching an app, using the hardware keys (Menu, Home, and Back) in conjunction with apps, switching among running apps, and exiting from an app. The information covered here applies to any app you encounter.

Launching an App

As with programs on a computer, you can launch phone apps directly or indirectly (by performing an action that requires the app to be running).

Directly Launching an App

To launch a particular app, you can do any of the following:

- On any Home screen page, tap the app's icon. (In addition to the app icons that are preinstalled on the Home screen pages, you may have added shortcuts to some of your favorite apps to make them more readily accessible.)

App icons

- At the bottom of any Home screen page, tap Apps. Ensure that the Apps tab is selected and then tap the icon of the app that you want to run.

Navigation
Because you probably have several pages of apps, you can move from page to page by swiping the screen to the right or left or by tapping a navigation dot below the app icons.

To display only the apps that you've downloaded, tap the icon in the upper-right corner of the screen, or press the Menu key and select Downloaded Applications.

Apps tab —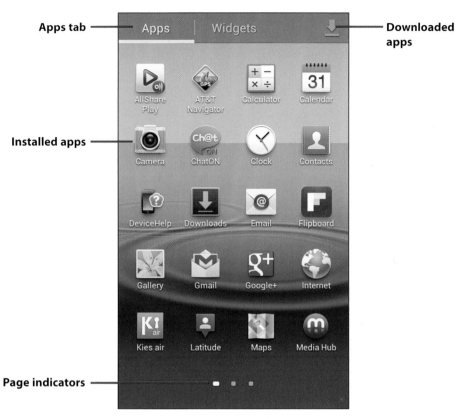

Installed apps —

Downloaded apps

Page indicators —

- On almost any screen, you can press and hold the Home key to display a list of recently run apps, as well as ones that are currently running. Scroll vertically until you see the app that you want to launch or to which you want to switch and then tap its thumbnail.

Recent and running apps

Indirectly Launching an App

In addition to tapping an app's icon, many actions that you perform on the phone can cause an app to launch. Consider these common examples:

- In any program or widget, tapping a link to material stored on the web, to an HTML (web) file stored on the phone, or to a particular web page or site causes the Internet app to launch to display the page. App help files are sometimes handled this way.

Facebook link

- Tapping a *mailto:* (email address) link on a web page or in an app causes Email to launch to create a new message to that address.

> For questions regarding this website contact *[webmaster].*— **mailto: link**
> *Last updated: January 11, 2011*

Not Just Links

In addition to tapping links, if you tap a phone number or fully formed email address on a web page, the number is entered into Phone in preparation for dialing or you can create a new Email/Gmail message to the address, respectively.

Compose Gmail or Email

- Tapping a file icon (such as a music, video, or photo file) in My Files, in Downloads, on the Home screen, or in a folder you created causes an appropriate app to launch and present the file's material. Tapping a document icon, such as a PDF or Microsoft Office document, may also cause an app to launch and display the file's contents. Either case depends on having an app installed that is capable of reading and displaying the file, such as Polaris Office.

PDF file

- Performing certain actions in an app can cause a related app to launch. For example, clicking the Contacts icon to select message recipients in Email or Messaging launches Contacts.

- Tapping certain entries in the Notifications panel, such as a new email notification, causes the appropriate app to launch.

Using the Hardware Keys

The three hardware keys at the bottom of the phone (Menu, Home, and Back) can be useful—and occasionally *essential*—when running apps.

Light 'em Up!

When the keys aren't in use, only the Home key—a physical button—is visible. Until you tap one of the three keys or the touchscreen, the Menu and Back keys are hidden. Whether or not you can *see* the keys, however, is irrelevant. If you tap the currently invisible Menu or Back key, the key still performs its function.

Accessing Menus

In programs that contain menus, you can press the Menu key on various screens to see the available options. Setting app-specific preferences is usually handled in this manner, for example. Note that menus are often context-sensitive—that is, they change depending on what you're currently doing.

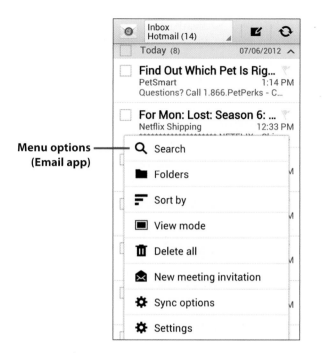

Menu options (Email app)

Other Menus

In addition to menus that are tied to the Menu key, apps may contain other menus. Some automatically appear onscreen (such as the Select menu in Gallery), whereas others are contextual menus that pop-up when you press and hold an item (such as a contact record in Contacts).

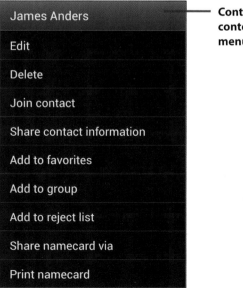

Contacts contextual menu

Returning to the Home Screen

To immediately exit the current app, press the Home key. The most recently accessed page of the Home screen appears.

Page indicator

Navigating Within an App

Within most apps, forward navigation options are obvious. You tap entries, icons, thumbnails, or buttons to go to the next screen or to perform an action. However, the method of *returning* to the previous section or screen isn't always as obvious. When it doesn't happen automatically, you can usually press the Back key. In addition to moving you back through sections or screens (when using the Internet to view web pages or when modifying phone settings, for example), you can also press Back to avoid making a selection in a dialog box or options menu, leave the Notifications panel, or dismiss the onscreen keyboard.

It's Not All Good

One Too Many Presses

Using the Back key has a major drawback. If you press it one too many times, you'll find that you've inadvertently exited the current program and are now staring at the Home screen. When this happens, simply relaunch the app.

Switching Among Running Apps

Although most apps automatically exit when you leave them (see the next task, "Exiting an App"), you can use the Task Manager to switch among those that are running.

1. On almost any screen, press and hold the Home button until the list of recent and active applications appears.

2. Tap the Task Manager button.

3. Ensure that the Active Applications tab is selected. To switch to any running app, tap its name.

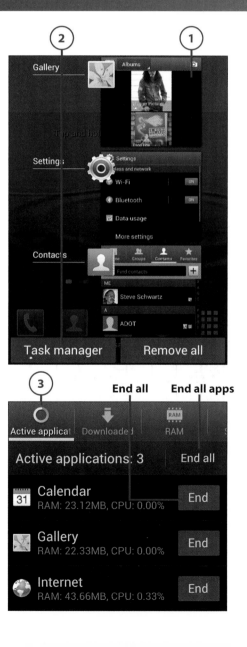

Exiting an App

If you're new to smartphones, you've probably noticed one big difference between phone apps and computer applications: *Most apps have no Quit or Exit command*. The few apps that do have such a command are typically those that, if left running, would run up data-related charges.

Whenever you perform an action that leaves the current app, such as powering off the phone, pressing the Back key, or pressing the Home key, the Android operating system decides whether to quit or suspend the app. Similarly, if app activities are causing the phone to run low on memory, Android performs these same functions as needed. However, if you want to quit an app *manually* to ensure that it's no longer running, draining the battery, using memory, or running up data transmissions, you can use the Task Manager.

1. As described in the previous task list, launch the Task Manager and tap the Active Applications tab (if it isn't currently selected).

2. To quit a specific app, tap its End button. To simultaneously quit all listed apps, tap the End All button.

Downloading and Installing Apps from Google Play

Formerly known as Android Market, Google Play is the most common place for you to find Android apps for your phone. In addition to apps, you can download ebooks, movies, and music from Google Play.

1. Launch Google Play by tapping its Home screen icon (Play Store) or by tapping Apps and then Play Store.

Play Store

First Launch
If this is the first time you've run Google Play, you'll be asked to agree to its Terms of Service before continuing. Tap the text link to read the Terms of Service and then tap Accept.

2. Tap Apps, Music, or another link on the main screen to indicate the type of material that you're seeking or want to browse.

3. Do one of the following:

   - To browse for apps, continue tapping links to focus your search.

   - If you know the name or type of app for which you're searching, tap the search icon at the top of the screen and begin typing. A drop-down list of potential matches appears as you type. Tap one or continue typing to further narrow the search.

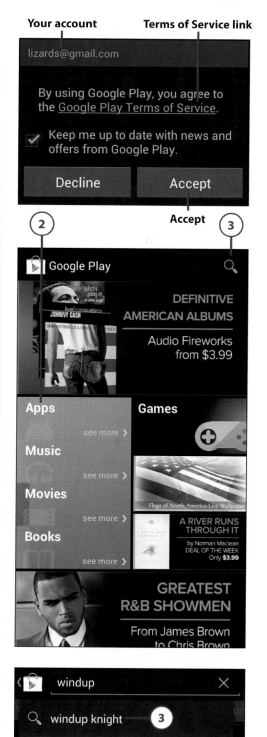

Your account

Terms of Service link

Accept

4. To view a listed app, tap its name.

5. Review the description and user ratings for the app. If desired, you can also do the following:

   • Tap the sample screen shots or videos at the top of the page. If multiple screen shots are available, you can view them by swiping left and right.

   • To learn more about the app, tap the link(s) to the developer's website (if provided).

6. If you want the app, tap the blue icon. If the app is free, the icon will read Install; otherwise, it will contain the price.

Charge It!

If the app isn't free, you can charge it to a credit card that you've registered with Google Play. Specify a registered credit card or add a new one and then follow the onscreen instructions to complete the purchase.

Adding a credit card creates a *Google Wallet* account for you. To learn about Google Wallet and where it's accepted, visit www.google.com/wallet/.

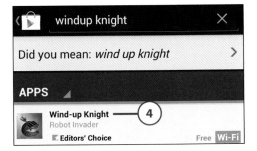

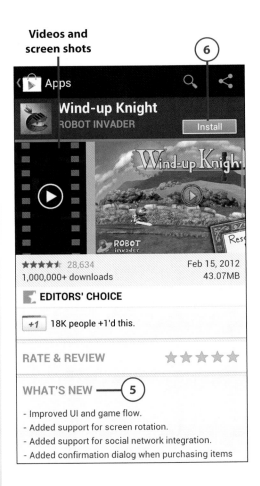

Videos and screen shots

7. Before starting the download, the app's Permissions screen appears, detailing how the app interacts with the operating system, system devices, and your personal information. If the permissions are acceptable to you, tap the Accept & Download button. The app is downloaded and installed on your phone, and its icon is added to Apps.

Add credit card

Angry Birds Space Premium
ROVIO MOBILE LTD. ✧

lizards@gmail.com
Add card

Total   US$0.99

Continue

⑦

‹ ▶ Apps

Wind-up Knight
ROBOT INVADER

lizards@gmail.com

Accept & download

PERMISSIONS

Storage
Modify/delete SD card contents   ›

Phone calls
Read phone state and identity   ›

Network communication
Full Internet access   ›

See all ⌄

Go Back

To step backward through Google Play to revisit previously viewed screens, press the Back key or tap the location information in the upper-left corner.

Current location

‹ ▶ Apps

>>>Go Further

REQUESTING A REFUND

Whenever you purchase an app from Google Play, you have 15 minutes to try it, decide whether you want to keep it, and, if not, request a refund. Do the following to request a refund:

1. Launch Google Play, press the Menu key, and tap My Apps.

2. The My Apps list of Google Play–installed apps appears. Tap the app that you just purchased and want to return.

3. If you're within the 15-minute window, you'll see a Refund button in the app's description window. Tap it to proceed.

4. The Refund button changes to Uninstall. Tap it to remove the app from your phone and initiate the refund to your account.

Customizing Google Play

Google Play has its own Settings screen that enables you to customize the way app updates are handled and provides an option to create a PIN that you can use to authenticate purchases.

1. In Google Play, press the Menu key and tap Settings.

My Apps
Accounts
Settings ——(1)
Help

2. The Settings screen appears. Following are the options you can change.

3. *Notifications.* When checked, an item appears in the Notifications panel when updates are available for apps and other material that you've downloaded from Google Play. You can download and install the updates by tapping the notification.

Check for Updates

To manually check for updates, launch Google Play, press the Menu key, and tap My Apps to display the list of your downloaded apps. Any app for which an update can be downloaded is marked Update Available.

4. *Auto-update Apps.* When checked, updates for apps are automatically downloaded and installed from Google Play as they become available.

Selective Auto-updates

For more control over which apps automatically update, go to each app's Google Play page and tap the Allow Automatic Updating check box.

5. *Update Over Wi-Fi Only.* When checked, updates are delivered only when your phone has an active Wi-Fi connection. That is, 3G or 4G is never used and the downloads don't count toward your data usage.

6. *Auto-add Widgets.* When this option is checked and you download a new app, a shortcut to the app will automatically be added to your Home screen.

7. *Clear Search History.* Tap this option to delete all previous searches that you've performed in Google Play.

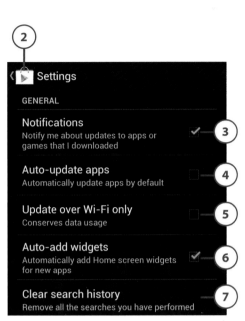

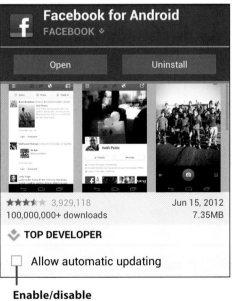

Enable/disable automatic updates

8. *Unlock Settings.* This option is available only when you've created a PIN for your account. Tap it to change or remove the PIN. (You must know the current PIN to change or remove it.)

9. *Content Filtering.* To prevent certain types of apps from being downloaded, tap Content Filtering, enter or remove check marks on the Allow Apps Rated For screen, and tap OK.

10. *Use PIN for Purchases.* This option is available only if you've created a PIN (see step 11). When it's enabled, Google Play requests your PIN each time you try to purchase an app, movie, song, ebook, or other content.

11. *Set or Change PIN.* Tap this option to create a Google Play PIN or to change an existing one. After you create and enable a PIN (see step 10), Google Play asks you to provide it whenever you make a purchase.

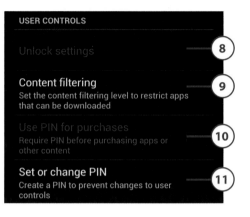

USER CONTROLS

Unlock settings — 8

Content filtering — 9
Set the content filtering level to restrict apps that can be downloaded

Use PIN for purchases — 10
Require PIN before purchasing apps or other content

Set or change PIN — 11
Create a PIN to prevent changes to user controls

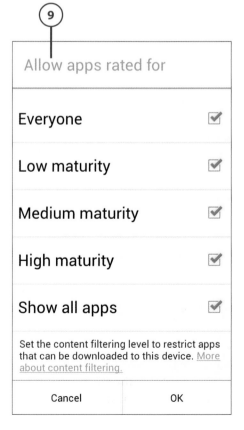

9

Allow apps rated for

Everyone ✓

Low maturity ✓

Medium maturity ✓

High maturity ✓

Show all apps ✓

Set the content filtering level to restrict apps that can be downloaded to this device. More about content filtering.

Cancel   OK

12. Google AdMob Ads. When this option is enabled, apps that display ads generate content based on what's known about you, such as your location, interests, and purchasing habits. When disabled, the apps still have ads, but they contain random, untargeted content.

> Type your PIN
>
> Create a PIN to control and lock settings:
>
> Type PIN
>
> Cancel   OK

⑪   ⑫

OTHER

Google AdMob Ads
Personalize ads based on my interests

Choose whether to personalize ads from Google and AdMob in mobile apps on this device. Learn more

USING THE GOOGLE PLAY WEBSITE

>>Go Further

In addition to using the Google Play app to choose apps and content for your phone, you can use your computer to access the Google Play website. The larger screen and convenient keyboard can be helpful when searching for apps and other material. Go to https://play.google.com/store, sign in to your Google/Gmail account (if required), and hunt to your heart's content. Any paid for or free app that you select will be downloaded to your phone. (Click the My Android Apps tab at the top of the screen to see a list of all apps that you've previously downloaded from Google Play.)

Enabling App Downloads from Other Sources

Google Play is the *official* source of Android apps. However, if you'd like to download and install apps from unofficial sources, such as developer websites or the Amazon Appstore (described in the next section), you must change one of your phone's settings.

1. On the Home screen, press the Menu key and tap Settings.

2. On the Settings screen, tap Security.

3. In the Device Administration section of the Security screen, tap the Unknown Sources check box. When it's checked, you can download apps from any source that you choose.

4. Confirm by tapping OK in the dialog box that appears.

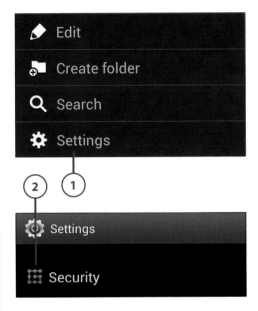

Using the Amazon Appstore for Android

In addition to Google Play, the popular online retailer Amazon.com provides another major source of free and paid Android apps. If you already have an Amazon.com account, you can use it to purchase apps for your phone, too. (If you haven't already done so, you must allow downloading of apps from *unknown sources*, as explained in "Enabling App Downloads from Other Sources.")

Installing the Amazon Appstore App

1. Using your computer's web browser, go to www.amazon.com, click the Shop by Department menu, and choose Appstore for Android, Apps.

2. Click the Get Started icon in the upper-right area of the page.

3. In the Get Started box, enter your mobile phone number or email address and then click the Go button. A text or email message is sent to your phone, depending on what you entered.

4. On your phone, open the text or email message from Amazon.com. Click the download link.

5. Wait a few moments and check the Notifications panel for the download. Tap it to continue.

6. The Appstore installation screen appears. Tap the Install button, and then tap Open on the screen that follows.

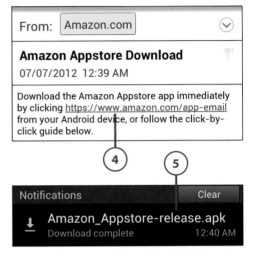

From: Amazon.com

Amazon Appstore Download
07/07/2012 12:39 AM

Download the Amazon Appstore app immediately by clicking https://www.amazon.com/app-email from your Android device, or follow the click-by-click guide below.

④ ⑤

Notifications	Clear

↓ Amazon_Appstore-release.apk
Download complete   12:40 AM

Appstore

Do you want to install this application?

Allow this application to:

- **Network communication**
  full Internet access

- **Your accounts**
  act as an account authenticator, manage the accounts list, use the authentication credentials of an account

- **Storage**
  modify/delete SD card contents

- **Phone calls**
  read phone state and identity

- **System tools**
  prevent phone from sleeping, retrieve running applications

Show all   ⌄

Cancel	Install

⑥

7. The Welcome screen appears. To associate this account with your Amazon.com account, enter your email address and Amazon password. On subsequent launches, the app will automatically know who you are. (If you don't currently have an Amazon account, you can create one on the Amazon.com main web page.)

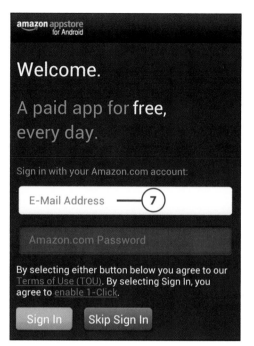

Downloading Apps from the Amazon Appstore

1. On the Home screen, tap Apps and then tap Appstore.

2. The Appstore opening screen appears.

3. *Browsing.* To find an app by browsing, tap to select a category in the scrolling list. (Categories scroll to the right and left, and the listings beneath them scroll up and down.) You can further filter some categories, such as games, by tapping a subcategory. Review the listing thumbnails and, if you don't see something of interest, tap a different category or subcategory or press the Back key to go up a level.

Paths to Better Browsing

You can quickly filter the apps by directly choosing a software category. Press the Menu key, tap the Categories icon, and then tap the category in the scrolling Categories menu. On the other hand, if you're at a loss concerning where to start, press the Menu key and tap the Recommended icon. Amazon displays a list of apps that might interest you, based on your previous downloads.

4. *Searching.* If you know the name or type of app that you want, you can perform a search. Tap in the search box and enter the search text. When sufficient characters have been typed, a Suggestions list appears. Tap to select a suggestion or continue typing to further filter the suggestions.

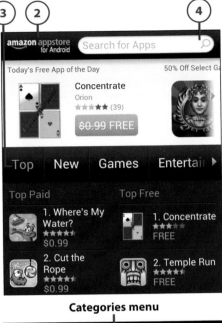

More Precise Searches

You can search all apps on the main screen or search within a category or subcategory by navigating to that category before beginning the search (refer to step 3).

5. When you see an app that interests you, tap its entry and review the product description, screenshots, and so on. (Tap any screenshot to see it at full size or to play a video. Tap any greater than (>) symbol to expand a section, such as Product Description or Customer Reviews.)

6. If you decide to download the app, tap its Free or price button.

First Download Only

Until you turn on Amazon's 1-Click ordering and specify a preferred payment method, you aren't allowed to download *any* apps—paid or free. The first time you attempt to download any item, you'll be stepped through the process of completing your Amazon account setup. To add a payment method to your account, use your computer's browser to visit www.amazon.com, log into your account, and go to Add a Credit or Debit Card.

7. The button's label changes to Get App (for a free app) or Buy App (for a paid app).

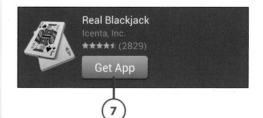

Expand
section

8. Tap the Get App or Buy App button to initiate the download, charging it to your designated credit card if it's not free.

9. The list of permissions the app requires is shown. If you agree with them, tap the Install button; otherwise, tap Cancel.

10. If you tapped Install, the app is now installed on your phone and its icon is added to Applications. If you'd like to run it now, tap Open; otherwise, tap Done.

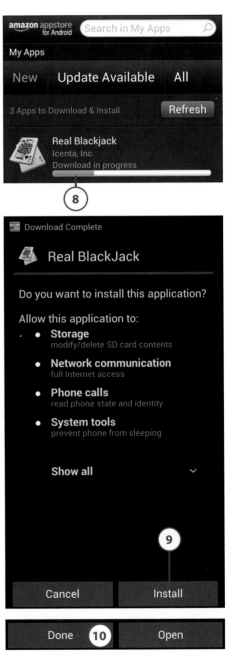

Check the Notifications Panel

Each app that you download from the Amazon Appstore adds an entry to the Notifications panel. In addition to launching the app by tapping its icon in Applications, you can tap its entry in the Notifications panel.

Customizing the Amazon Appstore

1. Press the Menu key and tap Settings. The Settings screen appears, enabling you to change the following options.

2. *Gift Cards.* If you have an Amazon. com gift card or a promotional code, tap this option to add it to your account (enabling you to apply the amount to app purchases). Enter the gift card or claim code and then tap Redeem.

3. *Use Wi-Fi When Downloading Apps.* To avoid using your 3G or 4G data connection to download large apps, tap this option to specify that apps larger than *X* MB should be downloaded only using Wi-Fi. (Apps smaller than the specified size can be downloaded using 3G/4G, if you don't have Wi-Fi access at that moment.)

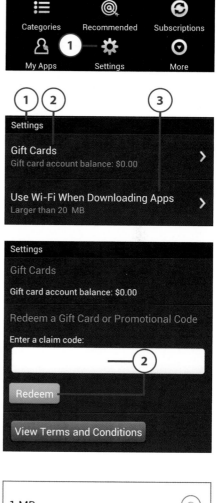

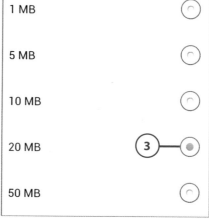

4. *Parental Controls.* When this option is enabled and the user attempts to purchase *in-app material* such as subscriptions or game add-ons, you must enter your Amazon.com password or a PIN. Tap Enable Parental Controls to enable the feature.

If Use PIN isn't checked, your Amazon.com password is requested for in-app purchases. If Use PIN is checked, you must enter a numeric PIN instead of the password.

5. *In-App Purchasing.* When this option is enabled, you can buy app add-ons or subscriptions from within any app that offers them. (This option is enabled by default. To disable it, you must enter your Amazon.com account password.)

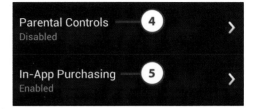

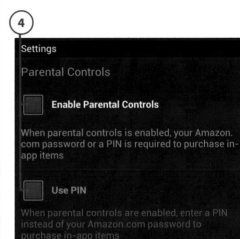

6. *Notifications.* Enable the various Notifications options to allow the Amazon Appstore to transmit notifications to the phone whenever something important occurs.

7. *Version and Release Notes.* Tap this option to view release notes for this version of the Amazon Appstore app and to check for newer versions of the app.

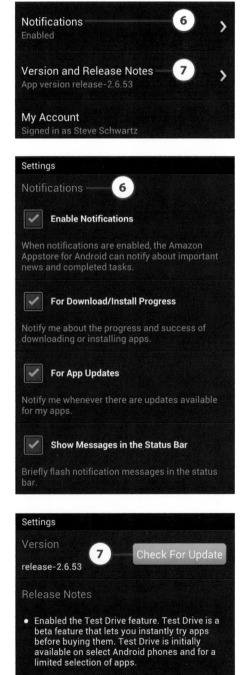

>>>Go Further

MORE AMAZON APPSTORE COMMANDS

You might find the following additional Appstore commands helpful:

- Press the Menu key and tap My Apps to get the list of apps that you've downloaded from the Appstore. Tapping a category on the My Apps screen enables you to view new downloads, all downloads, or only those for which an update is available. Tap a button to install, open, or update a listed app.

Categories —

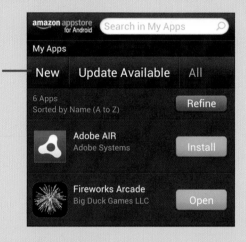

- When browsing for new apps, note that every app page has Save for Later and Share buttons. When viewing an app of interest, tap Save for Later to add the app to a list that you can view by pressing Menu, tapping More, and Saved for Later. Tap the Share button to forward information about the app to a friend via email or a text message.

Save for later —

Share with a friend

• If you didn't tap the Save for Later button when viewing an app, you can probably find the app again by pressing Menu, tapping More, and tapping Recently Viewed.

Recently viewed —

Managing Apps

You can manage your installed apps by creating Home screen shortcuts to your favorites and uninstalling the apps you no longer want or need.

Creating Shortcuts

To simplify the process of accessing your favorite apps, you can add Home screen shortcuts to them. You can accomplish this by using menus or by manually dragging them from Apps. (To learn more about moving and removing shortcuts, see "Customizing the Home Screen" in Chapter 17, "Customizing Your Phone.")

Home screen page

1. Navigate to the Home screen page where you want to add the app shortcut and then tap the Apps icon.

2. Press and hold the icon of the app for which you want to create a shortcut.

3. Drag it into position on the previously selected Home screen page (or to another page, if you like) and release the icon when it's in the desired spot.

Uninstalling Apps

If you're unhappy with an app or no longer need it, you can *uninstall* it, removing it from your phone and reclaiming the storage space it was using. Note, however, that only apps you've downloaded can be uninstalled; you can't remove the built-in apps.

Uninstalling Using the Application Manager

1. On the Home screen, press the Menu key and tap Settings.

2. On the Settings screen, tap Application Manager.

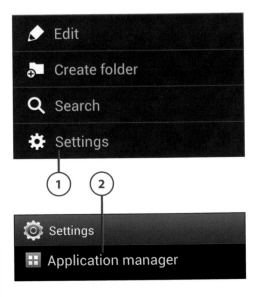

3. With the Downloaded tab selected, scroll to find the app that you want to uninstall and tap its entry.

4. Tap the app's Uninstall button. (Only apps that you are permitted to remove have an active Uninstall button.)

5. Tap the OK button on the confirmation screen that appears.

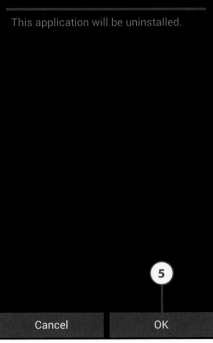

Uninstalling Using the Task Manager

1. On almost any screen, press and hold the Home button until the list of recent and active applications appears. Tap the Task Manager button.

2. Tap the Downloaded tab, scroll to find the app that you want to remove, and tap its Uninstall button.

3. Tap the OK button on the confirmation screen that appears.

Uninstalling Using Google Play

1. From the Home screen, launch Google Play by tapping Apps and then tapping Play Store. (On the center Home screen page, you may also have a Play Store icon that you can tap.)

2. Within Google Play, press the Menu key and tap My Apps.

3. On the My Apps screen, the list of apps downloaded from Google Play is presented. Tap the app that you want to uninstall.

4. On the app's Google Play page, tap the Uninstall button. (Although this button is available for most apps, it isn't presented for system apps.)

5. In the dialog box that appears, confirm the app's removal by tapping OK.

Play Store — 1

My Apps — 2

Accounts

Settings

Help

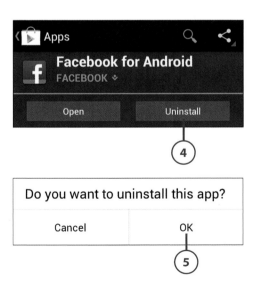

3

Facebook for Android
Facebook ✧
★★★✦☆   Installed

‹ ▷ Apps   🔍 ‹

Facebook for Android
FACEBOOK ✧

Open   Uninstall

4

Do you want to uninstall this app?

Cancel   OK

5

Updating Apps

Developers occasionally release newer versions of their paid and free apps (referred to as *updates*). When a newer version becomes available at Google Play, an update notification appears in the Notifications panel.

1. Open the Notifications panel and tap the update notification.

2. Google Play launches and opens the My Apps screen showing the apps for which updates are available.

3. Do either of the following:

   - To update an individual app, tap its Update text and tap the Update button on the screen that appears.

   - To simultaneously update all listed apps, tap Update *number* at the top of the list.

   The selected updates are downloaded and installed.

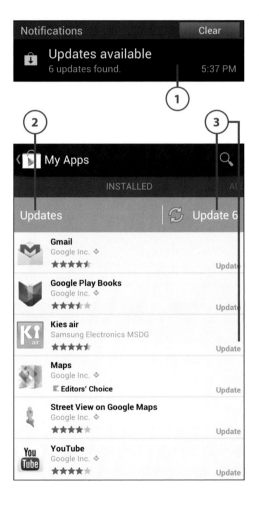

MORE ABOUT UPDATES

Here's some additional information about updating that you may find helpful:

- Updating apps from the Amazon Appstore works in much the same way as Google Play. When you tap an update notification, Amazon Appstore launches and takes you to the My Apps section. Select the Update Available tab to view the list of new updates and install one or all.

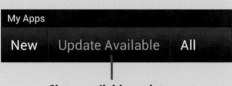

Show available updates

- You can manually check for Google Play or Amazon Appstore updates by launching the appropriate app, pressing the Menu key, and tapping My Apps.

- If you've downloaded an app directly from a developer's website, you should periodically revisit the site to check for newer versions.

>>>Go Further

In this chapter, you learn to use the phone's GPS chip in conjunction with several prein-stalled location-based apps. Topics include the following:

→ Enabling and disabling GPS
→ Obtaining driving directions from the current location to your destination

Using GPS Apps

The Galaxy S III has an embedded *GPS* (Global Positioning System) chip that enables the network to determine your phone's current location. When GPS is active, the phone can use E911 emergency location services to transmit your location, as well as run a variety of apps that display maps of your surroundings, provide turn-by-turn driving and walking directions, determine the distance to other locations, and show you where you are in relation to your friends.

Enabling/Disabling GPS

As with Bluetooth and Wi-Fi, you can enable and disable the phone's GPS as needed. Because the regular polling of the GPS drains the battery and consumes data, you can disable the feature when you aren't using it.

Use any of the following methods to enable or disable GPS:

- Pull down the Notifications panel and tap the GPS icon to toggle its current state.

Notifications panel

Enable/disable GPS

- On the Home screen, press the Menu key, tap Settings, and tap Location Services. Tap Use GPS Satellites to toggle its current state.

Location Services settings

- If you perform an action in an app that requires GPS (such as requesting navigation instructions) but GPS isn't enabled, you are usually asked to enable it in Location Services. After enabling GPS by tapping the Use GPS Satellites check box, press the Back key to return to the app.

Driving Directions

The most common use of GPS is to get turn-by-turn driving, bicycling, or walking directions from your current location (determined by the GPS) to a destination. Turn-by-turn directions are provided by Google Navigation. In addition to running this app directly, other apps such as Google Maps and Places/Local link to Navigation when navigation assistance is requested. (Note that some carriers, such as AT&T, provide their own navigation app that you can elect to use instead of Navigation.)

Google Navigation

1. Enable the GPS using one of the methods described in the previous section, "Enabling/Disabling GPS."

2. On the Home screen, tap Apps, followed by Navigation.

3. On Navigation's main screen, you can indicate your destination by speaking into the microphone, typing, or tapping the Go Home icon. Start by tapping the menu icon and specifying your mode of travel (Driving or Walking).

4. If the destination is your house, tap the Go Home icon.

Recent Destinations

If you've recently traveled to this destination using the GPS, you may be able to select it from the Recent Destinations list.

5. To set your destination by speaking, tap the Speak Destination icon and say where you want to go. If necessary, choose a location from the ones suggested.

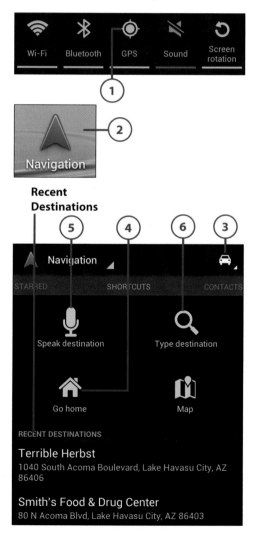

Notifications panel

Recent Destinations

6. To set your destination by typing, tap the Type Destination icon, enter a search string, and tap the Search key. If necessary, choose a location from the ones suggested.

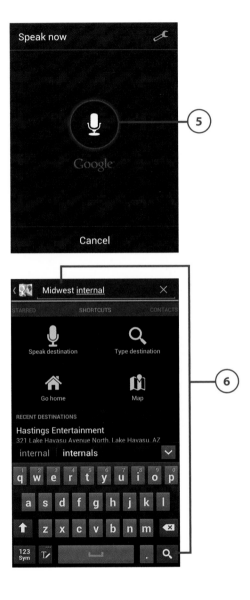

Use Navigation or the Provider's App?

As mentioned, some service providers include their own navigation app as an alternative to Navigation. Prior to displaying the map to your destination, a Complete Action Using dialog box appears. Tap the navigation app that you want to use for this trip. (After trying both apps, you can specify your *preferred* navigation app by tapping the Use by Default for This Action check box prior to picking the app to use for the current trip.)

7. The route appears. As you drive or walk, you receive audible instructions at each change in direction.

8. When you reach the destination, do one of the following:

   • To return to the main screen to set a new destination, press the Menu key or tap the menu icon (in the lower-right corner), tap More, and tap Set Destination.

   • If you're done using Navigation, press the Menu key and tap Exit Navigation. (As an alternative, you can press the Back key and tap OK in the Exit Navigation? dialog box that appears.) You can also disable the GPS, if you're done using it.

>>>Go Further

OTHER NAVIGATION OPTIONS

In addition to using Navigation's voice instructions to get to where you want to go, there are other options that you should explore:

- To get a list of text-based turn-by-turn directions, press the Menu key and tap Directions List.

Directions List

Via AZ-95 N

5.0 mi **10** min

↑ Head northeast on **Paso Dr** toward **Molly Gibson Dr**
Continue for 0.2 mi

↱ Turn right onto **S Acoma Blvd**
Continue for 0.4 mi

↱ Turn right onto **95** NORTH
Continue for 4.1 mi

↰ Turn left onto **Palo Verde Blvd S**
Continue for 150 ft

↱ Turn right onto **Pso Del Sol**
Continue for 0.2 mi

↰ **Pso Del Sol** turns left and becomes **El Camino Way**
Continue for 100 ft
Destination will be on the left

⊗ **Scotty's Broasted Chicken**

- To view alternate routes to your destination, press the Menu key and tap Route and Alternates. Tap the Alternate Routes icon at the bottom of the screen to display alternate route thumbnails. To view an alternate route, tap its thumbnail and then tap the Navigation icon.

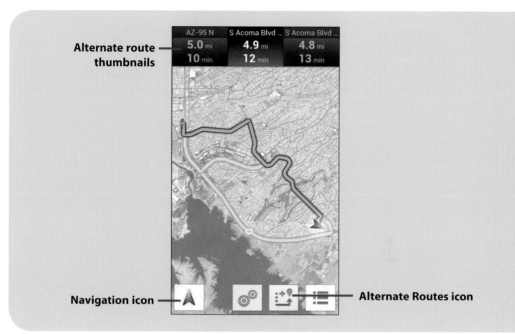

Alternate route thumbnails

Navigation icon

Alternate Routes icon

Google Maps

1. Enable the GPS using one of the methods described earlier in "Enabling/Disabling GPS."

2. On the Home screen, tap Apps, followed by Maps.

Location Services settings ①

Use GPS satellites
Location accurate to street level

3. A map of the surrounding area appears. Your location is indicated by the blue triangle.

4. Choose Navigation from the menu at the top of the screen.

5. Ensure that Navigation is set for the correct transportation mode: Driving, Walking, or Bicycling. The current mode is indicated on the icon.

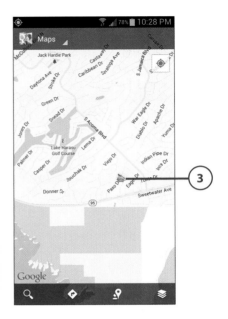

Menu

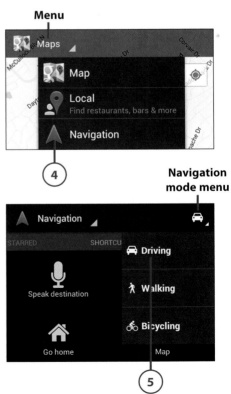

6. Continue with step 4 of the "Google Navigation" task list. When you reach your destination, you can return to Google Maps by pressing the Back key and then tapping OK in the Exit Navigation? dialog box.

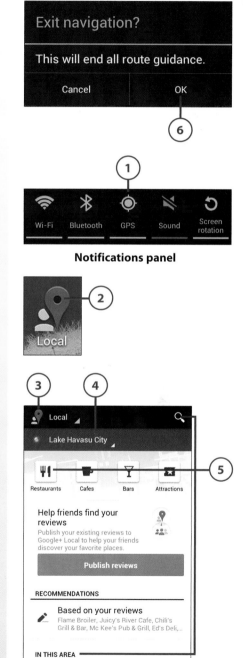

Google Local (Places)

1. Enable the GPS using one of the methods described earlier in "Enabling/Disabling GPS."

2. On the Home screen, tap Apps, followed by Local.

3. The opening screen of Local appears.

4. *Optional:* To start driving from a location other than your present one, tap the location indicator and select Enter an Address in the Choose Your Location dialog box. (To start from a location that's close to the one shown at the bottom of the screen, you can tap the At *location* text.)

5. To set your destination, tap an icon at the top of the screen or a text link in the In This Area section that represents the type of place you're seeking. Then select a place from the list that appears. If there's a *specific* place you have in mind, tap the Search icon.

6. Review the information that appears and do one of the following:

    •   To first see the place's location on a map, tap the Map icon. After viewing the map, press the Menu key and tap the Directions icon.

    •   To go directly to the Directions screen (skipping the map display), tap the Directions icon.

7. The Directions screen shows the starting point and destination. Select a transportation method (driving, public transportation, bike, or walking) by tapping its icon.

8. *Optional:* Tap the Get Directions button to view turn-by-turn instructions on the map. You can step through the route segments by tapping the next or previous icon.

Navigate from Get Directions

If you decide that you'd prefer audio instructions, tap the Navigation icon.

9. Tap the Navigation button for turn-by-turn audio directions. If a Complete Action Using dialog box appears, select Navigation or your service provider's navigation app.

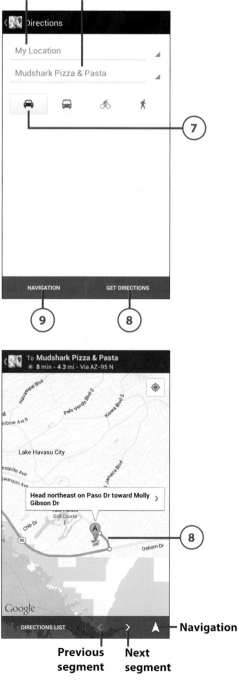

Start   Destination

Directions

My Location

Mudshark Pizza & Pasta

7

NAVIGATION   GET DIRECTIONS

9   8

To **Mudshark Pizza & Pasta**
8 min - 4.3 mi - Via AZ-95 N

Head northeast on Paso Dr toward Molly Gibson Dr

8

DIRECTIONS LIST   — Navigation

Previous   Next
segment   segment

10. The route appears. As you travel, you receive audible instructions at each change in direction.

11. When you reach your destination, press the Menu key and select Exit Navigation or Exit. You can also disable the GPS, if you want.

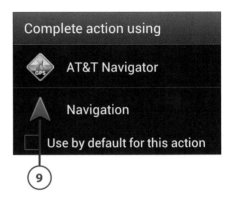

(9)

(10)

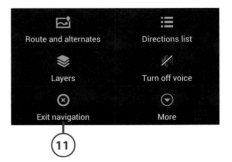

(11)

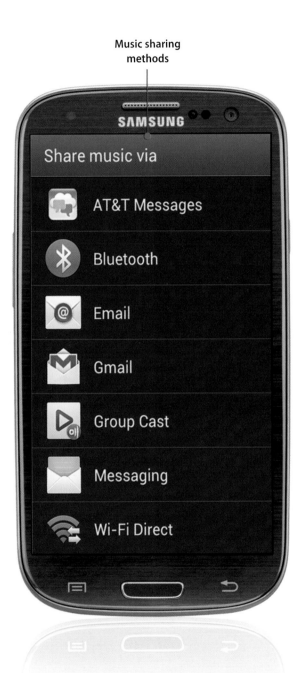

Music sharing methods

In this chapter, you learn how to copy selected files between your phone, a computer, and other phones. Topics include the following:

→ Using Kies Air to transfer files using Wi-Fi

→ Manually transferring files over a USB cable

→ Transferring files using Bluetooth

→ Emailing files to yourself

→ Using Wi-Fi Direct to transfer files between phones

→ Group Cast broadcasting

Transferring and Sharing Files

Although certain types of data, such as Calendar items and Contact records, can be automatically synchronized between the phone and a computer, most other file types—such as photos, videos, music, and various documents—must be manually moved from one device to another. Using the techniques and tools discussed in this chapter, you'll discover some of the ways that you can transfer files between your phone and your computer, as well as between a pair of phones. In addition, two new Galaxy S III techniques that enable others to *view* information on your phone are explained: Group Cast and Share Shot.

You can find instructions for synchronizing Calendar and Contacts data in Chapter 5, "Synchronizing Data."

Note

To use USB file transfer methods with a Windows PC, you must first install the Samsung USB drivers, as explained in "Tethering a Computer" in Chapter 18, "Powering Other Devices." Macs don't require any additional drivers.

Using Kies Air

If you have a wireless router or modem, you can use the phone's preinstalled Kies Air app to copy files between your phone and your computer (or any computer on your network). The computer component of Kies Air runs in a browser.

1. On the Home screen, tap Apps and then tap the Kies Air icon.

2. Tap the Start button at the bottom of the Kies Air screen.

3. Open your browser and enter the URL shown on the Kies Air Online screen.

Save the URL

To avoid having to manually enter the numeric URL each time you use Kies Air, save it as a browser favorite or bookmark. Although the URL may change slightly in later sessions, editing the URL is quicker than entering it from scratch.

4. Tap Allow in the Access Request dialog box that appears on the phone.

5. If an access request dialog box appears on your PC or Mac, click Run or Allow, respectively.

Mac

6. The Kies Air page displays on your computer, open to the default view. You can restore this view at any time by clicking the link for your phone in the upper-left corner. As explained in the Kies Air step lists that follow, file transfers can be from computer to phone (*uploads*) or from phone to computer (*downloads*).

7. When you're done using Kies Air, tap the app's Stop button and close the browser page on your computer.

Transferring Files from Phone to Computer

In Kies Air, file transfers from phone to computer are *downloads*. Each pane in the computer's browser window is an item category that shows material stored on the phone.

1. On the Kies Air browser page, find the pane that represents the type of file you want to transfer. If you prefer, you can dedicate the entire browser to that category by clicking its link in the left pane.

2. Select the files that you want to transfer by clicking their check boxes and then click the Download link.

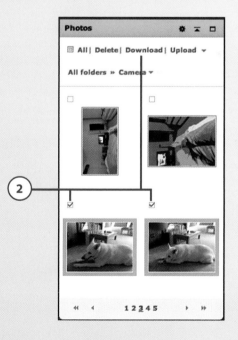

3. In the Download dialog box that appears on your computer, select the folder on the computer where the transferred files will be stored and then click the Download button.

PC

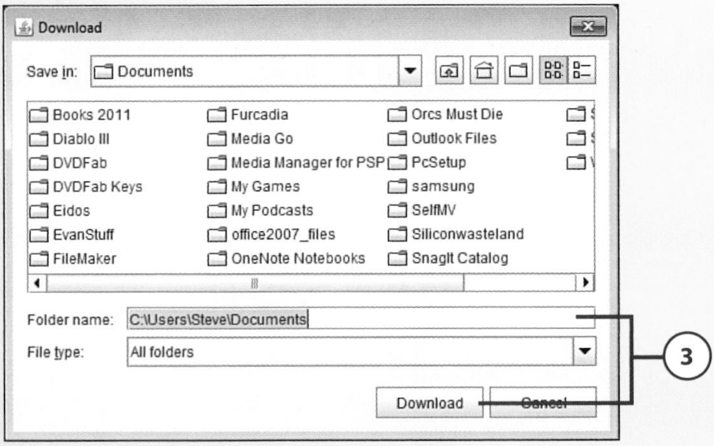

Mac

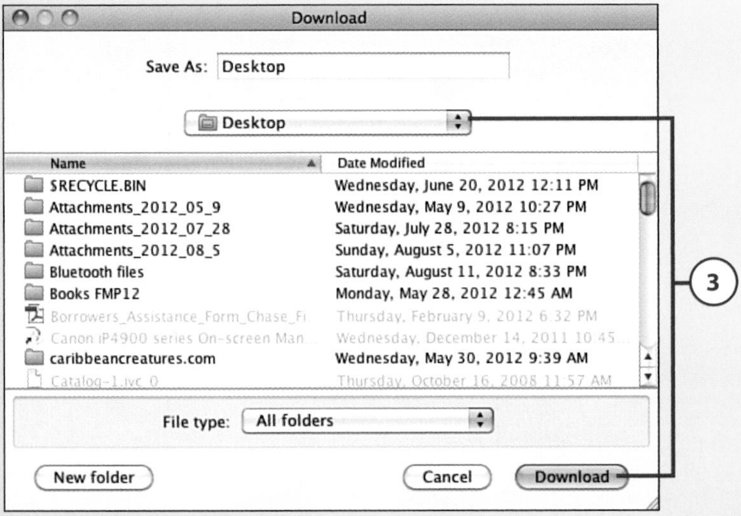

4. The transfer begins. When completed, a confirmation appears in the browser. Click OK.

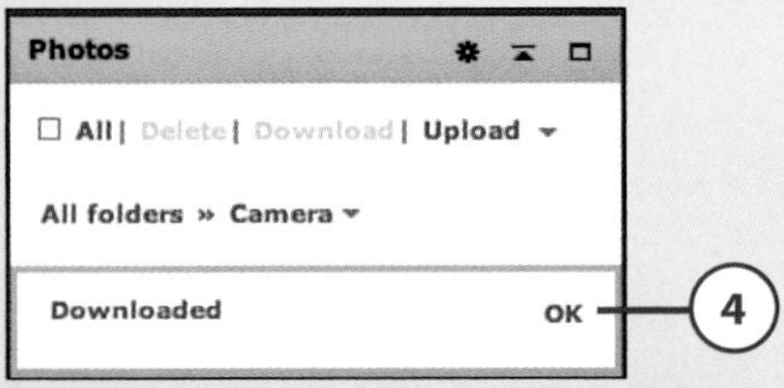

Transferring Files from Computer to Phone

In Kies Air, file transfers from computer to phone are *uploads*.

1. On the browser page on your computer, find the pane that represents the type of file you want to transfer. If you prefer, you can dedicate the entire browser to the category by clicking its link in the left pane.

2. Click the Upload link in the pane and choose Upload from the menu that appears. An Upload *file type* dialog box appears.

3. Navigate to the folder that contains the file or files you want to transfer to the phone. To select a single file, click its name or thumbnail. To select multiple files on a PC, Ctrl-click each file. To do the same on a Mac, Command-click each file.

4. Click OK to begin the file transfer.

PC

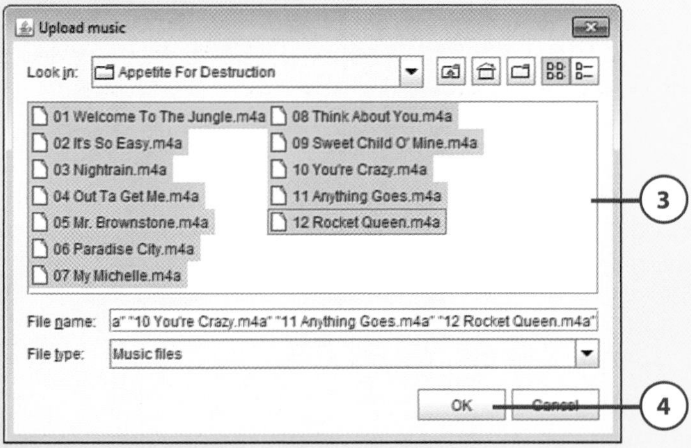

Mac

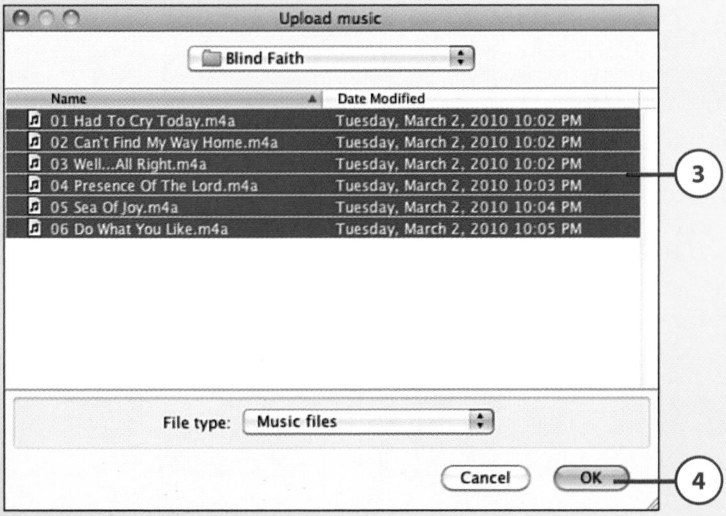

Where Are My Files?

The hardest part of transferring files from computer to phone is that you're expected to know where those files are stored on your computer. If you have no idea, try the Documents folder and its subfolders first. You may find it helpful to explore your hard drive *before* running Kies, making a note of the names and locations of relevant music, photo, and video folders.

If your photos are stored in iPhoto on your Mac, you may find it easier to transfer selected images to your phone if you first launch iPhoto and drag the image thumbnails to the Desktop. Transfer *those* images to the phone and then delete the Desktop copies.

5. When finished, a confirmation appears in the browser and thumbnails for the transferred items are added to the category. Click OK.

WHAT ABOUT THE DESKTOP KIES?

In addition to the wireless Kies Air, Samsung offers Kies 2.0, a free, more advanced PC and Mac application for handling transfers over USB (http://www.samsung.com/us/kies/). Although I wasn't a fan of Kies on the Galaxy S II, the current version works surprisingly well with the Galaxy S III.

For trouble-free file transfers, be sure to follow these simple launch, connect, and disconnect steps:

1. Launch Kies 2.0 on your Mac or PC.

2. Use the USB cable supplied with your phone to connect the phone to your computer. (If Kies doesn't see your connected phone, open the Notifications panel. There should be an entry in the Ongoing section that says "Connected as a media device." If it says "Connected as camera," tap the entry and select Media Device in the screen that appears.)

3. Perform file transfers in Kies 2.0.

4. In Kies's left panel, click the **x** beside the phone's name to disconnect it from the computer.

5. Disconnect the USB cable from the phone and computer.

6. Quit Kies 2.0.

Transferring Files over USB

Using the USB cable provided with your phone, you can connect the phone to a PC or Mac and freely copy files in either direction. The following steps temporarily turn your phone into the equivalent of a flash drive. (Note that if you're a Mac user, you must first download and install a free Mac application found at www.android.com/filetransfer.)

USB Transfers to and from a Mac

1. Using the phone's USB cable, connect the phone and the Mac.

2. Open the Notifications panel. In the Ongoing section, it should say Connected as a Camera. If it says Connected as a Media Device, tap the entry and select Camera (PTP) in the screen that appears.

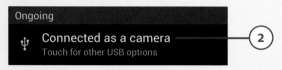

3. *First run only:* To launch Android File Transfer, open the Applications folder on the Dock and select Android File Transfer. (Android File Transfer should launch automatically in subsequent sessions.)

4. A window appears that lists all files on your phone. Transfer copies of files from the phone by dragging them to the Mac's Desktop or into a folder. Transfer copies of files from the Mac by dragging them into an appropriate folder on the phone.

5. When you're finished, disconnect the USB cable from the phone and the Mac. Android File Transfer should quit automatically.

Other Quit Options

If necessary, you can manually quit by pressing Command+Q or by choosing Android File Transfer, Quit Android File Transfer. If that fails, you can right-click the Android File Transfer icon in the Dock and choose Force Quit.

It's Not All Good

A Flaky Application

When Android File Transfers works properly, it's a joy to use. Using drag and drop to copy files is much easier and faster than picking files using dialog boxes. Unfortunately, the application regularly does unexpected things— for example, failing to automatically launch when the phone is connected, launching but failing to display the phone's file window, spontaneously quit-ting in the middle of a session, and ignoring the Quit command. Although Force Quit always works, it shouldn't be necessary and can occasionally have nasty consequences.

USB Transfers to and from a PC

1. If you haven't already done so, visit the Support section of the Samsung site (http://www.samsung.com/us/support/) and download the Windows USB driver for your car-rier's phone. You can find your model number by launching Settings, tapping About Device, and then tapping Model Number. Note that this is a one-time process.

2. Using the phone's USB cable, connect the phone and the PC. When the PC recognizes the connected phone, an AutoPlay dialog box appears. Click the option to Open Device to View Files.

Connect as Media Device or as a Camera?

Although Samsung recommends connecting the phone as a Media Device when transferring most types of files and as a Camera to transfer photos from phone to PC, my experience with Windows 7 shows that it doesn't make a difference. Both AutoPlay dialog boxes offer the option to Open Device to View Files, for example.

3. A file window opens. Double-click the Phone entry to view the folders and files on your phone. Transfer copies of files from the phone by dragging them to the PC's Desktop or into a folder. Transfer copies of files from the PC by dragging them into an appropriate folder on the phone.

4. When you're finished, disconnect the USB cable from the phone and the PC.

It's Not All Good

File Handling

In order to perform these USB transfers, you have to understand the Android filing system; that is, you need to learn where your photos, songs, and movies are stored. As such, you may prefer to use one of the file transfer programs and let it handle the file/folder management for you.

In addition to the options discussed in this chapter, you might want to investigate doubleTwist, a free desktop application available from http://doubletwist.com/ that enables you to selectively transfer or synchronize files between your Galaxy S III and a PC or Mac over USB.

Transferring Files Using Bluetooth

The Samsung Galaxy S III is a Bluetooth device and can use Bluetooth to wirelessly exchange data with any Bluetooth-equipped computer, such as an iMac or many current laptops.

Pairing the Phone with the Computer

To use Bluetooth for data transfers, the phone and computer must first be linked (known as *pairing*). The following steps show how to accomplish this one-time procedure on an iMac with its built-in Bluetooth support. If you have a different computer, refer to its Help for instructions on Bluetooth pairing.

1. On the Home screen, press the Menu key and tap Settings.

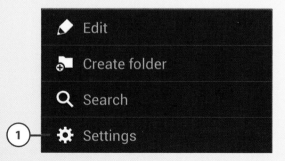

2.   In the Wireless and Network section of the Settings screen, ensure that the Bluetooth slider is On and then tap Bluetooth.

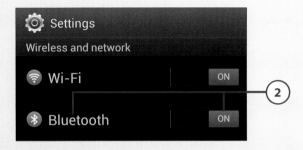

3.   On the Bluetooth screen, ensure that your phone is checked (making it visible to other devices, such as your iMac or laptop).

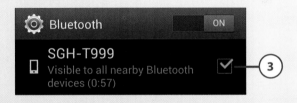

4.   On the iMac's Dock, click the System Preferences icon.

5.   In the Internet & Wireless section of the System Preferences dialog box, click the Bluetooth icon.

6. In the Bluetooth dialog box, ensure that On and Discoverable are checked, and then click the plus (+) button to add a new Bluetooth device.

7. The Bluetooth Setup Assistant launches. The phone is identified as a visible Bluetooth device. Select your phone in the Devices list and click Continue.

8. The Bluetooth Setup Assistant attempts to pair the phone with your Mac. In the Bluetooth Pairing Request that appears on the phone, tap OK if the number matches the one on the Mac's screen.

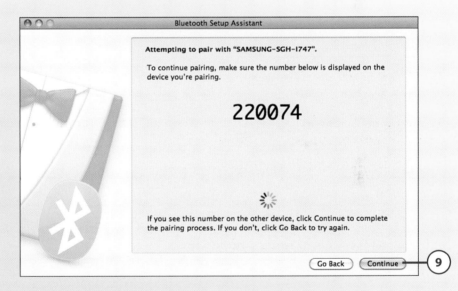

9. Click Continue in the Bluetooth Setup Assistant.

10. Click Quit to exit the Bluetooth Setup Assistant. Close the Bluetooth preferences dialog box.

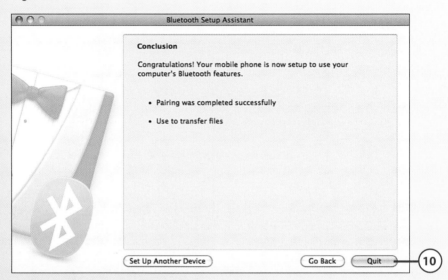

11. A phone-specific hierarchical menu is added to the Mac's Bluetooth menu.

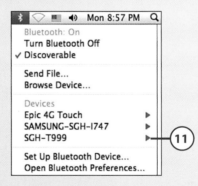

12. An entry also appears on the phone's Bluetooth settings screen showing that the phone is paired to the iMac. Whenever you perform a Bluetooth operation on the phone, you'll see this pairing information.

Sending Files from Computer to Phone

When the phone is paired with the computer, you can easily transmit selected files in either direction. This and the following step list show you how to transfer files from or to an iMac over Bluetooth.

1. From the Bluetooth menu, choose Send File from the *phone name* submenu.

2. Select a file in the Select File to Send dialog box. (To select more than one file, hold down the Command key as you click file-names.) Click the Send button.

3. The phone receives a Bluetooth Authorization Request. Tap Accept to transmit the file(s) to your phone.

Filing the Files

All files transmitted to the phone via Bluetooth are copied to the Bluetooth folder. To see the files, go to the Home screen, tap the Apps icon, tap My Files, and then open the Bluetooth folder.

Note that it isn't necessary to move these files from the Bluetooth folder into their normal folders. In general, Music Player, Gallery, and other apps should be capable of finding these new files without any heroic measures on your part—regardless of where they're stored.

Sending Files from Phone to Computer

Similarly, you can transmit files from your phone to a paired Bluetooth-equipped computer. For example, photos created with the phone's camera are convenient to send using Bluetooth. The following steps show how to send photo files to an iMac.

1. On the Home screen, tap the Apps icon and then tap the Gallery icon.

2. Tap the folder that contains the pictures that you want to send to the computer. (All image folders are shown, regardless of where on the phone they're found. The number beneath each folder name is the number of pictures in the folder.)

3. Thumbnails for the folder's images are displayed. To transmit a single photo, tap its thumbnail to view the image. If you want to transmit *multiple* photos, firmly press one of the thumbnails to select it (indicated by a blue selection rectangle) and tap the thumbnails of the other photos that you want to send.

4. Tap the Bluetooth icon at the top of the screen. (If the icon isn't present, tap the image once.)

Using Select All

If a folder contains many images and you want to transmit all or most of them, select any thumbnail and tap Select All at the top of the screen. Then tap the thumbnails of the photos that you do *not* want to send, removing their blue selection rectangles.

You can also select an entire folder of images by pressing and holding its thumbnail stack on the opening Gallery screen.

Select all images — Select all

---

5. On the Select Device screen, tap the name of your paired computer. That device will receive the transmitted files.

6. An Incoming File Transfer dialog box appears on the Mac.

7. If only one file is being transmitted, click Accept. If multiple files are being transmitted, click the Accept All check box and then click Accept. The file(s) are transmitted to the Mac and stored in the default folder.

8. Close the Incoming File Transfer dialog box by clicking the red button.

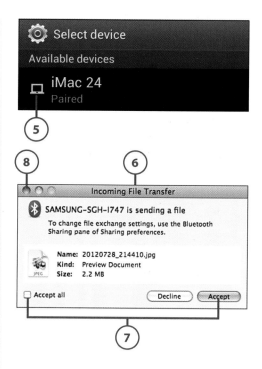

Select device

Available devices

iMac 24
Paired

Incoming File Transfer

SAMSUNG-SGH-I747 is sending a file

To change file exchange settings, use the Bluetooth Sharing pane of Sharing preferences.

Name: 20120728_214410.jpg
Kind: Preview Document
Size: 2.2 MB

Accept all   Decline   Accept

Send Versus Share

Depending on the app, the Bluetooth transfer command may be worded in a variety of ways. In Music Player, for example, it's Smart Bluetooth Share. Choose whichever command lets you specify Bluetooth as the transmission method.

>>>Go Further

PICK YOUR OWN DESTINATION FOLDER AND ACTION

When files are sent via Bluetooth to a Mac, the folder where they're stored is specified in Bluetooth preferences. The default folder is Documents. If you'd rather use a different folder, such as the Desktop, click the System Preferences icon in the Dock and then click the Bluetooth icon. In Bluetooth preferences, click the Sharing Setup button. Select Bluetooth Sharing in the Service list and choose Other from the Folder for Accepted Items drop-down menu. Select a new destination folder and click the Open button. (I created a folder on the Desktop called Bluetooth files for this purpose.)

In addition, if you get tired of responding to the Incoming File Transfer dialog box, you can specify that the incoming files are *automatically* transferred. From the When Receiving Items menu, choose either Accept and Save or Accept and Open.

Emailing Files

You can also use email to move files from your phone to your computer. As long as the final size of the attachment(s) doesn't exceed 10MB, your phone and most email systems allow the message to be transmitted. This means that if you restrict yourself to sending photos taken with the phone's camera or songs purchased on the phone, you can deliver them to your computer by emailing them to yourself. Of course, you can also use these same techniques to email your photos to friends and relatives.

Emailing Photos

The most direct way to email one or more photos from your phone is to use the Gallery app. The images can be sent from any email account that you've added to the Email app.

Work Directly in Email

You can also send photos by composing a new message in Email, tapping the Attach button (the paper clip), and selecting the photo(s) you want to send.

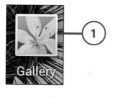

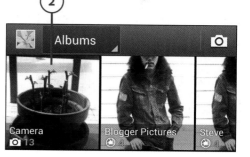

1. On the Home screen, tap Apps and then tap Gallery.

2. In Gallery, open the folder where the pictures are stored by tapping its thumbnail group.

3. Do one of the following:

   - To send a single photo, tap its thumbnail to view the photo.

   - To send multiple photos, press and hold the first thumbnail to select the photo. Then lightly tap each additional thumbnail that you also want to send. A blue selection rectangle appears around the thumbnail of each selected photo.

Send the Entire Folder

If you want to select every picture in the current folder, tap the Selection icon at the top of the screen and tap Select All.

---

4. Tap the Share icon, and then tap Email or Gmail. (If Email or Gmail aren't listed as choices, tap See All. If the Share icon isn't visible, tap the image once.)

5. The file(s) are added as attachments to a new email message. Specify your own email address in the To box.

6. *Optional:* Add a subject and message text.

7. Tap the Send icon.

8. When your PC or Mac's email program receives the message, save the photo files to any convenient location or drag them onto the Desktop.

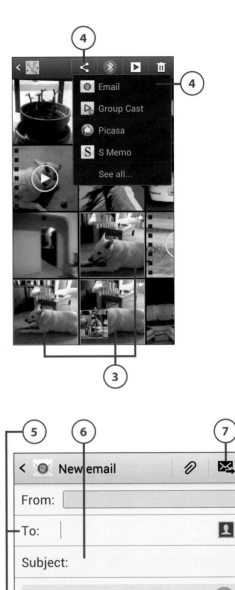

It's Not All Good

Potential Problems

Emailing photos doesn't always go as planned. Emailed photos are occasionally destroyed in the conversion process and arrive predominantly gray; others are occasionally delayed for hours or days, and some are *never* delivered. If emailing a particular photo doesn't pan out, try one of the other phone-to-computer transfer methods described in this chapter.

Emailing Songs

If you've purchased a song using your phone, you should be able to listen to it on your computer, too. You can email songs as attachments using the Email app or do so directly from the Music Player app, as described here.

1. On the Home screen, tap Apps and then tap the Music Player icon.

2. In Music Player, navigate to the song that you want to email.

3. Press and hold the song title until a dialog box appears. Tap Share Music Via.

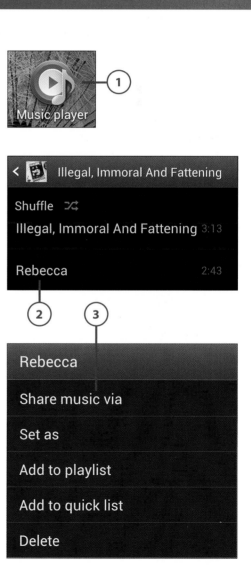

4. In the Share Music Via dialog box, tap Email or Gmail.

5. The song file is added as an attachment to a new email message. Specify your own email address in the To box.

6. *Optional:* Enter a subject and/or message text.

7. Tap the Send button.

8. When your PC or Mac's email program receives the message, save the song file(s) to any convenient location or drag the file(s) onto the Desktop. You can now add or import the song(s) into your music player application, such as iTunes or Windows Media Player.

Share music via

- AT&T Messages
- Bluetooth
- Email ──┐
- Gmail ──┘ ④
- Group Cast
- Messaging
- Wi-Fi Direct

⑤ ⑥ ⑦

< @ New email 📎 ✉

From:

├─To: 👤

Subject:

└─ ▶ 02 Rebecca.m4a 5.1 MB ⊖

Transferring Files Between Phones

By taking advantage of the Galaxy S III's Wi-Fi Direct support, there are several methods that you can use to transfer files between other Wi-Fi Direct-enabled phones, as well as view material on each other's phones.

Using Wi-Fi Direct

If two phones support Wi-Fi Direct, they can exchange files wirelessly. Here's how to do it with a pair of Galaxy S III's. The other user should enable Wi-Fi Direct on his or her phone while you're performing the following steps.

1. Both users must start by enabling Wi-Fi Direct. Open Settings, tap More Settings in the Wireless and Network section, and slide the Wi-Fi Direct slider to the On position. If you currently have a Wi-Fi network connection, it is automatically disabled.

Other Wi-Fi Direct-Capable Phones

Other phones that also support Wi-Fi Direct may have different procedures for enabling the feature.

2. Tap the Wi-Fi Direct text. The Wi-Fi Direct screen appears and the phone begins to scan for nearby Wi-Fi Direct enabled devices.

3. *Optional:* To give your phone a friendlier name, press the Menu key, tap Device Name, enter a new name in the Device Name dialog box, and tap OK.

4. When your phone displays the name of the phone to which you want to connect, tap its name.

5. An Invitation to Connect dialog box appears on the other phone. To allow the connection, the other person taps the Accept button. (Phones other than the Galaxy S III might have a different acknowledgment procedure.)

6. Each phone lists the other as a connected device.

7. To send a file (such as a photo, song, or video) from one phone to the other, select the item(s) in My Files or an appropriate app and issue a Share command, followed by Wi-Fi Direct. Tap the device to which you want to send the file(s) and tap Done.

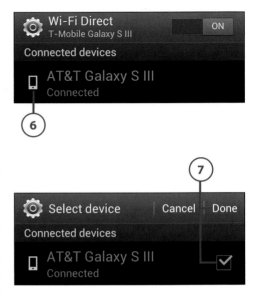

File Sharing Notes

Note the following when using Wi-Fi Direct to transmit files between devices:

- Files can be transmitted in either direction between connected devices.

- The wording of the Share command varies, depending on the type of selected material and the app you're using. It may be Share, Share Via, or Share Music Via, for example.

- If the recipient of a Wi-Fi Direct transmission is a Galaxy S III, image files are sent to the ShareViaWiFi folder and can be viewed in Gallery.

- Wi-Fi Direct file transmissions are listed in the Notifications panel.

8. When you're done sharing files with the other device, move the Wi-Fi Direct slider to the Off position.

Using S Beam

Using a combination of *NFC* (Near Field Communication) and Wi-Fi Direct, S Beam enables you to exchange files and other materials (such as songs, photos, videos, contact records, websites, maps, and YouTube videos) between a pair of Galaxy S III's. Note that NFC must be enabled on both phones and that the sending phone must have S Beam enabled.

1. On the Home screen, press the Menu key and tap Settings.

2. In the Wireless and Network section of Settings, tap More Settings.

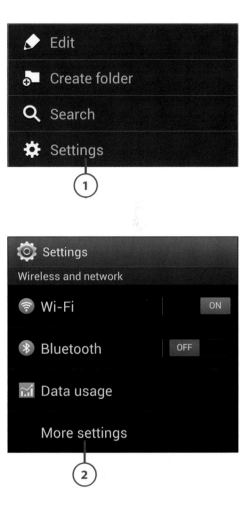

3. On the Wireless and Networks screen, enable NFC by tapping its check box.

4. If S Beam isn't enabled, tap its entry. On the S Beam screen, move the slider to the On position.

5. On the sending phone, launch the app that contains the material that you want to transmit and display the material.

Sending Multiple Gallery Items

You can simultaneously transmit multiple selected photos in Gallery. Open the folder that contains the photos, select the thumbnails, and then press the phones together.

NFC
Allow data exchange when device touches another device ✓ ③

Android Beam
Ready to transmit app content via NFC

S Beam ④
Off

⚙ S Beam ON ④

When this feature is turned on, you can beam files to other NFC and Wi-Fi Direct devices by holding the devices close together. For example, you can beam image/video files from the Gallery, music files from the Music player, and more. Just bring the devices together (typically back to back) and then tap your screen. The app determines what gets beamed

The Beatles
Here Comes The Sun ⑤
Abbey Road

7/17

00:05   03:07

6. Press the phones back to back, ensuring that both phones are active; that is, neither is displaying the lock screen. Within approximately 10 seconds, a Wi-Fi Direct connection is made between the phones and Touch to Beam appears on the sending phone's screen. Tap the displayed material to initiate the file transfer.

7. The material is transmitted. When the transmission ends, the material is displayed on the receiving phone in the appropriate app, such as Gallery, Music Player, or Video Player. Note that you can find transmitted images and videos in the SBeamShare folder.

8. When you're done transmitting material, the receiving phone can disable Wi-Fi Direct on the Wireless and Networks screen of Settings by moving the slider to Off.

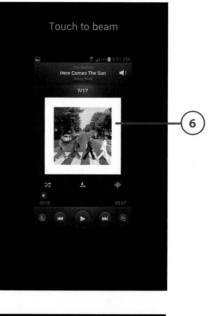

>>>Go Further

USING ANDROID BEAM

Think of Android Beam as S Beam's smaller sibling. Enabled by default on all Galaxy S III's, Android Beam works exactly the same as S Beam, but is designed to share smaller bits of information (such as the web page you're currently browsing or a map view in Maps) over shorter distances. Ensure that the lock screen isn't displayed on either phone, touch the phones back to back, and tap the Touch to Beam thumbnail that appears. The receiving phone automatically enables a Wi-Fi Direct link between the phones and the material is transmitted.

If the material is too large to send using Android Beam, a message appears informing you that S Beam must be enabled. Tap OK, enable S Beam on the sending device, and try again. A Wi-Fi Direct connection is made and the material is sent.

Using Share Shot

Share shot enables you to shoot photos with the Galaxy S III camera and—using Wi-Fi Direct—instantly transmit them to as many as five nearby friends. Before you proceed, instruct all participants to enable Wi-Fi Direct. Perform steps 1–3 of "Using Wi-Fi Direct," earlier in this chapter.

1. On the Wi-Fi Direct screen, the phone scans for nearby phones and devices that have Wi-Fi Direct enabled.

2. Do one of the following:

   • To share with one other phone or device, tap its name.

   • To share with multiple phones or devices, tap the Multi-Connect button, select the devices, and tap Done.

3. An Invitation to Connect appears on each screen. Each user must tap Accept.

4. On your phone, launch Camera by tapping its Home screen icon, tapping Apps and then Camera, or dragging the lock screen Camera icon upward.

5. In Camera, tap the Settings icon, Shooting Mode, and Share Shot.

6. The Share Shot dialog box appears. Tap OK.

7. Shoot the photos. As each picture is taken, it is stored in your ShareShot folder and transmitted to the recipients' RECV folder.

8. When you're done sharing, change the Shooting Mode to Single Shot (or any other mode) and disable Wi-Fi Direct on all phones.

Shooting Mode

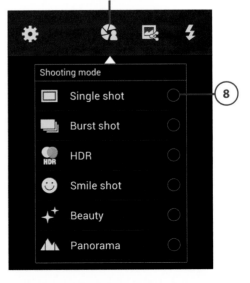

Broadcasting with Group Cast

In addition to transmitting material from one phone to another, you can create a group cast to allow others to view material that's on your phone. You can show or share selected Gallery images, PDFs, PowerPoint presentations, songs, and other material with one or more users. As you manually switch from one image, page, or slide to the next, the current item is broadcast to all group members' phones.

1. Open or select the material that you want to present. To begin a group cast, do one of the following:

    • In Gallery, tap the Share icon at the top of the screen and select Group Cast.

    • In Polaris Viewer, tap the Menu icon at the top of the screen, tap Send File, and tap Group Cast in the Send File dialog box.

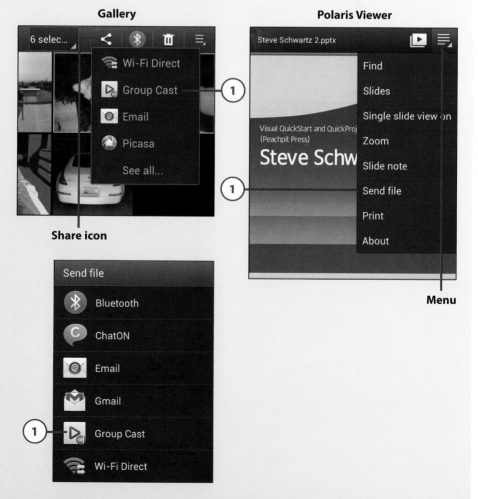

Choosing Material to Present

In Gallery, you can select image thumbnails within a folder or select an entire folder. To present a PDF or PowerPoint presentation, tap its filename in My Files or elsewhere to open it in Polaris Viewer.

2. Tap OK in the Notification dialog box that appears.

3. The AllShare Play – Group Cast screen appears. Using the keyboard, enter a PIN of up to six digits to secure the broadcast and then tap Done.

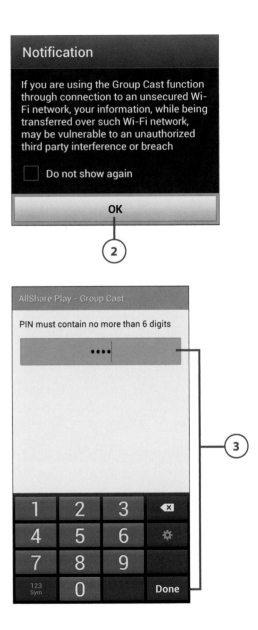

4. The selected material is listed at the top of the screen. Tell participants to launch the AllShare Play app and give them the PIN.

5. *Participants:* Launch AllShare Play by tapping its Home screen icon or by tapping Apps and then AllShare Play.

6. *Participants:* Within AllShare Play, press the Menu key and tap Join Group Cast.

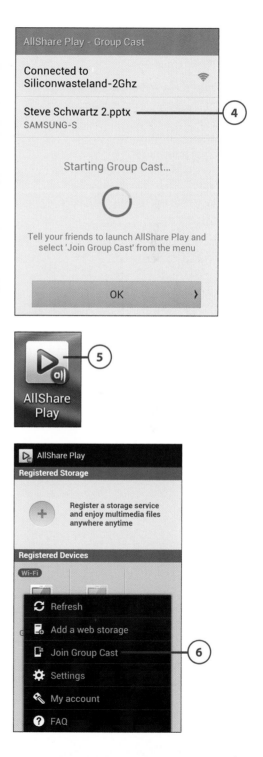

7. *Participants:* Tap the name of the presentation or material, enter the PIN, and tap Done.

8. After a few moments, the first image, page, slide, or item appears on each participant's screen. As the presenter, move from screen to screen by tapping the right arrow key. (If necessary, you can tap the left arrow key to return to the previous screen.)

9. *Optional:* You can draw on the screen to highlight important details.

Changing the Pen Color

To change the pen color, press the Menu key, tap Pen Settings, select a new color, and tap OK.

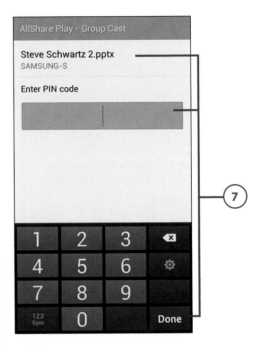

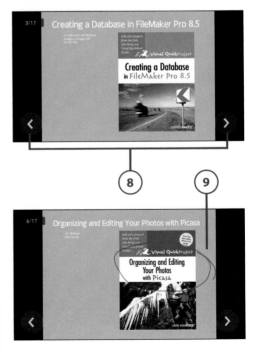

Pandora

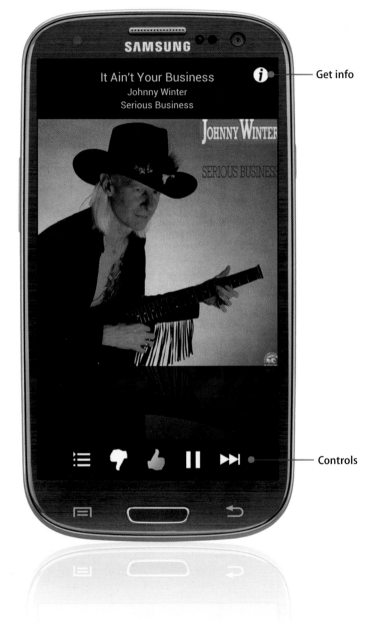

Get info

Controls

In this chapter, you learn how to play your favorite music on your phone. Topics include the following:

→ Using Music Player to play songs stored on the phone

Playing and Managing Music

If you're in the mood for some musical entertainment, your Galaxy S III is easily up to the task. In this chapter, you learn to use the built-in Music Player app to play songs and other tracks that are stored on your phone.

Playing Stored Music with Music Player

Chances are good that you've amassed a collection of your favorite tracks in iTunes, Windows Media Player, or another PC or Mac media organizer. Using the techniques in Chapter 13, "Transferring and Sharing Files," you can use USB, Wi-Fi, or Bluetooth to transfer many of those songs to your phone. With the included Music Player app, you can play these songs whenever you want.

1. On the Home screen, tap Apps and then tap Music Player.

2. To find the first song you'd like to hear, tap a tab at the top of screen. Tap All, Albums, or Artists to view an alphabetical list of songs, albums, or artists/groups. Tap Playlists to view any *playlists* (groups of songs) you've created, as well as the most played, recently played, and recently added tracks. (See the "Working with Playlists" section for additional information.)

Searching for a Song

You can *search* for music, too. Press the Menu key and tap Search to search for a song title, album, or artist that you want to hear.

3. If the specific song you want to hear isn't visible, continue tapping icons to narrow the results. For instance, when viewing the Artists list, you may need to tap an artist and then a specific album to see the song list. Then tap the song that you want to play.

Additional Options for the Selected Song

If you press and hold a song title in any list, a pop-up menu of options appears. You can delete the song from the phone (Delete), set it as your new ringtone (Set As), or add it to a playlist (Add to Playlist), for example.

> Maxwell's Silver Hammer
>
> Share music via
>
> Set as
>
> Add to playlist
>
> Add to quick list
>
> Delete

4. The song begins to play.

Song Selection Affects Playback

The song you initially select determines what other songs automatically play after the selected song ends, as well as what additional songs are available to you without returning to the main selection screen. For instance, if you select a song from an album, all additional songs from the album also play until the last track is completed.

The *order* in which the songs play is determined by the state of the shuffle icon. When there's a slash through it, songs play in listed order. If you tap the icon to remove the slash, the songs in the selection play in random order *(shuffled)*.

5. To pause or restart playback, tap the Play/Pause button.

6. To go forward or backward in the song, drag the playback slider.

7. If there are additional songs in the current selection (indicated by the pair of numbers at the top of the screen), tap the Previous or Next button or swipe the screen to the left or right to play the previous or next track, respectively.

8. To play a different song from the current selection, tap the List button. To make a *new* selection (such as choosing a different album), press the Back key until you reach the main Music Player screen.

9. To adjust the volume, press the volume control on the left side of the phone. If you prefer, you can tap the speaker icon and drag the slider that appears.

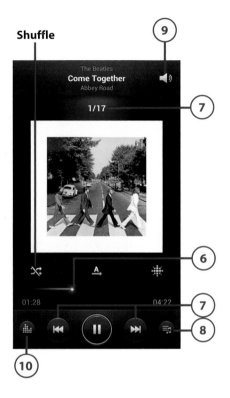

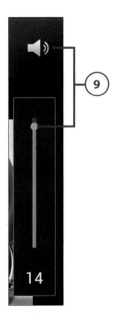

10. *Optional:* Select a new *SoundAlive* (equalizer) setting. Note that some settings, such as Virtual 7.1 ch, can only be applied when you're using earphones.

11. If you leave the Music Player screens (to run another app, for example), you can return to Music Player by tapping the Music Player app icon or the Music Player icon in the Notifications panel.

Basic Controls Available Outside of Music Player

If all you want to do is pause or restart play or switch songs within the current album, playlist, or other selection, you can do so from the Notifications panel. You can do the same with the Music Player widget—if it's installed.

12. When you're done listening to music, you can quit Music Player by pressing the Menu key and tapping End.

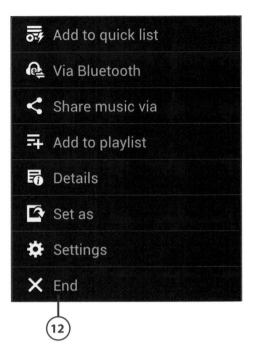

Working with Playlists

Sometimes playing a *specific* song or album isn't what you want to do. For such times, you can create special song selections called playlists. A *playlist* is any combination of tracks that you want to play together. For instance, you might create a playlist that includes all albums by a single group or songs from a genre (such as blues, techno, or classical) performed by a variety of artists.

Creating a Playlist

You can create a new playlist in many ways, but the simplest—and the one you're most likely to remember—is to start from Playlists view.

1. Within Music Player, press the Back key as many times as necessary to reach the main screen. Then tap the Playlists tab.

2. Press the Menu key and tap Create Playlist.

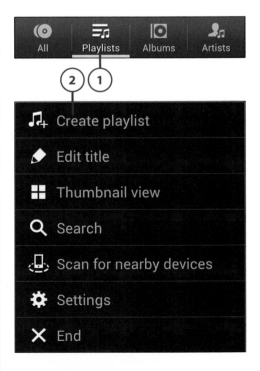

3. Name the new playlist and tap OK.

4. The new, empty playlist appears.

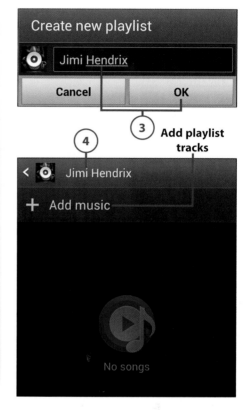

Add playlist tracks

Adding Songs to a Playlist

Following are some of the ways that you can add songs to a playlist.

- To select from an alphabetical list of all songs stored on your phone, open the playlist. Tap Add Music (for a newly created playlist) or press the Menu key and tap Add (for a previously created playlist). Select the desired songs/tracks and tap Done.

Selected song

Done

- To add entire albums or an artist to the playlist, tap a view tab (such as Albums or Artists) to help you find the material that you want to include in the playlist. Press and hold the artist or album, tap Add to Playlist in the dialog box that appears, and then tap the name of the playlist to which you want to add the material.

Selected album ——
Add song ——

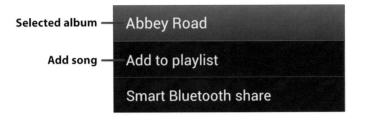

Scrolling Icons

The view tabs at the top of the screen scroll horizontally. Flick to the left or right to see the different tabs.

- While browsing the songs from an album or artist, you can add selected songs by pressing the Menu key, tapping Add to Playlist, selecting the songs, tapping Done, and then selecting the playlist.

- While playing a song, you can add it to a playlist by pressing the Menu key, tapping Add to Playlist, and selecting the playlist.

Playing song ——
Add song ——

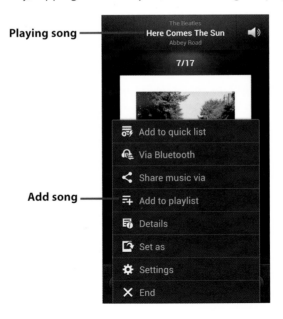

Built-in Playlists

In addition to the custom playlists that you create, Music Player includes several playlists that it automatically maintains for you: Quick List, Most Played, Recently Played, and Recently Added. Quick List is a catchall list to which you can easily add your favorite tracks while browsing songs. Press and hold a title, and then tap Add to Quick List.

Playing Songs from a Playlist

1. Return to the main Music Player screen by pressing the Back key as many times as necessary. Tap the Playlists tab to view the defined playlists and tap the playlist that you want to hear. (Your created playlists appear below the built-in ones.)

2. Tap the song that you want to hear first. (If you select the first song, the entire playlist plays.)

3. The selected song begins to play. When it's done, other songs from the playlist play in order until Music Player reaches the last song in the playlist or you halt playback.

4. *Optional*: Tap the shuffle icon to toggle between playing the songs in order (slashed icon) and playing them in random order (no slash).

Picking a Different Song

If you'd rather hear a different song from the playlist, tap the List button and select the new song.

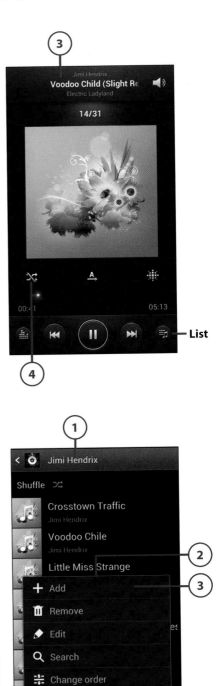

List

Managing Playlists

Using Menu options, you can add songs to or remove songs from the current playlist, change the playback order, or edit the playlist's title. You can also delete playlists that you no longer want.

1. Open the playlist that you want to modify. (On the main Music Player screen, tap Playlists and then tap the playlist's name.)

2. Press the Menu key to display the menu of playlist modification options.

3. *Add songs.* Tap Add to add songs to the playlist. Tap to select the desired songs/tracks and then tap Done.

4. *Remove songs.* Tap Remove to remove songs from the playlist. On the Remove screen, select each song that you want to remove and then tap the Remove button. (Note that removing a song from a playlist doesn't *delete* it from your phone; it just removes the song from the current playlist.)

5. *Edit the playlist title.* Tap Edit to change the playlist's title. In the dialog box that appears, modify the title and tap OK.

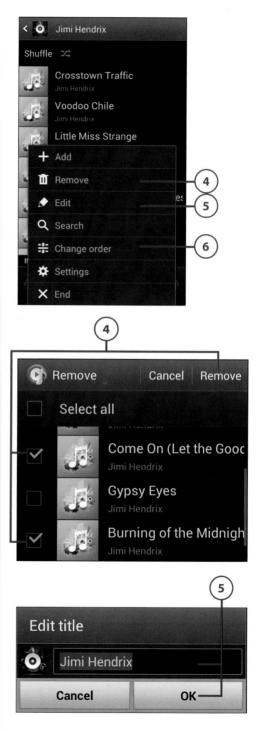

6. *Change song order.* Tap Change Order to set a new playback order for the songs in the playlist. To change a song's position, drag it up or down in the list by its dot pattern. When you're finished, tap Done.

Deleting a Playlist

You can delete any playlist that you've created by pressing and holding its name on the Playlists screen. Tap Delete in the dialog box. (*Caution:* The play list is deleted immediately; no confirmation dialog box appears.)

Delete playlist

MORE FUN WITH MUSIC PLAYER

To get the most from Music Player app, here are two additional tips to consider:

- The Galaxy S III's external speaker has similar fidelity to that of the inexpensive transistor radios that were common in the early 1960s. For better sound, place the phone on a solid surface, such as a desk or table. For *much* better sound, you can plug in earphones. (Note that whenever you connect earphones, the audio volume is automatically reduced to avoid possible hearing damage. You can increase the volume, if you like.)

- To get additional information about the song that's playing, tap the title—or press the Menu key and tap Details.

STREAMING MUSIC TO THE PHONE WITH PANDORA

In addition to playing songs that are stored on your phone, apps are available that enable you to *stream* music to the phone from the Internet or your own computer. (Streamed music resides on a server, not on your phone.) With the appropriate Android apps, you can listen to music transmitted over 3G/4G, Wi-Fi, or Bluetooth.

Pandora Internet Radio is one of the most popular Internet-based music streaming services. You define your favorite *stations* by selecting from presets (such as Blues or Southern Rock), or you can create more specific stations based on artists, groups, or particular songs. Pandora sets the content for each station according to your specifications, and adds songs and groups that it considers similar. To download and install Pandora, launch the Play Store App, tap the search icon, and begin typing **Pandora**. Select the Pandora Internet Radio entry.

>>>Go Further

>>>Go Further

Pandora station list

The free version of Pandora is ad supported. And there are *lots* of ads—so many, in fact, that it may remind you of using a browser without a pop-up blocker. Aside from the occasional voice advertisement, though, you can listen to several songs in a row without interruption.

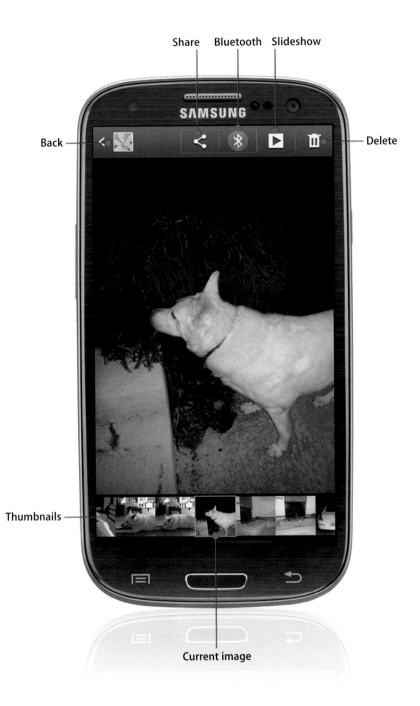

Share   Bluetooth   Slideshow

Back

Delete

Thumbnails

Current image

In this chapter, you learn to use the phone's cameras to shoot, edit, share, and manage photos of yourself and other subjects. Topics include the following:

→ Shooting self-portraits and photos of other subjects

→ Viewing, managing, and sharing the current photo

→ Viewing stored photos in Gallery

→ Using Photo Editor to make simple edits to your shots

Shooting, Editing, and Sharing Photos

If you keep your phone handy, you have no excuse for missing an unexpected photo opportunity. Using the Galaxy S III's pair of built-in cameras, you can easily shoot posed and candid high-resolution photos of friends, family, yourself, and anything else that catches your eye.

Shooting Photos

You can shoot photos of subjects in front of you using the 8-*megapixel* (MP) rear camera or take self-portraits with the 1.9MP front camera.

Shooting Self-Portraits with the Front Camera

Use *self-portrait mode* to take pictures of yourself—or yourself and a friend or two. Note that you can't use the flash or zoom in this mode.

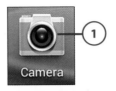

1. Tap the Camera shortcut on the Home screen (if you haven't removed it). Otherwise, tap Apps and then tap Camera.

Lock screen icon

Lock Screen Launch Options

You can also launch Camera from the lock screen by doing either of the following:

- Slide the Camera icon upward.

- While holding the phone upright (in its normal position), press the screen and rotate the phone into landscape mode. (To enable this option, launch Settings, tap Security, tap Lock Screen Options, and enable Camera Quick Access.)

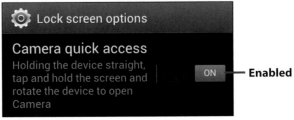

Enabled

---

2. On the viewfinder screen, determine whether the rear or front camera is active. If the rear camera is active, switch to the front camera by tapping the Self Portrait icon. (You can also tap the Settings icon and then tap Self Portrait in the menu that appears.)

3. Ensure that the Camera/ Camcorder Mode selector at the bottom of the screen is set for Camera. (Camera mode is for shooting photos; Camcorder mode is for shooting videos.)

4. *Optional:* Tap the Settings icon to review or adjust the camera settings that will be used for the shot. For additional information about Settings, see "Changing the Camera Settings," later in this section.

5. When you're ready to take the picture, tap the Shutter release.

Where's the Photo?

To review all photos taken with the Galaxy S III's camera, launch the Gallery app and open the Camera folder. To go directly to the most recent photo you've taken, tap its thumbnail in the lower-left corner of the viewfinder screen in the Camera app.

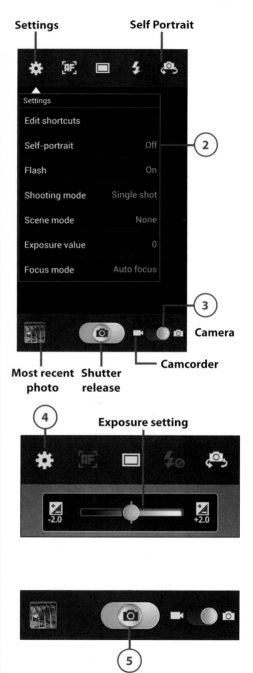

GPS Tagging

You can optionally enable *GPS tagging* for the photo (allowing location information to be stored with the image file). If the GPS isn't currently active, enable it
by going to the Home screen, dragging down the Notifications panel and tapping the GPS icon. In Camera, tap the Settings icon and set GPS Tag to On.

GPS enabled

Shooting Photos with the Rear Camera

Of course, most of the photos you'll
shoot with your Galaxy S III will be of
other people and subjects. Shooting
photos of others is similar to shooting self-portraits, but it uses the
higher-resolution rear camera and
has many additional options.

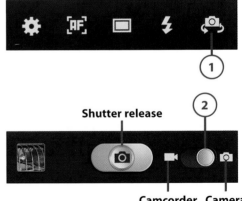

1. Launch the Camera app and
   determine whether the rear or
   front camera is active. If the front
   camera is active, switch to the
   rear camera by tapping the Self
   Portrait icon.

2. Ensure that the Camera/
   Camcorder Mode selector at the
   bottom of the screen is set for
   Camera. (Camera mode is for
   shooting photos; Camcorder
   mode is for shooting videos.)

Shutter release

Camcorder Camera

3. *Optional*: You can zoom in or out by pressing the volume button on the side of the phone. You can also zoom by touching the viewfinder screen and spreading your fingers apart (zoom in) or pinching them together (zoom out).

4. *Optional:* Tap the Settings icon to review or adjust the camera settings that will be used for the shot. For additional information about Settings, see "Changing the Camera Settings," later in this section.

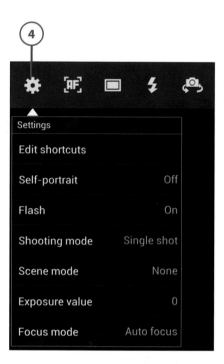

Settings	
Edit shortcuts	
Self-portrait	Off
Flash	On
Shooting mode	Single shot
Scene mode	None
Exposure value	0
Focus mode	Auto focus

Portrait or Landscape Mode

Whether you're using the front or rear camera, you can take any photo in portrait (right-side up) or landscape (sideways) mode. To shoot in landscape mode, turn the phone sideways.

5. *Optional*: To set the focus to a particular area, tap that spot on the viewfinder screen. The focus rectangle turns green when the lighting and focus is sufficient to snap the photo.

6. When you're ready to take the picture, tap the shutter release.

Avoid Odd Angles for Faces

When shooting portraits of yourself or others, you can avoid misshapen faces by holding the camera at the same angle as that of your subject. If your results are subpar, try another shot while ensuring that camera isn't tilted—even slightly.

Changing the Camera Settings

Before taking a photo, you can apply optional settings to adjust the focus, exposure, resolution, ISO, and so on. (Note that certain settings are available only when using the rear-facing camera—not for self-portraits.) To reveal the Settings menu, tap the Settings icon at the top of the screen. Available Settings options include the following:

- *Flash.* Options are Off, On, and Auto Flash. Select Auto Flash if you want the camera to determine whether flash is needed, based on the current lighting.

- *Shooting Mode.* For each shot or series of shots, choose one of these options:

  - Single Shot is the default mode and snaps a single normal photo.

  - Burst Shot quickly takes multiple shots in succession as you hold down the shutter button.

Burst Shot's Best Shot

With Burst Shot enabled, you can optionally instruct Camera to select the best shot of the bunch by tapping the Best Shot button in the upper-left corner. After taking the shots, tap thumbnails of the photos that you want to save and then tap Done. (The photo that Camera judges to be the best is marked with a thumbs-up icon.)

Best shot button — Select best photos to save — ✕ Cancel ✓ Done — **Save selected shots**

Best shot

- HDR takes photos in *HDR* (High Dynamic Range) mode, increasing the amount of detail.

- Smile Shot zooms in on the subject's mouth and takes the picture when a smile appears.

- Beauty smooths the subject's facial features.

- Panorama takes multiple shots as you pan across a scene and then stitches them together. Tap the shutter button to start the shot, slowly pan the camera, and then tap the shutter again to conclude the process.

Panorama

- Cartoon adds a cartoonish appearance to the entire photo. The effect is shown on the viewfinder screen before the shot is taken.

Cartoon shot

- Share Shot enables you to share the photo with other Wi-Fi Direct-enabled phones that are nearby. See "Transferring Files Between Phones" in Chapter 13 for information on using Wi-Fi Direct.

- Buddy Photo Share uses facial recognition to email the current photo to people who are in the shot.

Reset the Shooting Mode

The most recent shooting mode is retained. After shooting in any of the special modes, remember to reset the mode to Single Shot. Many other settings are also retained and should be reset as needed.

- *Scene Mode.* Although None works fine for most photos, you can choose a particular scene (such as Night or Firework) for special subjects and lighting conditions from this scrolling menu.

- *Exposure Value.* Drag the Exposure value slider to the right to adjust for a dark scene or to the left for an overly bright scene.

- *Focus Mode.* Use Auto Focus for the majority of shots; in this mode, the camera sets the focus. Use Macro for close-ups (when shooting a tiny subject). Use Face Detection when you want the camera to search for a face in the shot and optimize the focus for the face.

Macro mode

- *Timer.* To instruct the camera to snap a picture after a preset delay, select a 2-, 5-, or 10-second delay.

Timer Shots

On a 35mm or digital camera, you'd use its timer to give yourself a few seconds to dash into a photo. With your Galaxy S III, however, using the timer assumes that you have some way to make the phone stand on its own. You can prop it up or mount it in a tripod designed for smartphones.

- *Effects.* Choose Negative to reverse blacks, whites, and colors; choose Grayscale to create a black-and-white photo (shades of gray only—no colors); or choose Sepia to create a traditional *duotone* (two-tone) image. (If you shoot a photo normally, you can apply these same effects in most image-editing programs.)

Sepia effect

- *Resolution.* To shoot at the default resolution of the camera, select 8M (3264×2448). If you're running out of storage space or intend to share the photo on the web or in email, you can select a lower resolution.

Alter the Resolution after the Shot

Using almost any image-editing program (such as Photoshop), you can reduce the resolution *after* shooting the photo.

- *White Balance.* To adjust shots for current lighting "temperature" and how white will be displayed, select Auto (allow the camera to determine the best setting), Daylight, Cloudy, Incandescent, or Fluorescent.

- *ISO.* The ISO setting is for film speed or sensitivity to light. You can use a lower ISO for shots taken on a bright, sunny day and use a higher ISO for dimly lit shots or ones taken in dark settings. Options include Auto (allow the camera to set the ISO), 100, 200, 400, and 800.

- *Metering.* This setting determines how the camera meters the light source. Options include Center-Weighted, Spot, and Matrix.

- *Antishake.* When enabled, antishake adjusts shots for unintended blur caused by a shaky hand.

- *Auto Contrast.* When enabled, auto contrast normalizes contrast in shots that have extreme differences in lighting conditions—for example, shooting a subject that is brightly lit in places and dimly lit or shaded in others.

- *Guidelines.* When enabled, white guidelines divide the screen into a 3×3 grid to make it easier to center and frame the subject matter.

- *Image Quality.* Select Superfine, Fine, or Normal. Superfine is the default setting. Each reduction in quality reduces the resulting file size.

- *GPS Tag.* When enabled, image files contain data that shows where the shots were taken.

- *Shutter Sound.* When enabled, pressing the shutter results in a shutter-like sound effect.

- *Reset.* Select this option and tap Yes in the confirmation dialog box to reset all settings in the Settings menu to their default values.

Settings Shortcuts

To quickly change your most frequently used settings, you can add four short-cut icons at the top of the screen. When you tap one of the icons, the appropri-ate Settings menu appears. To add, remove, or change the four shortcut icons, tap the Settings icon and choose Edit Shortcuts. You can press and drag up to four icons into the slots at the top of the screen.

Reviewing Photos

After taking a photograph, you can immediately examine and perform vari-ous actions on it, such as sharing, deleting, or renaming the shot.

1. To review the photo in Gallery, tap the photo's thumbnail in the lower-left corner of the viewfinder screen. If tool icons aren't visible at the top of the screen, you can make them appear by tapping anywhere on the screen. Note that you can review any photo in portrait or landscape orientation by simply rotating the screen.

2. To share the photo via Email, Messaging, Facebook, or another means, tap the Share icon and then choose a sharing method from the scrolling menu. (Tap See All to view all supported methods.) Options include the following:

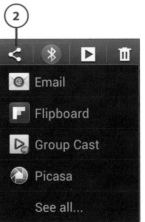

Camera thumbnails

   • *Email, Gmail.* Send the image file as an email attachment using one of your email accounts or Gmail. See "Emailing Files," in Chapter 13 for instructions.

   • *Flipboard.* Post the photo as a status update to your Facebook, Twitter, or similar account using the Flipboard app. For information on using Flipboard, see Chapter 10, "Social Networking and Socializing."

   • *Group Cast.* Share the photo with Wi-Fi-connected group cast participants. To set up a group cast, see "Transferring Files Between Phones" in Chapter 13.

   • *Picasa.* Upload the photo to Picasa Web Albums (associated with your Google account). To view the uploaded photo, visit https://picasaweb.google.com.

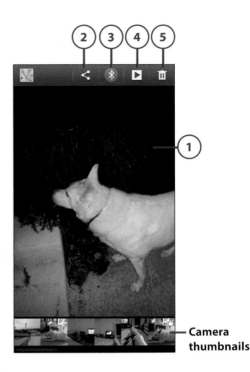

- *S Memo.* Use the photo as a basis for a new S Memo that you can save and share.

- *Wi-Fi Direct.* Send the photo to another cell phone within range of yours that supports Wi-Fi Direct. See "Transferring Files Between Phones" in Chapter 13 for information on using Wi-Fi Direct.

- *Messaging.* Transmit the photo as part of a Multimedia Message. See "Composing a Multimedia Message (MMS)" in Chapter 7, "Text and Multimedia Messaging," for instructions.

- *ChatOn.* Share the photo with ChatOn buddies.

- *Google+, Twitter, Facebook.* Post the photo as a status update to your account.

3. To transmit the photo to a Bluetooth-paired device (such as an iMac or a Bluetooth-equipped laptop), tap the Bluetooth icon and then tap the destination in the list of Bluetooth-paired devices. See "Transferring Files via Bluetooth" in Chapter 13 for instructions.

4. Tap the Slideshow icon to generate a slideshow from all images in the Camera folder. See "Creating a Slideshow," later in this chapter, for instructions.

5. To delete the photo from the phone's internal memory or added memory card, tap the Delete icon. Tap OK in the confirmation dialog box.

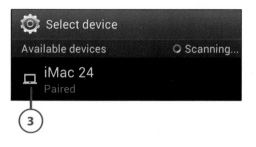

6. Press the Menu key to see additional options. You can do the following:

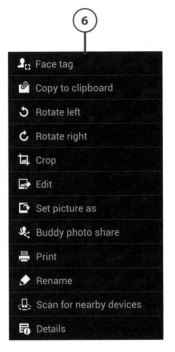

- *Face Tag.* Enable or disable face tagging for this image.

- *Copy to Clipboard.* Copy the image so you can paste it elsewhere, such as into an email message.

- *Rotate Left, Rotate Right.* Rotate the image 90 degrees in the specified direction.

- *Crop.* By dragging the selection rectangle that appears and its handles, specify the portion of the image that you want to retain and then tap Done.

- *Edit.* If you've installed Samsung's Photo Editor (available as a free download from Play Store/Google Play), tap Edit to edit the image. See "Using Photo Editor," later in this chapter, for instructions.

- *Set Picture As.* Select this option to use the photo as the person's contact icon, the Home screen wallpaper, or the Lock screen wallpaper. Tap to select an option in the Set Picture As dialog box.

- *Buddy Photo Share.* Use facial recognition to share the photo with friends who are in the shot.

- *Print.* Print the photo on a compatible Samsung wireless printer.

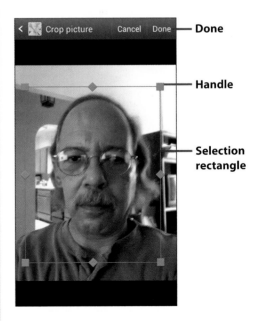

Done

Handle

Selection rectangle

- *Rename.* Change the default name assigned to the photo to something meaningful. In the Rename dialog box, enter a new filename and tap OK.

- *Details.* Display the image's title, dimensions, file size, storage location, and other properties.

New name

Rename

New file name

Steve 7-31-12

Cancel   OK

Viewing Photos in the Gallery

All photos stored on the phone—regardless of whether you took them with Camera—can be viewed in the Gallery app.

1. From the Home screen, launch Gallery by tapping the Apps icon, followed by the Gallery icon. You can also launch it by tapping a Gallery shortcut on the Home screen—if you have one.

2. On the main Gallery screen, tap the folder that holds the pictures you want to view. The Camera folder, for example, contains photos you've taken with the Galaxy S III cameras. (Note that *all* folders that contain photos or videos are automatically listed in Gallery, regardless of the files' sources or whether they're on the main or add-in memory card.) The number beside each folder indicates the number of files in the folder.

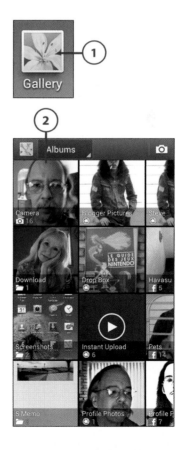

3. Thumbnails of the photos and videos contained in the folder appear. To view a photo, tap its thumbnail.

Overflowing Folders

Depending on how many photos you've shot, received, or transferred to your phone, some folders may contain *many* photos. You can scroll through their thumbnails by flicking or dragging to the right and left, or by dragging the navigation control at the bottom of the screen.

4. You can view photos in portrait or landscape mode by rotating the phone to the desired orientation. (Note that you must have Settings, Display, Auto-rotate Screen enabled.)

Folder name ③ **Launch Camera app** **Slideshow**

Portrait

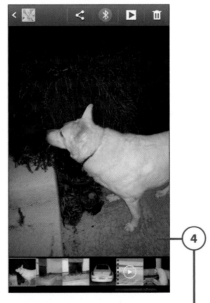

Landscape

5. You can zoom the current photo by doing any of the following:

- Touch the screen and pinch your fingers together (zoom out) or spread them apart (zoom in).

- Double-tap the image to view it at its full size. Repeat to shrink it to its previous size in the current orientation (portrait or landscape).

- If Tilt to Zoom (a Motion setting) is enabled, you can zoom in and out by tilting the phone.

Enabling Tilt to Zoom

When Tilt to Zoom is enabled, you can tilt the screen in Gallery to zoom in or out on the current picture. To enable this feature, go to the Home screen, press the Menu key, tap Settings, and then tap Motion. On the Motion screen, enable motion by tapping Motion Activation and then move the Tilt to Zoom slider to the On position.

To use Tilt to Zoom in Gallery, press two fingers on the screen and tilt the phone toward you to enlarge the photo you're viewing; tilt it away from you to reduce the photo's size.

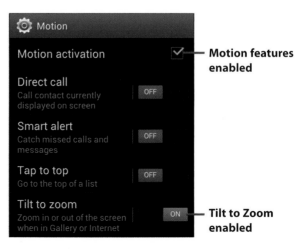

6. To view additional images in the current folder, swipe the screen to the left or right. As an alternative, you can tap the thumbnail of the specific image that you want to view. (If the thumbnails aren't visible, tap the current image once to reveal them.)

7. To view images in a different folder, press the Back key repeatedly until the main Gallery screen appears; then go to step 2.

Thumbnails

Current image

>>>Go Further

IMAGE MANAGEMENT AND OTHER OPTIONS

Gallery enables you to do more than view stored photos and videos. The Menu key has two command sets that enable you to perform image-management, editing, and viewing tasks. Available commands depend on whether you're on the folder-selection screen, on the image-selection screen, or are viewing a photo.

- *Folder-selection screen.* On this screen, you can delete an entire unwanted folder or transmit all its files with a single command. Firmly press the folder and release; a blue-green selection rectangle appears around the folder. Then tap the Share, Bluetooth, or Delete icon.

  If you want to transmit or delete *multiple* folders, tap to select the additional folders before tapping a command icon. (To simultaneously select all folders, tap the Selection menu in the upper-left corner and choose Select All.) The Share, Bluetooth, or Delete command is performed on all selected folders.

Selection **Bluetooth**
menu **Share** | **Delete**

Folder-selection —
screen

Selected folder —

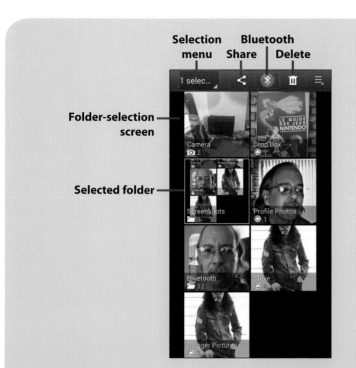

- *Image-selection screen.* After opening a folder, you can select one or more files on which to perform a command. Firmly press and release an image thumbnail to select it; a blue-green selection rectangle appears around the thumbnail. To select additional files, tap their thumbnails or choose Select All from the Selection menu.

  To transmit the selected files, tap the Share icon and choose a command from the pop-up menu that appears or tap the Bluetooth icon and select a paired Bluetooth device. To delete the selected files, tap the Delete icon, followed by OK. To rotate all the images in the same direction or to view a slideshow based only on the selected images, tap the menu icon and choose the appropriate command.

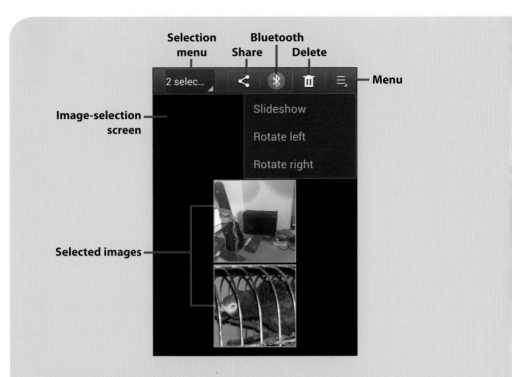

Different Options for Different Folders

Not all actions can be performed on every folder. For example, you can share and transmit Picasa folders via Bluetooth, but you can't delete them. And you can't perform any of these actions on Facebook image folders.

- *Image-viewing screen.* When viewing a selected photo, tap the image once to make the command icons appear at the top of the screen. To transmit the image file, tap the Share icon and choose a command from the pop-up menu that appears or tap the Bluetooth icon and select a paired Bluetooth device. To delete the image file, tap the Delete icon, followed by OK. Tap the Slideshow icon to view a slideshow consisting of all images in the current folder.

  To access other image-related commands, press the Menu key. For a description of these commands, refer to step 6 of "Reviewing Photos," earlier in the chapter.

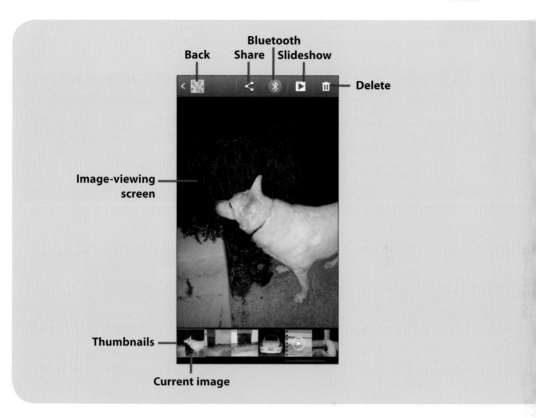

Back

Bluetooth
Share | Slideshow

Delete

Image-viewing screen

Thumbnails

Current image

Running a Slideshow

You can create a slideshow with transition effects and music using all or selected images from any folder. The show will play in portrait or landscape mode, depending on the phone's rotation. (Note that when you're reviewing a photo that you just took with Camera, the Camera folder is automatically used as the basis for the slideshow.)

1. In Gallery, open the folder that you want to use as the basis for the slideshow. (Note that certain folders' images, such as those from Facebook or Picasa, cannot be viewed as a slideshow.)

2. *Optional:* To restrict the slides to specific photos, press and hold one of the thumbnails to select it and then tap the additional image thumbnails that you want to include. (It isn't necessary to select *any* thumbnails if you want to use all photos in the show.)

3. Tap the Slideshow icon at the top of the screen. (If you've prese-lected specific thumbnails, you can find the Slideshow command in the menu.)

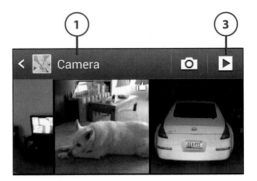

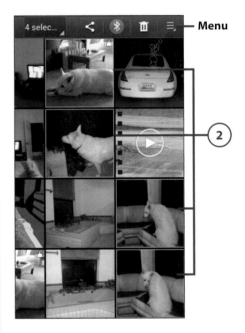

4. Review or set options for the show in the dialog box that appears:

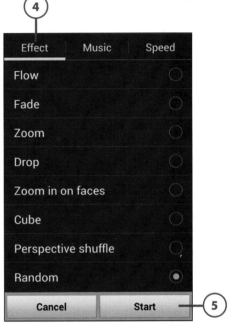

- On the Effect tab, select an effect to use when transitioning between slides.

More Effects
If you want to see some spectacular transition effects, try Random.

- On the Music tab, select the music track that will accompany the show and then tap Done. (If you have players installed in addition to Music Player, you'll be asked to select a player to use.) To run the show without music, set the track selection slider to Off.

Changing Songs
To choose a different song to use, tap or double tap the currently selected song's title.

- On the Speed tab, specify the amount of time that each slide will be shown.

5. Tap the Start button to begin the show.

6. To immediately end the show or change its settings, tap any slide or press the Back key.

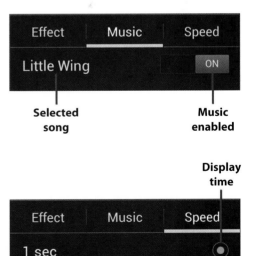

Selected song

Music enabled

Display time

Using Photo Editor

If you don't need the feature set of a dedicated Mac or PC image-editing program, you can download Samsung's Photo Editor app to perform basic edits on any image that's stored on the phone, as well as initiate edits from within Gallery. To locate the app in the Play Store/Google Play, search for Samsung Photo Editor.

1. To launch Photo Editor, do one of the following:

   - From the Home screen, tap Apps and then tap Photo Editor.

   - To edit the photo you're currently viewing in Gallery, press the Menu key and tap Edit. Jump to step 3.

2. If you launched Photo Editor by tapping its icon, its main screen appears. Do either of the following:

   - To open a picture in the default folder (Camera) for editing, tap its thumbnail from the horizontally scrolling list.

   - To edit a picture from a different folder, tap Select Picture. Gallery opens, displaying all image folders. Open the desired folder and tap the thumbnail of the image you want to edit.

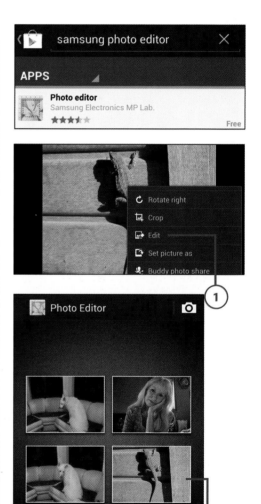

3. The photo displays in Photo
   Editor. Editing tools are above and
   below the photo.

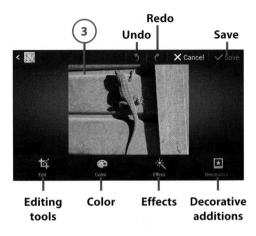

Redo

Undo

Save

Orientation and Magnification

You can edit in portrait or landscape mode by turning the phone
to the desired orientation. To
change the magnification, spread
your fingers apart (zoom in) or
pinch them together (zoom out).
Another way to quickly zoom in
or out is to double tap the photo.
It's useful to zoom in when making precise edits.

Editing tools   **Color**   **Effects**   **Decorative additions**

4. *Move.* When the photo is zoomed
   in, you can drag the image to
   view areas that are off-screen.

5. *Resize.* If desired, you can reduce
   the size of the image—in preparation for emailing or posting on
   the web, for instance. Tap Edit (or
   Transform), tap Resize, tap a percentage icon, and tap Done.

6. *Rotate.* Tap Edit (or Transform) and
   then tap Rotate to rotate or flip
   the image. The Rotate Left and
   Right icons rotate the image in
   90-degree increments with each
   tap. You can also rotate the image
   manually by dragging over it with
   your finger. The Flip Horizontal
   and Flip Vertical icons reverse the
   image horizontally (left-to-right)
   or vertically (top-to-bottom). Tap
   Done when you're satisfied with
   the changes, or tap Cancel to
   revert to the original orientation.

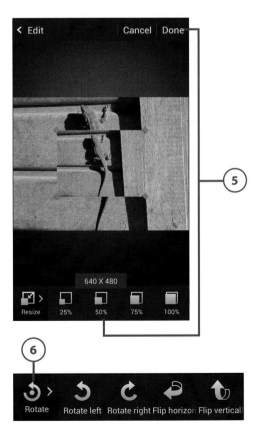

7. *Crop.* Use the Crop tool to retain only a selected portion of the image, while discarding the rest. Tap Edit (or Transform), Crop, and then tap the Square (rectangular selection) or Lasso (irregular-shaped selection) tool.

- *Square tool.* When you choose Square tool, a blue selection rectangle appears. By default, you can freely change the rectangle's dimensions and angle. To restrict the dimensions to a particular ratio, tap the Square icon again and choose an option from the menu that appears. To specify the cropping area, drag the rectangle's edge and corner handles to change the size of the selection, drag the rotation handle to change the rectangle's rotation angle, and drag the center of the rectangle to reposition it on the image.

- *Lasso tool.* Use your fingertip to draw around the area that you want to crop.

  When you've selected the part of the image that you want to retain, tap Done.

Square crop

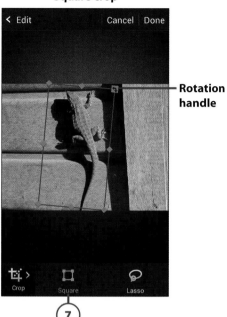

Rotation handle

Lasso crop

8. *Color.* Use Color to adjust contrast, brightness, saturation, and other attributes of the entire image. Tap Color and then tap an attribute icon in the horizontally scrolling list. Most icons require that you manipulate one or more sliders— to increase or decrease contrast, for example. Tap Done to apply the Color modification(s) to the image.

9. *Effect.* Tap the Effect icon and select a special effect to apply from the horizontally scrolling list. Some effects are applied instantly; others (such as Twirl) require you to indicate how and where to apply the effect. Tap Done to apply the effect to the image.

Choose brush

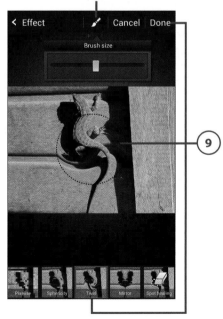

10. *Decoration.* Tap the Decoration icon to apply decorative embellishments to the current photo, such as adding a frame or a sticker. Tap an icon (Frames, Sticker, Multi-grid, or Drawing), apply the item to the photo, and tap Done.

Frame Sticker

The Pen and Eraser

Use the Pen and Eraser tools together to do freehand drawing or writing on the image. If you want to correct part of the Pen's drawing, you can remove it using the Eraser.

Undo Redo

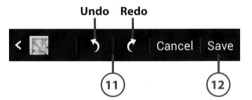

11. *Undo, Redo.* Tap the Undo icon to step back through your edits one by one. Tap Redo to move forward through the edits, reapplying them to the image.

12. When you're done editing, you can save your work as a new image file. Tap Save, name the edited image, and tap OK. The edited image is saved in the PhotoEditor folder. (If you don't want to save the edited image—discarding all your edits during the current session, tap Cancel.)

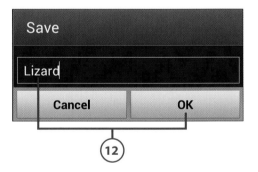

Which Version Do I Want to Save?

You can save the edited image at *any* edit stage. If you've been experimenting and want to save only the first few edits, tap Undo until the image is displayed at the proper stage, and then issue the Save command.

13. *Optional:* To edit another image, press the Menu key and tap Select Image. Respond to the Save dialog box by tapping Yes (save edits made to the current image), No (ignore edits made to the current image), or Cancel (continue editing the current image).

Shortcuts

Camcorder
selected

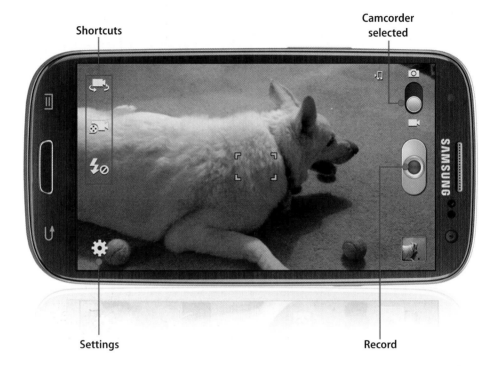

Settings

Record

In this chapter, you learn to use your phone for viewing videos from a variety of sources, as well as for shooting, trimming, and sharing your own videos. Topics include the following:

→ Streaming video over the Internet to your phone
→ Using the Video Player app to play videos
→ Recording videos with the rear and front cameras
→ Using dedicated video chat apps

Videos from Movies, TV, and Other Sources

With the Galaxy S III's pair of internal cameras, you can record videos of yourself, others, and anything that moves. The phone's high-resolution screen makes it ideal for viewing those videos, as well as movies and TV shows that you've extracted from DVDs, rented or purchased online, or streamed to special video player apps.

Streaming Video to the Phone

Streaming video is sent to your phone as a stream of data that plays as it's transmitted. Unlike material that you download, streaming requires an active Internet connection and doesn't result in a file that's permanently stored on your phone. If you want to watch the same video again, you'll need to stream it again. You can access streaming video through dedicated apps or by clicking web page links.

Streaming with a Dedicated App

The two most common classes of streaming video apps are sub-scription based and free. Examples of subscription-based apps include Netflix, HBO Go, and Max Go (for Cinemax). To access Netflix movies, you must be a Netflix streaming subscriber. To access HBO or Cinemax, you must currently receive HBO or Cinemax through a supported satellite or cable TV provider.

After installing and launching any of these apps, you sign in with the username and password that you use to log on to the provider's website at www.netflixcom, www.hbogo.com, or www.maxgo.com. The apps are designed to remember this login information, so future launches won't require you to reenter it.

Netflix login ———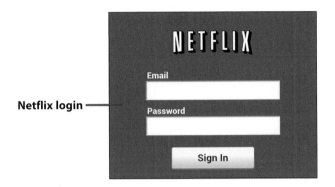

Many other apps for streaming video don't require a subscription. Examples include YouTube, MTV News, and Adult Swim.

Adult Swim app

Depending on how the streaming app was designed, when you select a video to view, it plays in a dedicated player or in Video Player, an app that's preinstalled on the Galaxy S III. The controls most players provide are similar to the ones in Video Player. In the Adult Swim player, for example, you can tap the screen at any time to display the playback controller and then do any of the following:

Adult Swim player

- To start/restart or pause playback, tap the Pause/Play button.

- To jump forward or backward within the current video, drag the position marker to the approximate spot.

- If the current video is split into multiple segments, you can go to the next or the previous segment by tapping a segment icon.

- To review information about the video you're watching, tap the Information icon.

- To share the video with others, tap the Share icon and choose a sharing option from the pop-up menu that appears.

- To adjust the playback volume, press the volume control on the left side of the phone.

- To exit the current video, press the Back key.

- Press the Menu key at any time to assist in your search for videos, clips, games, and scheduling information.

Adult Swim menu

Streaming from Web Pages

Video clips are embedded in many web pages. When viewed in the Internet app, these clips play in a similar manner to what you'd see in a computer browser—although the controls might be different. For example, some embedded clips display only a progress bar. However, if you search carefully, you might find a Full Screen or similarly worded link that enlarges the video and adds normal playback controls.

Embedded clip (CNN)

Playing Videos with the Video Player App

Regardless of whether a video was downloaded, bundled with or converted from a DVD, sent by a friend, or rented or purchased online, all compatible videos stored on your phone play using the Video Player app.

1. From the Home screen, tap Apps and then tap Video Player.

2. Select a video to watch by tapping its title or thumbnail.

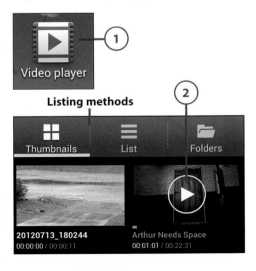

Video Selection Assistance

To make it easier to find the video that you want to watch, tap an icon at the top of Video Player's opening screen to display video thumbnails, a list of video titles, or the folders in which videos are stored. If you have many stored videos, you can specify a different sort order for the thumbnails or list by pressing the Menu key and tapping List By.

You can also select a video in Gallery, My Files, or another app that uses Video Player as its player. Doing this launches Video Player and begins playing the selected movie or clip—effectively skipping steps 1 and 2.

Sort options ——

3. The controller appears and the video begins to play. Rotate the screen to the desired orientation: landscape or portrait.

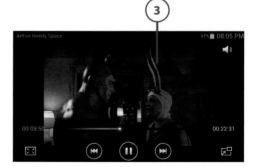

Partially Viewed Videos

When examined on the video selection screen, videos that you halted partway through playback have a blue progress bar that shows approximately where you left off. When you select one of these videos, it will restart at that point rather than at the beginning.

4. While playing the video, you can use the controller to do the following:

- To start/restart or pause playback, tap the Pause/Play button.

- To jump forward or backward within the current video, drag the position marker to the approximate spot.

- Tap the Rewind button to jump to the beginning of the current video or, if you're at the beginning, to the previous video in the Videos list. Press and hold the Rewind button to scroll backward through the current video.

- Tap the Fast Forward button to jump to the beginning of the next video. Press and hold the Fast Forward button to scroll forward through the current video; the longer you hold the icon, the faster it scrolls.

- To adjust the playback volume, tap the Volume icon and drag the slider that appears. (You can also change volume by pressing the volume control on the left side of the phone.)

- To exit the current video, press the Back key twice. To exit Video Player, press the Home key.

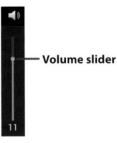

Title · Position marker · Volume

Video size · Rewind or prev. video · Pause or Play · Fast Forward or next video · Picture in Picture

Volume slider

Adjusting the Image Size

You can tap the Video Size icon in the lower-left corner to change the way the video is sized to fit the phone's screen. Depending on how the video was encoded and the display type for which it was intended, some sizes may stretch the image in one direction and others may clip the image horizontally or vertically to fit. Tap the icon repeatedly to see all display options.

Picture in Picture (or Pop Up Play)

If you want to continue viewing a video while doing other things on your phone (such as reading email), tap the Picture in Picture icon. Your Home screen appears, but contains a miniature, movable version of the playing video. You can use your fingertip to move the video to any part the screen. If you launch or switch to a different screen or app, the Picture in Picture video moves with it. (This feature is only available for unprotected videos.)

To end Picture in Picture, press and hold it and then tap the red minus (–) icon that appears on the video. To return to Video Player, tap the Picture in Picture video.

Picture in Picture ————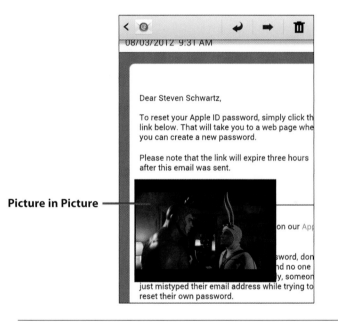

Using the Video Player Menu

While running Video Player, you can press the Menu key at any time and select from these options:

Video Player menu

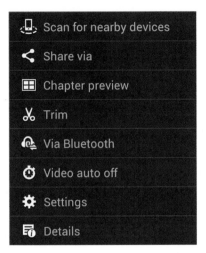

- *Scan for Nearby Devices.* Scan for eligible devices within range with which media can be shared.

- *Share Via.* Transmit the video to others (Messaging, Email, Gmail) or another device (Bluetooth, Wi-Fi Direct), or post it on a social networking or chat site (YouTube, ChatOn, Google+, Facebook). Note that many videos are too large to be shared via text messaging, email, or Gmail.

- *Chapter Preview.* Display thumbnails of chapter breakpoints. When you tap a thumbnail, the video resumes at that point. (Note that if you pause the video before choosing the Chapter Preview command, it will also be paused after you tap a thumbnail.)

Chapter previews

- *Trim.* Trim extraneous material from the beginning and/or end of the current video. Drag the beginning and end markers to select the part of the video that you want to retain, use the Preview icon to ensure that the selection is accurate, tap the Trim icon, and then save the trimmed material over the original video or as a new video.

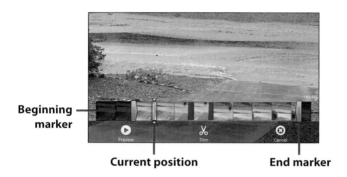

Beginning marker — **Current position** — **End marker**

- *Via Bluetooth.* Transmit the audio to a paired Bluetooth headset.

- *Video Auto Off.* Like the sleep timer on a TV, choose this command to automatically turn off video playback after a specified period (such as 30 minutes) or when the current video ends.

- *Settings.* Change display settings for the video.

Settings menu

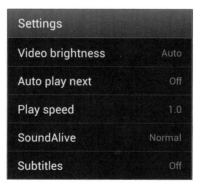

- *Details.* Display information about the video, such as its file format, resolution, and size.

Details list

Details

Name
Arthur Needs Space

Size
292MB

Resolution
544x408

Duration
22:31

Format
video/mp4

Date modified
08/03/2012

Close

Converting DVD Videos for Playback on the Phone

Many programs enable you to extract video content from DVDs for playback on the Galaxy S III. The following task shows how to extract video using DVD Ripper, a DVD-to-mobile conversion utility for Windows and Mac OS X from www.dvdfab.com. Each extracted movie or TV show results in a single MPEG-4 (.mp4) file that you can view with the Video Player app.

1. Launch DVDFab on your computer.

2. Select DVD Ripper in the left pane and select a device type, such as Android or Samsung. (If the device type isn't visible in the pane, choose it from the More submenu.)

3. Insert the DVD that contains the material you want to extract, and wait for the program to scan and analyze the DVD's file structure.

4. Choose a profile from the Profile drop-down menu at the bottom of the window. The profile sets the initial resolution, display size, and audio settings so they are compatible with the phone.

About Profiles

Although DVD Ripper comes with dozens of profiles, it doesn't currently have an official Galaxy S III profile. You can wait for the official profile to be included in an update, use the Profile Editor application to create a profile, use a similar profile (such as the iPod touch or the Galaxy S II), or check for a user-contributed profile at http://profile.dvdfab.com.

5. In the center pane, select the material that you want to convert for playback on the phone by doing one of the following:

   • If this is a movie DVD, the movie automatically is selected. (Generally, the movie will have the longest Play Time of the items on the DVD.)

   • If this is an *episodic* DVD (one containing multiple episodes of a television show, for example), click the check box of each episode that you want to convert. The application reanalyzes each episode that you check.

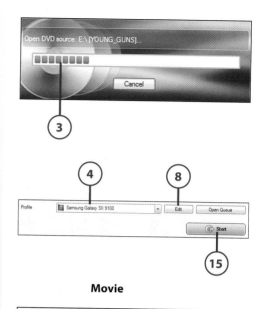

Open DVD source: E:\ [YOUNG_GUNS]...

Cancel

3

4   8

| Profile | Samsung Galaxy SII 9100 | | Edit | Open Queue |

Start

15

Movie

Title(Ang...	Play Time	Chapter	Aspect R...	Format
11	0:11	2	16:9	MPEG2
12	1:46:40	26	16:9	MPEG2
13	0:13	2	16:9	MPEG2
15	30:55	2	16:9	MPEG2
7	1:23	2	4:3	MPEG2
4	2:08	2	4:3	MPEG2
5	2:08	2	4:3	MPEG2
6	1:43	2	4:3	MPEG2
14	2:09	2	4:3	MPEG2
8	1:26	2	4:3	MPEG2

5

TV episodes

Title(Ang...	Play Time	Chapter	Aspect R...	Format
1	22:31	6	4:3	MPEG2
2	22:29	6	4:3	MPEG2
3	22:33	6	4:3	MPEG2
4	22:30	6	4:3	MPEG2
5	22:24	6	4:3	MPEG2
6	22:13	6	4:3	MPEG2
7	22:33	6	4:3	MPEG2
17	0:16	2	16:9	MPEG2
8	0:24	2	4:3	MPEG2
9	0:24	2	4:3	MPEG2
10	0:14	2	4:3	MPEG2
11	0:14	2	4:3	MPEG2
12	0:34	2	4:3	MPEG2

5

Using the Preview Window

Regardless of a DVD's contents, you can preview each movie, episode, and other material (such as bloopers and deleted scenes) in the Preview window. Previewing can help ensure that you've selected the correct video(s).

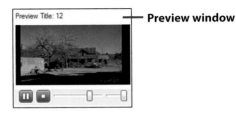

Preview window

6. In the top-right pane, select an audio option. Be sure to preview the material to ensure that you've chosen normal dialogue instead of director commentary.

7. Use the bottom-right pane to enable or disable subtitles, if the disk includes them. Do one of the following:

   - To display normal subtitles throughout the video, select a Subpicture language.

   - To disable normal subtitles, ensure that no languages are checked.

   - To ensure that important subtitles are displayed (when an actor is momentarily speaking in a foreign language), select Display Only Forced Subpicture.

8. You can set the resolution for a movie or each episode that you're extracting. Click the Edit button to review the current settings in the Conversion Settings window (see p. 445).

Options for Episodes

If you're converting multiple TV episodes, each can have different options (although you'll normally want them all to be the same). To change options for a particular episode, select the episode in the title list and then make the desired changes. To ensure consistency, be sure to apply these same settings to *every* episode.

9. You can edit the File Name and Title entries in the File Type section of the Conversion Settings window.

   - The filename automatically ends with a `.mp4` extension, so you can safely delete the `.mpeg4` suffix. In addition, the filename need not be in capital letters and can contain spaces. However, avoid using special characters, such as slashes and colons.

   - The Title is the text that identifies the movie or video when it's listed in Video Player or other players. Edit it to something more descriptive. In this example, I changed it to *Young Guns*.

⑨

```
┌─File Type: mp4 ─────────────────────────────┐
│  File Name      YOUNG_GUNS.mpeg4            │
│  Title          YOUNG_GUNS.Title12.DVDRip   │
│  Author                                     │
└─────────────────────────────────────────────┘
```

10. You can change Encoding Method and/or Bitrate to improve the visual quality of the video.

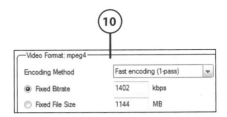

- Encoding Method can be 1-pass or 2-pass. The latter improves the quality but increases the time required to perform the encoding because it makes two passes through the source video.

- If you want to experiment with higher-quality output, try increasing the Fixed Bitrate setting. If you see a noticeable difference from the same video encoded at the default bit rate and you don't mind that the output results in a larger file, you might want to do the same with most videos.

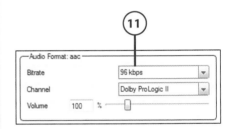

11. To improve the audio quality and clarity, you can choose a higher setting (such as 128 or 160 kbps) from the Bitrate menu in the Audio Format section of the Conversion Settings window. (Available Bitrate options are profile-dependent.)

12. Select a different frame resolution, if you want. (Note that the maximum resolution that can be displayed on the Galaxy S III is 1280×720.) To see how different settings affect the resulting video, click the Video Effect Settings button.

Another Path

You can also reach the Video Effect Settings window by clicking the Video Effect Settings button in the main window.

13. Click the OK button to return to the main screen when you're done reviewing and changing settings in the Conversion Settings window.

14. The Target box at the top of the main window shows the *path* (disk/folder) where the resulting MPEG-4 video file will be saved. To specify a different location, click the down arrow to the right to choose a location that you've previously used or click the folder icon to specify a new location.

Previous folders

Source: E:\ [YOUNG_GUNS]

Target: D:\captures\Galaxy S II\

(14)

Different folder

15. When you're satisfied with the settings, convert the selected video(s) by clicking the Start button (see p. 445).

(see p. 445)

When you're finished extracting videos, transfer them to your phone using any of the file-transfer techniques described in Chapter 13, "Transferring and Sharing Files." The new files will appear in the Video Player file list.

>>>Go Further

MORE VIDEO SOURCES

In addition to extracting videos from your personal DVD collection, there are other sources of ready-to-play (or *almost* ready-to-play) videos for your Galaxy S III. You can rent or purchase videos using the Play Store, Play Movies and TV, Media Hub, and Amazon Appstore apps; some recent movies include a version for phones and similar multimedia devices; and you can install software (such as Jaksta from www.jaksta.com) that can convert streaming video to MPEG-4 videos that will play on your phone.

Recording Videos with the Phone

Using your phone's cameras, you can create movies that are suitable for posting on websites, emailing to friends, and playing on your phone or a flat-screen TV.

1. Launch Camera by doing one of the following:

   - Tap the Camera shortcut on the Home screen.

   - On the Home screen, tap Apps and then Camera.

   - On the lock screen, slide the Camera icon up.

   - On the lock screen, hold the phone upright (in its normal position), press the screen and rotate the phone into landscape mode. (To enable this option, launch Settings, tap Security, tap Lock Screen Options, and set Camera Quick Access to On.)

2. Slide the switch at the bottom of the screen to the Camcorder position—to indicate that you're about to shoot a movie rather than a photo.

3. *Optional:* To switch between the rear-facing and front-facing cameras, tap the Self Portrait icon.

4. Decide whether to shoot the video in portrait or landscape orientation and, if necessary, rotate the phone.

5. Set the zoom level by placing two fingers on the screen and spreading them apart or squeezing them together. Note that you can change the zoom level as you're recording, if it's desirable.

Camera

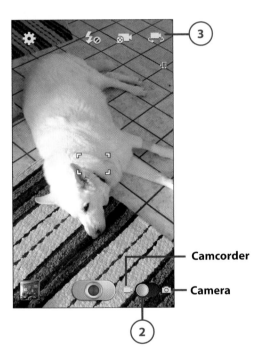

Camcorder

Camera

6. Tap the Settings icon at the top of the screen to review or change settings for the recording. (Many of the Settings options are identical to those available to you when shooting photos, as explained in "Changing the Camera Settings" in Chapter 15, "Shooting, Editing, and Sharing Photos.") When you're done making changes, dismiss the menu by tapping anywhere else onscreen or by pressing the Back key.

7. When you're ready to begin recording, tap the Record button.

8. When you're done recording, tap the Record button again. The MPEG-4 video is automatically stored in the DCIM/Camera folder in the phone's built-in memory or the memory card, depending on the setting for Storage in step 6.

9. If you want to view the video now, tap its icon in the lower-left corner of the screen. The Video Player app launches and plays the new video. Refer to Chapter 15 for options for sharing your video masterpieces.

Important Settings

In addition to the settings for shooting photos that were explained in Chapter 15, two camcorder-specific settings are important:

- *Recording Mode.* Specify a normal recording or a highly compressed one that's suitable for attaching to an MMS (Multimedia Messaging Service) message.

- *Resolution.* Select a resolution that's based on the video's intended use. Each resolution setting specifies the horizontal by vertical dimensions (in pixels). For playback on a flat-screen TV, select 1920×1080 or 1280×720, depending on whether the set is capable of 1080 or only 720. Select a lower resolution for playback on the web or for video that you intend to email. (See "Mirroring the Phone on an HDTV," in Chapter 18, "Powering Other Devices," for instructions on using the optional Samsung HDTV Universal Adapter to transmit video, music, games, and other media from your phone to an HDTV.)

Resolution submenu ———

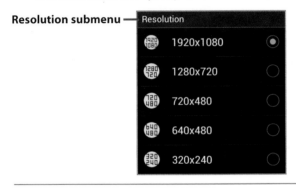

>>>Go Further

VIDEO EDITOR

Other than using Video Player's Trim feature to "crop" a video to create a selective or reduced-sized clip, the Galaxy S III doesn't provide any video-editing capabilities or apps. For those of you who've upgraded from the Galaxy S II, however, you may be pleased to learn that Samsung's Video Maker app has been retooled for the Galaxy S III. Video Maker enables you to combine video clips and photos into a multimedia slideshow that you can export as an MPEG-4 movie. You can download your free copy of this Samsung app from Play Store by searching for *Video Maker.*

Video Chats

A final video-related use for your front (and, occasionally, the rear) camera is conducting *video chats*—Internet conversations that combine voice and video. Not only can you hear each other, but you can see the other person's expressions as he or she talks, as well as what's happening nearby. Because of the high amount of data exchanged during video chats, they're best conducted over Wi-Fi or between users who have steady, high-speed 4G connections and unlimited data plans.

To get started with one-on-one or group video chats, launch Google Play (Play Store) and search for *video chat*. As you read the app descriptions, you'll note that most require you and your friends to use the same app and be on the same platform: that is, Android, not Apple's iOS. Some apps also let you connect to desktop or tablet versions of the app. Regardless, to test any of the apps (other than those that permit uninvited chat requests from strangers), you need someone willing to download and try them with you. Some popular video chat apps to consider include Skype, ooVoo Video Call, Fring, Yahoo! Messenger (with video add-ons), and Qik.

Search results

S Voice

Enable/disable
voice prompt

Help

Microphone
(new question)

In this chapter, you learn how to customize your phone by populating the Home screen with widgets, shortcuts, and folders; change the default wallpaper; set default and contact-specific ringtones; issue voice commands and questions; and more. Topics include the following:

17

- → Customizing the Home screen with new wallpaper, shortcuts, folders, and widgets
- → Setting an Apps view
- → Changing system settings
- → Setting default, contact-specific, and group ringtones
- → Securing the lock screen
- → Configuring and using voice services (S Voice, Voice Commands for Apps, and Google Search) to find information and perform actions
- → Choosing accessories for the phone

Customizing Your Phone

Nothing prevents you from using the phone exactly as it was when you first opened the box—keeping the default wallpaper, installing no additional widgets, downloading no new apps, and ignoring Settings for the operating system and apps. But the fun of having a powerful smartphone is in *customizing* it—personalizing the phone in ways that make it easier, more efficient, and fun to use.

Customizing the Home Screen

The easiest and most obvious way to personalize the phone is to customize its Home screen. In fact, many of the Home screen customization options, such as changing the wallpaper, adding widgets, and adding shortcuts to your favorite apps, are what users do first with their new phones.

Selecting Wallpaper

The simplest way to customize the phone is to change its Home screen background (called *wallpaper*) by selecting an image that's aesthetically pleasing, amusing, or touching. Wallpaper can be a static image or a *live,* moving image. The image you choose is applied to all Home screen pages.

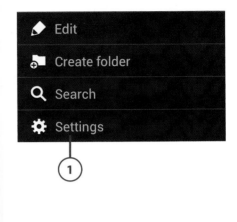

1. On the Home screen, press the Menu key and tap Settings (or tap the Settings shortcut).

Wallpaper Shortcut

As an alternative, press and hold any empty spot on a Home screen page, select a wallpaper option in the Home Screen dialog box, and jump to step 4.

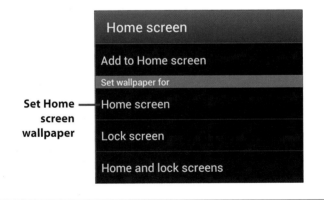

2. On the Settings screen, tap Wallpaper.

3. On the Wallpaper screen, tap Home Screen, Lock Screen, or Home and Lock Screens— depending on the screen(s) that you want to customize.

4. In the Select Wallpaper From dialog box, select the type of wallpaper that you want to use. Options include Gallery (a cropped area of a photo or other image stored in Gallery), Live Wallpapers (images that move), and Wallpapers (static, full-screen images).

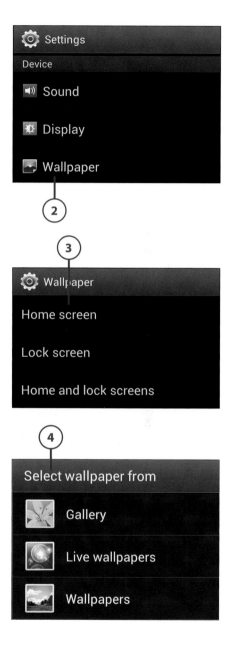

- *Wallpapers.* Tap a thumbnail in the horizontally scrolling list and tap Set Wallpaper.

- *Gallery.* Open the folder that contains the image. Tap the image thumbnail, resize and move the selection rectangle to select the desired area, and tap the Done button.

- *Live Wallpapers.* Tap a wallpaper style to see a preview. If a Settings button is presented, tap it to set display options. To complete the process, tap the Set Wallpaper button.

Static Versus Live Wallpaper

Live wallpaper contributes more to battery drain than a static Wallpaper or Gallery image. If you find that you're running out of power too quickly, consider replacing your live wallpaper with static wallpaper.

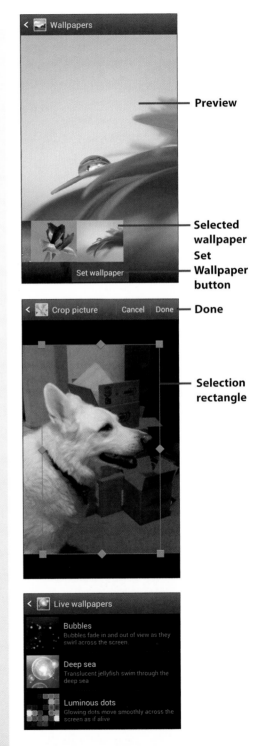

Preview

Selected wallpaper

Set Wallpaper button

Done

Selection rectangle

Rearranging, Removing, and Adding Home Screen Pages

The default Home screen has seven horizontally scrolling pages. You can rearrange the pages, remove ones that you don't need, or add new pages (up to the maximum of seven).

1. On the Home screen, press the Menu key and tap Edit.

2. To change the position of a page, press and hold its thumbnail and then drag it to a new location in the array.

3. To delete a page, press and hold its thumbnail and then drag it onto the trash icon. If the page contains one or more items, a confirmation dialog box appears. Tap OK to confirm the deletion.

Effects of Deleting a Page

As indicated by the confirmation dialog, deleting a page also removes the items on that page, such as widgets and shortcuts. Of course, you can recreate those items on the remaining or new pages.

First screen

Main screen

Last screen

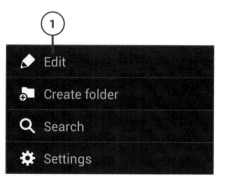

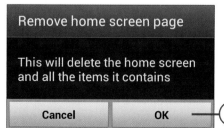

4. To add a new page, tap any thumbnail that contains a plus (+) symbol (representing a previously deleted page). You can optionally change the location of the new page, as described in step 2.

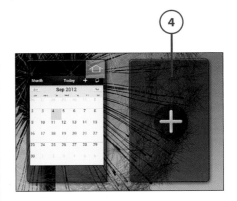

5. When you're done editing, complete the process by returning to the Home screen—press the Back or Home key, or tap a Home screen page thumbnail.

Adding Shortcuts

You can place shortcuts to your favorite apps on the Home screen. When you tap an app shortcut, the app that it represents launches. An Android *shortcut* is the equivalent of a Mac alias or a Windows shortcut.

1. *Optional*: Navigate to the Home screen page to which you want to add the shortcut, ensure that it has an open space for the shortcut, and tap the Apps icon. (You can add the shortcut to any page, but the current one is initially offered as the destination.)

Fast Way to Add a Shortcut

To quickly add a new app shortcut to a Home screen page, press and hold any open spot on the page. The Home Screen dialog box appears. Tap Add to Home Screen and then select Apps. Press and hold the app icon and drag it to its destination on the page.

Add to Home Screen

> Home screen
>
> Add to Home screen
>
> Set wallpaper for
>
> Home screen
>
> Lock screen
>
> Home and lock screens

2. On the Apps screen, ensure that the Apps tab is selected. Locate the app for which you want to create the shortcut, scrolling horizontally as needed.

3. Press and hold the app's icon, drag it into an open spot on the current Home screen page, and release the icon.

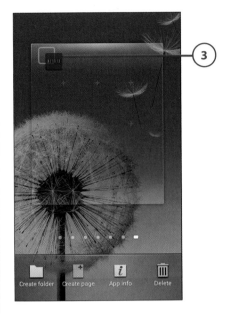

Repositioning or Removing a Shortcut

After creating a shortcut, you can reposition it on the current or a different Home screen page. Press and hold the shortcut, and then drag it to the desired position.

To remove a shortcut that you no longer need, press and hold it, and then drag it onto the Delete (trash can) icon. Removing a shortcut doesn't affect the item that it represents.

Creating a Bookmark Shortcut

You can also create shortcuts to your favorite web pages. In Internet, open the page or site for viewing. Press the Menu key and tap Add Shortcut to Home. The bookmark is added to a Home screen page.

Bookmark shortcut

Adding Widgets

A *widget* is an application that runs on the Home screen. Many, such as Weather, aren't interactive or are only minimally so. For example, you can tap the refresh icon on the Weather widget to force an update of the weather info. Otherwise, such widgets simply provide continuously updated information. Other widgets, such as Music Player, are designed for interaction. By tapping its buttons, you can pause or restart playback, and skip to the next or previous song.

You can add a widget in any free space on a Home screen page, as long as there's room for it. Widgets come in a variety of sizes, from one- or two-section widgets to full-screen ones. In addition to the widgets supplied with your phone, downloaded applications sometimes include their own widgets.

To add a widget to a Home screen page, follow the steps listed in "Adding Shortcuts." In step 2 on the Apps screen, select the Widgets tab rather than the Apps tab. Under each widget name is the number of screen sections (horizontal x vertical) required by the widget.

Widgets tab

WIDGET SHORTCUTS

Shortcuts in previous incarnations of Android weren't restricted to just apps and bookmarks. They're just as flexible in Android 4.x, but they're created by adding a special widget that's linked to a file, record, or operating system element. For instance, you can create a Direct Dial shortcut that, when tapped, automatically dials a person's phone number. After adding the Direct Dial widget to a Home screen page, you tap the person's contact record to link it to the shortcut.

Here are some other widget-based shortcuts you might want to add:

- *Bookmark*. Links to a web page selected from your stored bookmarks.

- *Contact (1x1 and 4x1)*. Links to a person's record in Contacts, enabling you to easily call, message, or email the person.

- *Direct Message*. Enables you to create a new text or multimedia message to a specific person in Contacts.

- *Email Account*. When tapped, this widget displays the Inbox of a selected account in Email.

- *Settings Shortcut*. Opens a Settings category that you frequently access.

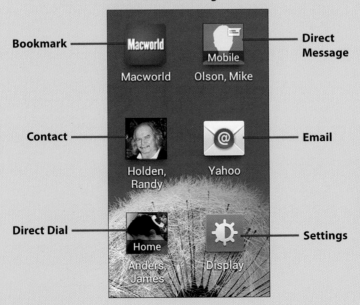

Shortcut widgets

Creating Folders

To help organize your Home screen items, you can add folders in which to store them.

1. On the Home screen, navigate to the page to which you want to add the folder and do either of the following:

   - Press the Menu key and tap Create Folder.

   - Press and hold any open spot on the page. In the Home Screen dialog box, tap Add to Home Screen. In the Add to Home Screen dialog box, tap Folder.

2. Tap the untitled folder that appears. Enter a name for it in the Unnamed Folder box and tap Done.

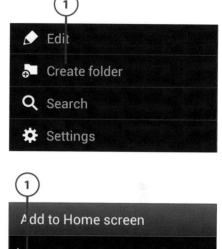

WORKING WITH FOLDERS

Of course, creating a folder is just the first step. Adding and organizing shortcuts within the folders is what makes them useful.

To insert an item into a folder, press and hold the item's icon and then drag it onto the folder. Tap the folder to access its items. In the pop-out contents list that appears, tap an item to launch or open it.

To remove an item from a folder, tap the folder to open it, press and hold the item's icon, and then drag it to any location outside of the folder. (To delete an app shortcut that's in a folder, drag the app's icon onto the Delete icon at the bottom of the screen.)

Finally, like other Home screen items, you can reposition a folder by pressing and holding its icon, and then dragging it to its destination on the current or a different page.

Folder

Select a folder item

Repositioning and Removing Home Screen Items

Part of the fun of setting up your Home screen pages is that you can freely rearrange items. And because many items are shortcuts, removing them from the Home screen has no effect on the actual items they represent. Follow these steps to reposition or remove Home screen items.

1. On the Home screen page, press and hold the item that you want to reposition or remove.

2. To *remove* the item, drag it onto the Delete (trash can) icon that appears at the bottom of the screen. When you release the item, it is removed.

3. To *reposition* the item, drag it to an empty spot on the current or another Home screen page. When you release the item, the move is completed.

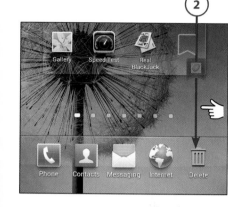

Moving Between Pages

When moving an item between Home screen pages, don't let up on the finger pressure until the destination page appears. If you inadvertently release the item on the wrong page or in the wrong spot, press and hold the item again and finish the move.

>>>Go Further

REARRANGING AND REPLACING THE PRIMARY SHORTCUTS

At the bottom of every Home page screen are the five *primary shortcuts:* Phone, Contacts, Messaging, Internet, and Apps. If desired, you can rearrange or replace any of the first four.

- To *rearrange* the primary shortcuts, press and hold the one that you want to move, drag it to the left or right, and then release it when it's in the desired position.

- To *replace* a primary shortcut, press and hold it, and then drag it into any blank spot on the current Home screen page. Find the replacement shortcut on a Home screen page and drag it into the empty slot in the primary shortcuts. (If the desired app shortcut isn't already on a Home screen page, you must first create a shortcut for it as described earlier in "Adding Shortcuts.")

New primary shortcut

Setting the Apps View

The default method of viewing your installed apps is an alphabetical, multi-page grid. Because you'll spend a lot of time in Apps, you may prefer to change this display to show your apps as an alphabetical scrolling list or as a custom grid arranged in any fashion and order that you like.

1. On the Home screen, tap the Apps icon.

2. On the Apps screen, select the Apps tab. Press the Menu key and tap View Type.

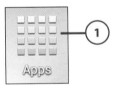

3. In the View Type dialog box, tap one of the following:

    - *Alphabetical Grid*. This is the default display style, presenting all app icons alphabetically on a series of 4×5 grid pages.

    - *Alphabetical List*. Select this option to present the apps in an alphabetical, vertically scrolling list—like the contact list in Contacts.

    - *Customizable Grid*. This option enables you to create additional grid pages and arrange the app icons however you like, such as putting all games together, placing the most frequently used apps on the first page, and creating folders in which to store certain apps.

4. If you chose Customizable Grid in step 3, you can customize the grid by pressing the Menu key and tapping Edit. (Be sure to choose the Edit command. Otherwise, changes made are to Home screen pages rather than Apps pages.) Then do any of the following:

    - To change an icon or folder's position, press and hold the item and then drag it to a new position on the current or another page. Surrounding icons move to make room for the item.

Name the folder   **Folder**

Add apps

    - To create a folder, press and hold an icon that you want to move into the folder and drag it onto the folder icon at the bottom of the screen. To name the new folder, tap the folder, tap the Unnamed Folder text, enter a new name, and tap the Done key. To add other apps to the folder, tap the plus (+) symbol, select the apps to add, and tap the Done button.

- To remove a folder, press and hold it and then drag it onto the X icon at the bottom of the screen. Tap OK in the Remove Folder confirmation dialog. Apps within the deleted folder are restored to the Apps pages.

- To add a new page, navigate to the page after which you want to insert the new page. Press and hold an icon that you want to add to the new page and drag it onto the page icon at the bottom of the screen.

When you're done making changes to the Apps pages, tap the Save button or tap Cancel to ignore all changes.

Delete

Add page

Save edits

Changing System Settings

By changing preferences in Settings, you can make the phone look and work to match your needs. Although system and app settings are discussed throughout the book, this section points out some settings that aren't mentioned elsewhere but are important in customizing your phone.

To access system settings, go to the Home screen, press the Menu key, and tap Settings. To access an app's settings (for those that provide them), press the Menu key and tap Settings.

Settings (System)

Settings

Wireless and network

Wi-Fi   ON

Bluetooth   ON

Data usage

Settings (Internet)

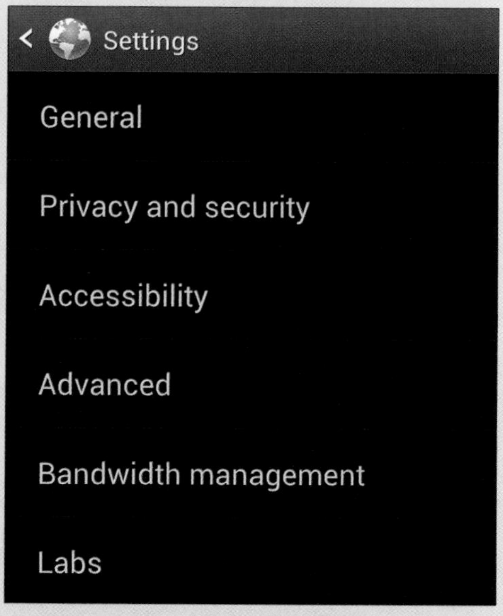

< Settings

General

Privacy and security

Accessibility

Advanced

Bandwidth management

Labs

Date and Time

In Date and Time Settings, when the Automatic Date and Time and Automatic Time Zone settings are enabled, date, time, and time zone information is automatically obtained from the network. If necessary, you can override this information by disabling the two Automatic settings and then making changes to the Set Date, Set Time, and Select Time Zone items. Tap Select Date Format if you want to change the format for displaying dates.

Date and Time Settings —

⚙ Date and time

Automatic date and time
Use network-provided time   ☐

Automatic time zone
Use network-provided time zone   ☐

Set date
09/05/2012   ⊙

Set time
7:31 PM   ⊙

Select time zone
GMT-07:00, Mountain Standard Time

Use 24-hour format
1:00 PM   ☐

Select date format
12/31/2012   ⊙

Ringtones

A *ringtone* is an audible event notification, such as a sound effect or a snippet of music. You can specify default ringtones for incoming calls and text messages, as well as set person-specific ringtones for anyone with a Contacts record.

Setting the Default Incoming Call Ringtone

Unless overridden by a personal or group ringtone, the default ringtone plays to notify you of an incoming call.

1. On the Home screen, press the Menu key and tap Settings (or tap the Settings shortcut).

2. In the Device section of Settings, tap Sound.

3. On the Sound screen, tap Device Ringtone.

4. All built-in, created, and downloaded ringtones are presented in the Device Ringtone scrolling list. Tap an entry to play it. When you're satisfied with your choice, tap OK.

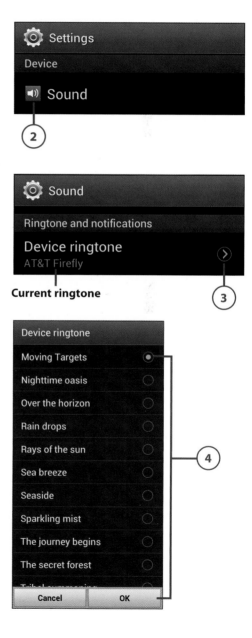

Current ringtone

Setting the Default Notification Ringtone

Unless overridden by a personal or group ringtone, the default notification ringtone plays to signify new email, a text message, a missed call, a waiting voicemail, or an upcoming Calendar event. Unlike call ringtones, notification ringtones are brief and less intrusive.

Default notifications
Whistle

2

Default notifications

Harmonics

Join Hangout

Join Hangout

Knock

On time

Opener

Postman

Pure bell

Temple bell

Tickety-tock   **3**

Whistle

Cancel   OK

1. Perform steps 1 and 2 from the previous task ("Setting the Default Incoming Call Ringtone").

2. On the Sound setting screen, tap Default Notifications.

3. All notification ringtones are presented in the Default Notifications scrolling list. Tap an entry to play it. When you're satisfied with your choice, tap OK.

Assigning a Ringtone to a Contact

To make it easier to quickly recognize an incoming call from a person, you can associate a distinctive ringtone with his or her record in Contacts.

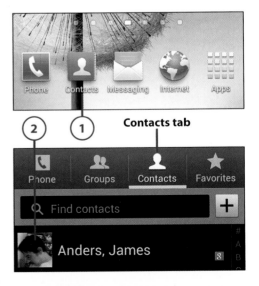

Contacts tab

Phone   Contacts   Messaging   Internet   Apps

2   **1**

Phone   Groups   Contacts   Favorites

Find contacts   **+**

Anders, James

1. On the Home screen, tap the Contacts icon.

2. With the Contacts tab selected, find the person's record by scrolling or searching. Tap the record to open it.

3. Scroll to the Ringtones section of the record and tap the ringtone entry.

4. In the Ringtones dialog box, select one of the following:

- *Default*. Replace the ringtone currently assigned to this contact with the default ringtone (see "Setting the Default Incoming Call Ringtone").

- *Ringtones*. All built-in, created, and downloaded ringtones are presented in the Ringtones scrolling list. Select one and tap OK.

- *Go to My Files*. Using the Android file system, you can select any audio file that's stored on the phone—including complete songs. After selecting a file, tap Done.

Where Are My Sound Files?

Although audio files can be stored anywhere on the phone, you might start by looking in the Media and Music folders. Downloaded ringtones and sound effects are often stored in the distributor's folder (zedge, for example).

5. The selected ringtone is associated with the person's contact record.

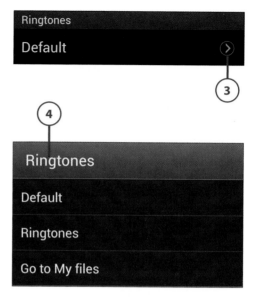

Ringtones
Default ⟩

3

4

Ringtones
Default
Ringtones
Go to My files

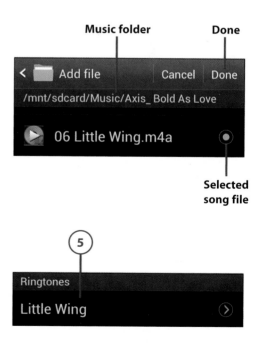

Music folder   **Done**

‹ 📁 Add file   Cancel   Done

/mnt/sdcard/Music/Axis_ Bold As Love

▶ 06 Little Wing.m4a   ⦿

Selected song file

5

Ringtones
Little Wing ⟩

Assigning a Ringtone to a Contact Group

You can also associate a distinctive ringtone with all members of a contact group. (To learn about groups, see "Working with Contact Groups" in Chapter 3, "Managing Contacts.")

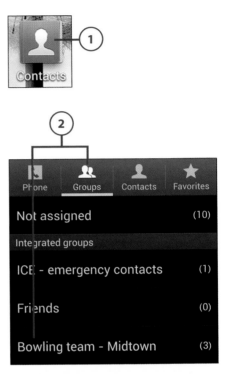

1. On the Home screen, tap the Contacts icon.

2. On the Groups tab, select a group from the list by tapping its name.

3. Press the Menu key and tap Edit.

4. Tap the Group Ringtone item.

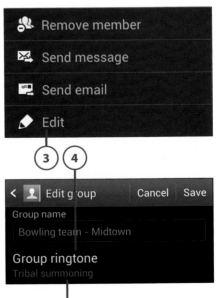

Current ringtone

5. Select a ringtone, as described in step 4 of the previous task ("Assigning a Ringtone to a Contact ").

6. Tap the Save button.

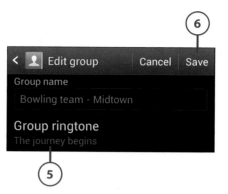

WHICH RINGTONE HAS PRECEDENCE?

>>>Go Further

After reading the material in this section, you might be wondering what happens when a person is associated with *multiple* ringtones. For instance, although Bob may have been assigned a personal ringtone, he may also be a member of a group that has a different ringtone associated with it. The answer is that *a contact record ringtone always has precedence.*

Thus, if a caller has no personal ringtone and doesn't belong to a group that has a ringtone, his or her calls are announced by the default ringtone. If the person belongs to a group with a ringtone and he or she doesn't have a personal ringtone, the group ringtone plays. Finally, if a person belongs to a group with a ringtone and he or she also has a personal ringtone, the personal ringtone plays.

Assigning a Default Messaging Ringtone

You can also select a ringtone to announce new text and multimedia messages.

1. On the Home screen, tap the Messaging icon.

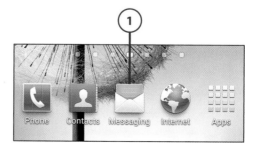

2. On the main Messaging screen, press the Menu key and tap Settings.

3. On the Settings screen, scroll down to the Notification Settings section and tap Select Ringtone.

4. Select a sound effect from the Select Ringtone scrolling list and tap OK. (If you'd rather not have a messaging ringtone, tap the Cancel button or select Silent.)

②

Q Search

⚙ Settings

🗑 Delete threads

Notification settings

Notifications
Make sounds and show icon in status bar when you receive messages ☑

Select ringtone
Pure bell ⟩

Current ringtone | ③

Select ringtone

Harmonics ○

Join Hangout ○

Join Hangout ○

Knock ○

On time ○

Opener ○

Postman ⦿

Pure bell ○

Temple bell ○ ④

Tickety-tock ○

Whistle ○

Cancel | OK

>>>Go Further

CREATING RINGTONES FROM SONGS

You can also use a song that's stored on your phone as a ringtone.

1. Launch Music Player, and press and hold the song title.

2. In the dialog box that appears, tap Set As.

Song title ——
Set As ——

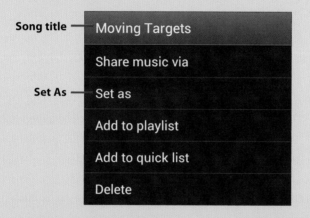

3. In the Set As dialog box, tap Phone Ringtone to use the song as the default ringtone for incoming calls. Tap Caller Ringtone to play the song whenever you receive a call from a particular person in Contacts.

Set As ——
dialog box

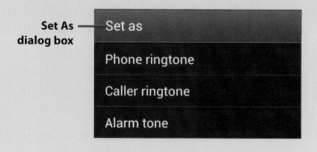

Enabling Motion Settings

You can selectively enable Motion settings to control phone features by tilting, shaking, or making special movements with the phone.

1. On the Home screen, press the Menu key and tap Settings (or tap the Settings shortcut).

2. In the Device section of Settings, tap Motion.

3. The Motion settings screen appears. To use any of the motion features, you must enable Motion Activation by tapping its check box. Similarly, you can simultaneously disable all motion features by removing the check mark.

4. When enabled (On), the individual Motion settings in the main section work as follows:

   • *Direct Call.* When viewing a person's contact record, you can move the phone to your ear to place a call to the person.

   • *Smart Alert.* When you pick up the phone, you're notified of missed calls or messages.

   • *Tap to Top.* Double-tap the top edge of the case to scroll to the beginning of some lists, such as Contacts.

   • *Tilt to Zoom.* When viewing an image in Gallery or a web page in Internet, place two fingertips on the screen and tilt the phone toward you to zoom in or away from you to zoom out.

   • *Pan to Move Icon.* When you press and hold a Home screen shortcut or widget, you can tilt the phone to the left or right to quickly move the item to another page.

   • *Pan to Browse Images.* Press and hold an onscreen image to pan within it by tilting the phone up, down, left, and right.

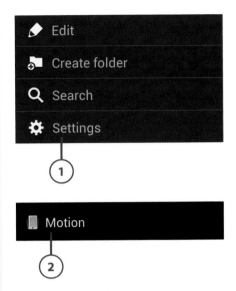

- *Shake to Update*. Shake the phone to scan for new Bluetooth devices, Wi-Fi networks, and the like. This feature requires that you be working in an appropriate phone setting, such as the Bluetooth or Wi-Fi Settings screen.

- *Turn Over to Mute/Pause*. Mute incoming call ringtones or pause playing media by turning the phone over.

5. The Hand Motions section of Motion Settings includes these options:

   - *Palm Swipe to Capture*. Create screen captures by placing the edge of your hand on the screen and dragging across it. Captured screens are saved in the Screenshots folder. (You can also create screen captures by simultaneously pressing the Home key and Power button.)

   - *Palm Touch to Mute/Pause*. Mute audio or pause video by covering the touchscreen with your palm.

5

Hand motions

Palm swipe to capture
Capture screen by swiping it from right to left or vice versa with the side of your hand ☑

Palm touch to mute/pause
Mute or pause sounds by covering screen with your hand while playing media with the screen on ☑

Securing the Phone

Do you occasionally leave your phone unattended? If you don't like the idea that someone might easily be able to use your phone and see everything you've stored on it, you can secure it.

Securing the Lock Screen

Whenever you turn on the phone or restore it from a darkened state, you normally see the *lock screen*. Its purpose is twofold. First, when the phone is idle, the lock screen appears, providing a bit of privacy from casual observers. Second, you can secure the phone by requiring that a pattern, PIN, password, or face unlock be supplied to clear the lock screen. As with the Home screen wallpaper described earlier in this chapter, you can customize the lock screen wallpaper by choosing a different image to display.

Setting a Lock Pattern

A *pattern* consists of four or more connected dots traced on a 3×3 grid to unlock the phone.

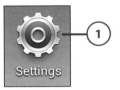

1. On the Home screen, press the Menu key and tap Settings (or tap the Settings shortcut).

2. In the Personal section of Settings, tap Security.

3. On the Security screen, tap Screen Lock.

4. On the Select Screen Lock screen, tap Pattern. (If you're currently using a secure lock method, you'll be asked to perform the current unlock action before continuing.)

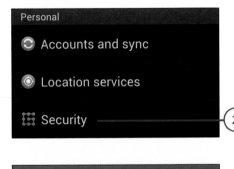

Personal

○ Accounts and sync

◎ Location services

▦ Security ——— ②

☼ Security

Screen security

Screen lock ——— ③
Swipe

Lock screen options

☼ Select screen lock

Swipe
No security

Motion
No security

Face unlock
Low security

Face and voice
Low security

Pattern ——— ④
Medium security

PIN
Medium to high security

Password
High security

None

5. Read the instructions for creating a pattern and tap Next.

6. Use your fingertip to draw an unlock pattern that connects at least four dots. Tap Continue.

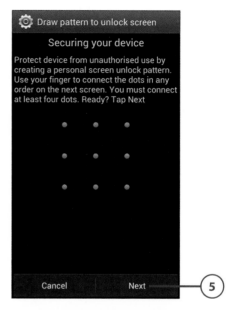

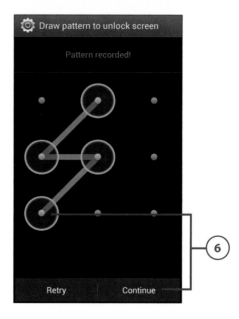

7. To confirm that you know the pattern, trace it again and tap Confirm.

8. As a precaution, enter a backup PIN to use if you forget the pattern. Tap Continue.

9. To confirm that you know the PIN, reenter it and tap OK.

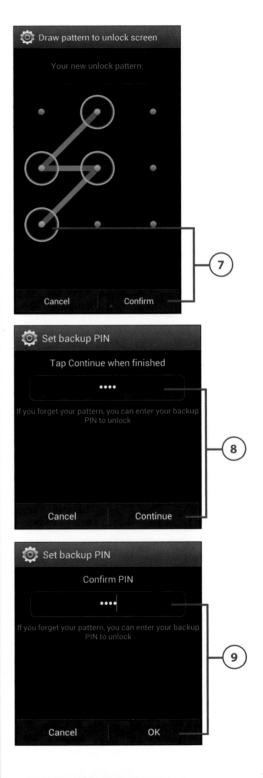

Current Lock Setting

You can always view the current lock setting on the Security screen. It's displayed in the Screen Lock item.

Security

Screen security

Screen lock

Current lock setting — Secured with PIN

Setting a Lock PIN

A *PIN* is a number of four or more digits that you enter on the onscreen keyboard to unlock the phone.

1. Perform steps 1–3 of the "Setting a Lock Pattern" task. On the Select Screen Lock screen, tap PIN. (If you're currently using a secure lock method, you're asked to perform the current unlock action before continuing.)

2. Use the keyboard to enter a PIN containing at least four digits. Tap Continue.

Oops!

If you make a mistake while entering your PIN, you can tap the Delete key to backspace over the incorrect character(s).

Delete

3. To confirm that you know the PIN, enter it again and tap OK.

Setting a Lock Password

A *password* is a combination of uppercase and lowercase letters, numbers, and special characters that's used to unlock the phone.

1. Perform steps 1–3 of the "Setting a Lock Pattern" task. On the Select Screen Lock screen, tap Password. (If you're currently using a secure lock method, you're asked to perform the current unlock action before continuing.)

2. Use the keyboard to enter a password containing at least four characters. Tap Continue.

Case Counts

If your password contains letters, be aware that letter case counts. *Knot*, *knot*, and *KNOT* are considered different passwords.

3. Confirm the password by entering it again, and then tap OK.

Enabling Face Unlock

Face Unlock uses the front-facing camera to determine whether you or someone else is attempting to unlock the phone.

1. Perform steps 1–3 of the "Setting a Lock Pattern" task. On the Select Screen Lock screen, tap Face Unlock. (If you're currently using a secure lock method, you're asked to perform the current unlock action before continuing.)

Face + Voice
If desired, you can choose Face and Voice to augment the facial recognition unlock by adding voice recognition. Each time the phone is locked and it recognizes your face, you're prompted to say the unlock phrase.

---

2. Read the two informational screens. To continue, tap the Set It Up button and the Continue button.

3. When the Setup Face Unlock screen appears, hold the camera level with your face. When your face is successfully captured, the oval of dots turns green.

4. The Face Captured screen appears. Tap the Continue button.

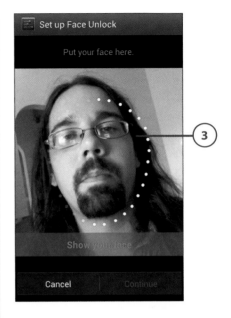

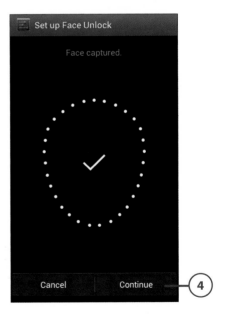

5. Tap Pattern or PIN to create an alternative unlock method that will be used in instances when your face isn't recognized. (See "Setting a Lock Password" or "Setting a Lock PIN" in this section for instructions.) Tap OK to dismiss the final screen.

Setting a Nonsecure Unlock Method

In addition to setting one of the previously described secure methods for locking the screen, you can select Swipe or Motion to simply *hide* the screen or select None to dispense with the lock screen altogether.

1. Perform steps 1–3 of the "Setting a Lock Pattern" task.

2. On the Select Screen Lock screen, tap one of the following:

- *None.* Select None to make the screen turn black following a screen timeout. When restored, the most recent screen is instantly displayed.

- *Swipe.* This is the default lock screen setting. When restoring from a dark display, the lock screen wallpaper appears. Dismiss it by swiping right, left, up, or down.

- *Motion.* Motion is a Swipe variant that displays the normal lock screen wallpaper. Restore the screen by pressing and holding anywhere on the lock screen wallpaper and tilting the phone toward you.

Unlocking the Screen

The manner of clearing the lock screen depends on whether you've set a secure lock method or have left the screen unprotected. When the lock screen is cleared, it reveals the Home screen or whatever you were doing when the screen darkened—working in Email, for example.

- *Swipe.* Using your finger, swipe the lock screen in any direction, dragging it off-screen.

- *Motion.* Press and hold anywhere on the lock screen and tilt the phone toward you.

- *Pattern.* Trace your unlock pattern, connecting dots in the correct sequence. Don't lift your finger from the screen until you complete the pattern.

- *PIN.* Using the keyboard, enter your PIN and tap OK. If you make a mistake while entering the PIN, you can tap the Delete key to backspace over the incorrect character(s).

- *Password.* Using the keyboard, enter your password and tap Done. As previously noted, if the password contains letters, make sure that you use the correct letter case for each one. If you make a mistake while entering the password, you can tap the Delete key to backspace over the incorrect character(s).

Lock screen (Swipe)

Lock screen (Pattern)

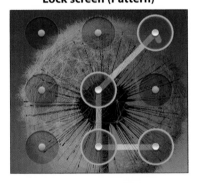

Lock screen (PIN)

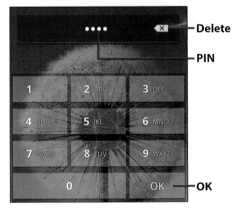

Delete

PIN

OK

- *Face Unlock.* Hold the phone at eye level parallel to your face. If the phone determines that it's you, the screen unlocks. Otherwise, it requests the backup PIN or pattern that you designated.

Lock screen (Password)

Password

Delete

Done

IF AT FIRST YOU DON'T SUCCEED …

>>>Go Further

You are allowed five attempts to correctly enter your unlock pattern, PIN, or password. If all fail, an alert appears, explaining that the phone will remain locked for the next 30 seconds. Tap the OK button. A countdown timer near the top of the lock screen shows the seconds remaining until you can try again.

You have incorrectly drawn your unlock pattern 5 times. —— Invalid unlock attempts

Please try again in 30 seconds.

OK

Setting Lock Screen Options

The lock screen can optionally display informational material, such as the time, weather, and stock quotes.

1. On the Home screen, press the Menu key and tap Settings (or tap the Settings shortcut).

2. In the Personal section of Settings, tap Security.

3. Tap Lock Screen Options.

Lock Screen Options Is Grayed Out

To set Lock Screen Options, the current screen lock method must be Swipe or Motion or, if you're using a secure lock method (PIN, password, pattern, or face unlock), With Swipe Lock must be enabled.

4. On the Lock Screen Options screen, enable options by setting sliders to On and tapping check boxes. To change settings for a lock screen option that allows it, tap the option's text. Press the Back key when you're done making changes.

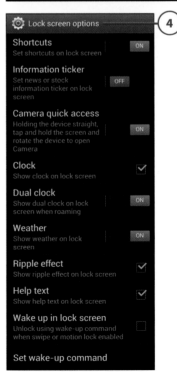

Displaying Owner Information

You can optionally display horizontally scrolling owner information on the lock screen, such as your name, phone number, and so on. Tap Owner Information on the Security screen. On the Owner Information screen, enable Show Owner Info on the Lock Screen, enter the owner information (or any other text that you like) in the text box, and press the Back key.

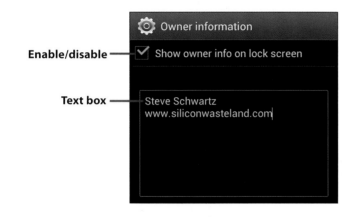

Enable/disable

Text box

Showing/Hiding Passwords and PINs

If you're concerned that people might peek as you enter passwords or PINs, you can disable Make Passwords Visible to obscure the characters as you type. Conversely, when enabled, this setting briefly shows each character that you type and then quickly replaces it with a bullet.

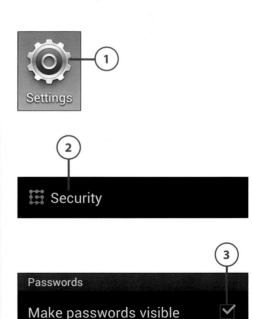

1. On the Home screen, press the Menu key and tap Settings (or tap the Settings shortcut).

2. On the Settings screen, tap Security.

3. In the Passwords section of the Security screen, remove the check mark from Make Passwords Visible.

Using Voice Services

If you don't like tapping and typing (or are driving, making such activities dangerous and probably illegal), you can use S Voice, Voice Command for Apps, and Google Search/Voice Actions to control the phone. Note that Voice Command for Apps and Google Search run independently of S Voice.

S Voice

S Voice is a voice app that allows you to ask questions in natural language ("Where can I find pizza?") and launch apps ("Open Calculator"). The result may be a direct answer, a web search, or the launch of an appropriate app, such as Maps.

1. *First Run Only*: Launch S Voice by tapping Apps, followed by S Voice or by tapping an S Voice shortcut on the Home screen.

Subsequent Launches

You can configure S Voice so that you can subsequently launch it by double-tapping the Home key, as well as by tapping the S Voice icon. With S Voice running and onscreen, press the Menu key, tap Settings, and enable Launch S Voice.

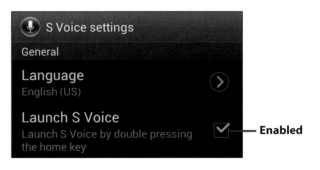

2. The S Voice screen appears. Say your first question or command. For example, you might ask, "What's the weather like today?" to see the weather forecast for your city.

3. To ask S Voice the next question or give it a new command, tap the microphone button or say the wake-up phrase ("Hi, Galaxy" is the default phrase).

S Voice Command Help

If you want assistance with question phrasing and app commands, tap the Help icon on the main screen; say "Help"; or press the Menu key, tap Settings, and tap Help on the S Voice Settings screen.

Be sure to check out the other settings, too. You can change the wake-up command, show or hide offensive words, and set your home address, for example.

What's the weather like today ②

Here is the forecast for today for Lake Havasu City, Arizona

Lake Havasu City, Arizona
Wed, 12 Sep

89 °F   97° 80°
Clouds giving way to some sun

AccuWeather.com

Say 'Hi Galaxy' to wake me up

— **Help**

Enable/ ③
disable
voice
prompt

Voice Command for Apps

When Voice Command for Apps is enabled, you can use voice commands to control Phone, Clock, Camera, and Music Player.

1. On the Home screen, press the Menu key and tap Settings (or tap the Settings shortcut).

2. In the Personal section of the Settings screen, tap Language and Input.

Settings ①

②

Ⓐ Language and input

3. To enable or disable Voice Cmd for Apps, drag the slider to the On or Off position, respectively.

4. To specify the apps that you want to control, tap the Voice Cmd for Apps text and add or remove check marks.

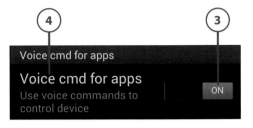

Supported Voice Commands

Review the screen for examples of supported voice commands, such as Pause, Play, and Next in Music Player. Note that you must launch the appropriate app and make it active before saying commands; they don't work from the Home screen or within other apps.

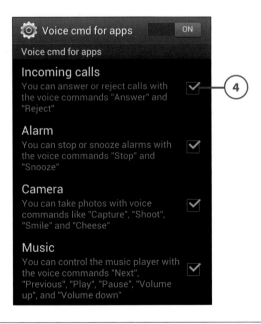

Google Search

Using the voice input feature of Google Search, you can perform a web search, find people in Contacts, or issue commands to apps called *voice actions*.

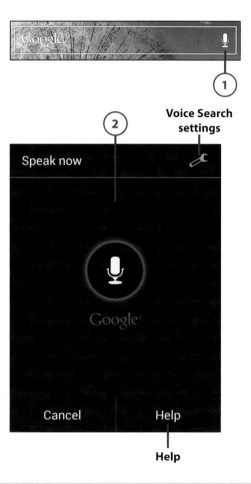

Voice Search settings

Help

1. On a Home screen page that contains the Google Search widget, tap the microphone icon to its right.

2. Say the search text, such as "Samsung Galaxy S III" or "Stephen R. Donaldson," or issue a voice action command, such as "Listen to Talking Heads," "Call Jameson Auto Body," or "Navigate to Fairview Apartments."

>>>Go Further

MORE VOICE ACTIONS

In addition to Google Search's search capabilities, you can use it to perform many of the actions that Voice Command for Apps supports. All you have to do is preface your request with a supported keyword or phrase, such as "send email," "send text," "call," "directions to," or a contact's name. For examples of other supported phrases, tap the Help button and then Tutorial.

I'm especially impressed by the "note to self" command. Whatever you say is emailed to your Gmail account as an audio attachment and as speech converted to text.

Accessorize!

Another way to customize your phone is to add accessories and devices. If you're thinking of decking out your Galaxy S III, consider these add-ons:

- *Case.* Even with a two-year contract, the Galaxy S III represents a significant expense. A case that protects the phone if it slips out of your hands is a solid, inexpensive investment. Be sure to pick one that's specifically designed for the phone. Although others may fit, it's important that the case provide easy access to all phone controls, features, and the entire screen. If you're checking out brands on the Internet, search for "Samsung Galaxy S III cases."

- *Headset.* For the sake of clarity, privacy, and fewer traffic tickets, consider using a headset. If you just want to listen to music and videos, a wired headphone will suffice. If you also want to use it for phone calls, you'll need a headset (a device that also includes a microphone). There are two kinds of headsets: wired and wireless. Note that almost all Bluetooth wireless headsets provide audio to only one ear, making them poor choices for listening to music. See "Bluetooth Headset" in Chapter 1 for information on connecting and using a Bluetooth headset.

- *Samsung HDTV Universal Adapter.* With this optional adapter, you can mirror whatever's on your phone on an HDTV. See "Mirroring the Phone on an HDTV" in Chapter 18 for instructions on using the Samsung HDTV Smart Adapter to transmit video, music, games, and other media from your phone to an HDTV.

Hot spot activated icon

Enabled

Hot spot name

Connected device name

Connection instructions

Mobile HotSpot — ON

Galaxy S III_t-mobile
Allow all devices to connect

Connected device

Acer17
90:a4:de:00:77:84
192.168.43.35

How to connect to your Mobile HotSpot

1. Activate Wi-Fi on the device
2. Find Galaxy S III_t-mobile in Wi-Fi network list
3. Connect to Galaxy S III_t-mobile by entering frankzappa as the password
4. Enjoy your Mobile HotSpot

Allowed device list   Configure

In this chapter, you learn how to transmit data from your phone to other devices. Topics include the following:

→ Creating a Wi-Fi hotspot with the phone
→ Using a USB cable to tether your phone to a Windows PC
→ Using the optional Samsung HDTV Universal Adapter to mirror the phone's screen on a television

Powering Other Devices

If your laptop or desktop computer currently lacks Internet access— when traveling or during a provider outage, for example—you can use your phone as the equivalent of a USB (*tethering*) or wireless (*mobile or portable hotspot*) modem. And if you've purchased the optional Samsung HDTV Universal Adapter, you can connect the phone to a flat-screen TV to mirror whatever is displayed on the phone.

Creating a Mobile HotSpot for Wi-Fi Devices

Using the phone's Tethering and Mobile HotSpot settings in combination with your 3G or 4G data connection, your phone can become a *hotspot* through which up to eight Wi-Fi devices can simultaneously connect to the Internet. (Note that some carriers call this a *mobile* hotspot, while others call it a *portable* hotspot.)

It's a Plan Add-On

Creating a hotspot and tethering (discussed in the next section) normally aren't part of a data plan; they're an add-on. Sprint, for example, charges an additional $29.99 per month for these capabilities and limits you to 5GB of data. If you use this feature only sporadically (such as while traveling), you can add it to your plan when needed and then cancel at the end of the month. If you're interested in creating a hotspot or using tethering, you need to contact your carrier and determine the cost, limits, and so on.

1. Open Settings by doing one of the following: tap the Settings icon on the Home screen, tap the Notifications panel icon, press the Menu key and tap Settings, or tap Apps followed by Settings.

2. In the Wireless and Network section of Settings, tap More Settings.

3. Tap Tethering and Mobile HotSpot.

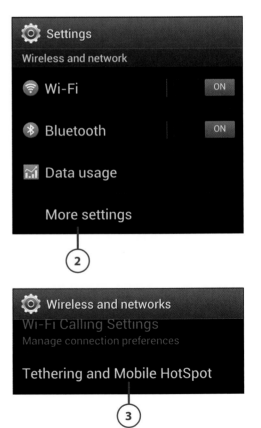

4. On the Tethering and Mobile HotSpot screen, drag the Mobile HotSpot slider to the On position.

Or Simply Launch the App

Some carriers, such as T-Mobile, provide an app that—when launched—takes you directly to the Tethering and Mobile HotSpot settings. It's not special software; it's simply a shortcut that takes you directly to this step with a single tap.

T-Mobile's Mobile HotSpot icon

5. If Wi-Fi is currently enabled for the phone, an Attention dialog appears. Tap OK to turn Wi-Fi off. (The hot spot runs only over 3G or 4G, not Wi-Fi.)

6. If the Mobile HotSpot screen doesn't automatically appear, tap Mobile HotSpot.

7. The Mobile HotSpot screen shows the current connection settings. You can optionally edit the default settings—changing the connection name, selecting a security protocol, and setting a password—by tapping Configure.

8. Make any desired changes to the settings and then tap Save.

HotSpot enabled

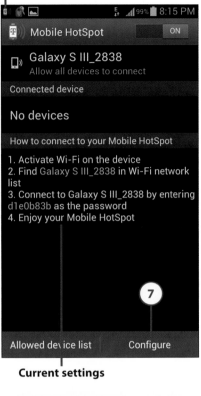

Current settings

9. Connect up to eight Wi-Fi-enabled devices (laptops, tablets, iPods, and so on) to the hotspot network by selecting the hotspot network's name on each device and entering the password when prompted.

10. When you're finished, deactivate the hotspot by dragging the Mobile HotSpot slider to the Off position (see step 4). Mobile HotSpot quits, all connected devices are disconnected, and Wi-Fi is automatically re-enabled—assuming a Wi-Fi network is available.

Not connected

Connections are available

Wireless Network Connection   ∧

Galaxy S III_t-mobile ———— 9

Red Dragon's Lair

suddenlink.net-F239

Roan-Family

grodt

Your Getaway

wireless

Open Network and Sharing Center

8:18 PM

Enter password

Connect to a Network

Type the network security key

Security key: frankzappa

☐ Hide characters

OK   Cancel

Successful connection

Currently connected to:

Galaxy S III_t-mobile
Internet access

Wireless Network Connection   ∧

Galaxy S III_t-mobile   **Connected**

10

⊛ ⚋ ↑ ▭   ✳ E↓↑ ▁ 48% ▮ 6:49 PM

🔲)) Mobile HotSpot   ON

▯)) Galaxy S III_t-mobile
Allow all devices to connect

It's Not All Good

Test Your Connection Speed

As with other cellular connections, the faster the network and the better your signal strength, the more usable a hotspot connection will be. Before enabling a hotspot and committing to the monthly fee, you might want to use your phone's current data connection to run a speed test at http:// speedtest.net.

Living in an area without 4G, my results over a 3G connection were abysmal—think extremely slow dialup modem: 98 kbps download, 80 kbps upload. Repeating the test using the Mobile HotSpot resulted in a dramatic drop to 3 kbps for downloads. To put this into perspective, my normal cable Wi-Fi results are around 15,000 kbps (download) and 1,600 kbps (upload)—150 times faster than 3G and 5,000 times faster than using the Mobile HotSpot.

Although it's sufficient for sending text-only email, I wouldn't want to do anything that required large amounts of data to be transmitted. For example, sending an email message with a 2 MB attachment took more than 10 minutes. Before committing to the Mobile HotSpot fee, consider where you'll be when using it and what networks will be available to you.

Tethering the Phone and a PC

Another way to provide Internet access to a computer is to connect the phone and computer with the phone's USB cable (referred to as *tethering*). Unlike a mobile hotspot, tethering is restricted to only one computer at a time and is currently available only for Windows and Linux-based computers.

Bluetooth Tethering

In addition to USB tethering, Sprint supports wireless tethering using Bluetooth.

1. *Windows users only:* Visit the Support section of the Samsung site (http://www.samsung.com/us/support/), and download and install the USB driver for your carrier's phone. You can find your model number by going to Settings, About Device, Model Number on your phone. Note that this is a one-time process.

T-Mobile Samsung Galaxy S III

Finding Your Model Number

To find your phone's model number, go to the Home screen, press the Menu key, tap Settings, and then tap About Device.

> Model number
> SAMSUNG-SGH-I747

AT&T Samsung Galaxy S III

2. Connect the phone's USB cable to the phone and to one of the PC's USB ports.

3. Open Settings by doing one of the following: tap the Settings icon on the Home screen, tap the Notifications panel icon, press the Menu key and tap Settings, or tap Apps followed by Settings.

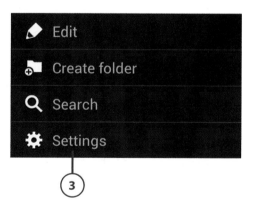

4. In the Wireless and Network section of the Settings screen, tap More Settings.

5. On the Wireless and Networks screen, tap Tethering and Mobile HotSpot.

6. On the Tethering and Mobile HotSpot screen, enable tethering by tapping USB Tethering.

7. After the computer recognizes the phone, you can use the PC's browser and other Internet applications.

8. When you're finished using the phone as a USB modem, remove the check mark from USB tethering (see step 6), eject the phone hardware in the same way that you do with other connected USB devices, and disconnect the USB cable.

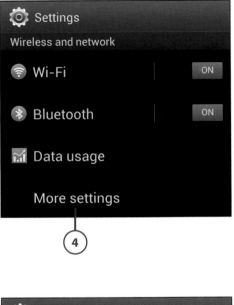

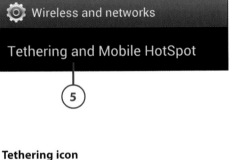

Tethering icon

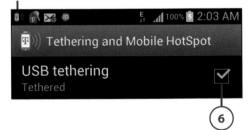

An Extra Step

In Windows, you may see a notice that the necessary drivers are being installed. When installation finishes, an AutoPlay dialog box appears, asking what you want to do with the new connected device—the phone. Click Open Device to View Files.

Open Device

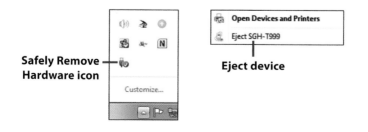

Disconnection Details

You should never simply unplug a USB data device. Click the Safely Remove Hardware icon at the far right of the Windows task bar, choose the Eject *phone model* command from the pop-up menu that appears, and then—when you're told that it's safe to do so—disconnect the USB cable.

Safely Remove —— **Hardware icon**

Eject device

Mirroring the Phone on an HDTV

With Samsung's optional HDTV Universal Adapter (11-pin), you can use your flat-screen TV to display whatever is shown on the phone.

1. Plug an HDMI cable into the HDTV Universal Adapter.

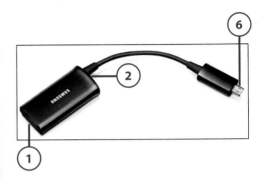

Adapting the Samsung HDTV Smart Adapter

If you purchased the Samsung HDTV Smart Adapter for a Galaxy S II, you can purchase a Samsung adapter tip—the HDTV Adapter Tip (5 to 11 Pin Converter)—so you can also use it with the Galaxy S III.

2. Plug the USB charger cable into the HDTV Universal Adapter. (The adapter must receive continuous power to work.)

3. Connect the other end of the HDMI cable to your flat-screen television.

4. Plug the USB charger into an electrical outlet.

5. Using your television's Input menu, select the HDMI input to which the HDTV Universal Adapter is connected.

6. Plug the HDTV Universal Adapter's cable into your phone's USB port. A tone plays to signify that the connection is active.

7. On the phone, run any application that you want to display on the TV.

>>>Go Further

HDTV SMART ADAPTER TIPS

Note the following when using the Samsung HDTV Universal Adapter:

- *Playing music.* Depending on the quality of your television's speakers, stored and streamed songs may sound excellent.

- *Viewing videos and movement.* Video quality can vary greatly, depending on its source and the application. For example, streamed video using an app, such as HBO Go, is generally encoded for playback on the phone's diminutive screen rather than on a large, flat-screen TV. Expect the quality to be only passable. Games, on the other hand, may look wonderful. Experimentation will teach you what displays well and what doesn't.

- *Viewing photos.* Multi-megapixel photos may look fine when displayed on a TV. When viewing pictures, you can rotate the phone to switch from portrait to landscape display.

- *Viewing slide shows.* Slide shows don't have to be silent or dull. When playing a Gallery photo folder as a slide show, you can select a song to accompany the show and a transition effect to use when switching to each new slide.

Time since restart

Remaining charge

Refresh

In this chapter, you learn to use your phone more efficiently by managing your plan, available storage, and memory; adding a memory card; updating system software; and performing basic troubleshooting. Topics include the following:

→ Using Task Manager to manage memory
→ Conserving the battery manually and by enabling Power Saving mode
→ Making the most of your talk and data plans
→ Viewing and expanding current storage
→ Performing system updates
→ Troubleshooting and resetting the phone

Optimizing and Troubleshooting

There's more to understanding your Galaxy S III than being able to make phone calls and master a handful of favorite apps. This chapter delves into material that you don't need to commit to memory or even read immediately—but when you need it, you'll be happy to have it.

Managing Memory with the Task Manager

You've probably noticed that most apps don't have a Quit or Exit command. That's because the Android operating system is designed to handle memory management behind the scenes. If free memory is running low, for example, unnecessary processes automatically shut down. However, if you occasionally feel the need to take a hands-on approach to quitting apps and freeing memory, you can use the Task Manager.

1. Launch the Task Manager by pressing and holding the Home key and then tapping the Task Manager button.

Switching to a Recent or Active Application

When you press and hold the Home key, the vertically scrolling list of thumbnails represent currently active and recently run apps. To switch to or launch one of these apps, tap its thumbnail.

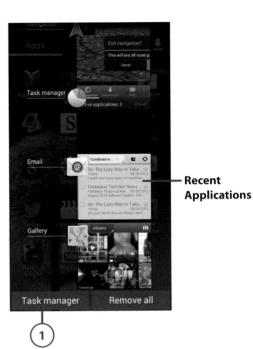

Recent Applications

2. In Task Manager, tap the Active Applications tab to view the currently running applications. To close a listed app, tap its End button; to simultaneously close all running applications, tap End All.

Active Applications

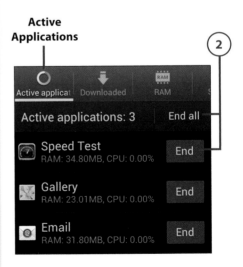

3. *Optional*: If exiting running applications doesn't resolve your memory issue, tap the RAM tab and then tap Clear Memory to clear all inactive and background processes. Note the change in the memory bar.

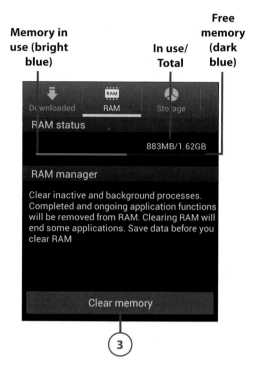

Memory in use (bright blue)

In use/ Total

Free memory (dark blue)

Clear Memory Consequences

As is the case with using the Force Stop command (described later in this chapter), Clear Memory can have consequences other than simply freeing memory that unnecessary processes are using. As the RAM screen explains, "Completed and ongoing application functions will be removed from RAM." This causes running apps to abruptly quit and background processes to halt.

Conserving the Battery

Depending on how frequently you use the phone and what you typically do with it, you can automatically help conserve the remaining charge by enabling Power Saving mode.

If you prefer to take the manual approach, you can disable features that aren't currently needed or change certain default settings so that less power is drawn. To monitor how various apps and the operating system use the battery, you can run the Battery app.

Show the Battery Percentage

Although the battery indicator in the status bar gives you a rough indication of the remaining charge, you can alter it to show the exact percentage remaining. Open Settings, tap Display, and enable Display Battery Percentage.

Configuring and Enabling Power Saving Mode

When Power Saving mode is enabled and a low battery level is detected, selected features are automatically changed or disabled to extend the remaining charge.

1. On the Home screen, press the Menu key and tap Settings, or tap the Settings shortcut.

2. In Settings, scroll to the Device section and tap the Power Saving text.

3. The Power Saving screen appears.

4. To enable Power Saving mode, ensure that the Power Saving switch is in the On position.

5. Enable or disable power-saving options by tapping check boxes. To view a brief explanation of what each option does, tap Learn about Power Saving.

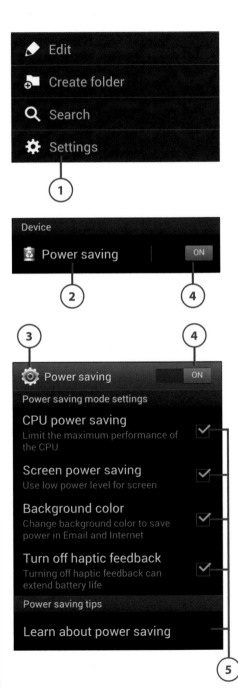

Using the Notifications Panel

If you don't need to change the Power Saving settings, you can quickly enable or disable Power Saving mode by opening the Notifications panel, scrolling the icons to the right, and tapping the Power Saving icon.

Power Saving icon

Tips for Manually Conserving the Remaining Charge

If the battery is generally draining too quickly or you want to extend usage time when the battery is almost depleted, you can manually change certain settings as needed or set new defaults.

- If you aren't currently using some services, such as Wi-Fi, GPS, or Bluetooth, disable them in the Notifications panel by tapping their icons. Turn them back on only when you need them.

- The phone's screen draws considerable power. Consider reducing the Screen Timeout value or Brightness (in the General section of the Display Settings). And whenever you're done using the phone for a bit, tap the Power button to instantly darken the display—rather than waiting for the Screen Timeout.

Service icons

Display Settings

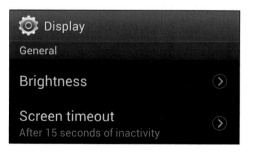

- Consider checking less frequently for new email. For unimportant email accounts, you could set the frequency to Once a Day or Never, for example. You can still perform manual refreshes as often as you want. To change the retrieval frequency, launch Email, press the Menu key, tap Settings, and tap the account that you want to manage. Scroll to the Data Usage section, tap Email Check Frequency, and select a new frequency.

- Avoid battery-intensive activities. Playing videos and games prevents the display from timing out. Streaming videos or music transfers large amounts of data to the phone, requiring that the connection be constantly running.

- In standby mode, the phone consumes little battery power. Although it may be sacrilege to suggest this, you can take things a step further by powering off the phone when you won't need it for an extended period. For instance, if you *never* answer the phone after you go to bed, consider turning it off nightly—or leave it on while you charge it during this period.

Data usage
Email check frequency ⊙
Every 5 minutes

Email Check Frequency

Plug It In

Before the battery dies, you can continue a conversation and other activities by quickly plugging the phone into a wall outlet or USB port. The phone charges as you continue to work. When your call or app activity concludes, power off the phone and allow the battery to charge normally.

It's Not All Good

Why Is This App Using GPS?

It's amazing and rather sad that so many apps now have a GPS component (given that it contributes to battery drain and data usage and frequently seems an unnecessary feature). For example, although a game might use GPS information to pair you with or show nearby players, is the feature essential? Will the app function without it? My attitude is that, unless enabling GPS benefits *me*, I'd rather not play "Where in the World Is Steve Schwartz?"

You have several options with GPS-enabled apps. First, turn off GPS and see whether the app still functions or whether GPS is forced back on. Second, if the app has a Settings command, you may be allowed to disable the GPS component or substitute a manually entered location. Third, enable GPS while using the app and quickly disable it when you're done. Fourth, decide whether the app is *really* important to you. If not, uninstall it and search for a similar app that doesn't require GPS. Fifth, suck it up and reconcile yourself to recharging more frequently. If an app is critical to your business or life, it's probably worth the battery drain.

Viewing Battery Usage by Features and Apps

If you want to get a handle on which features and applications are draining your battery the most, you can find the answer in Settings.

1. On the Home screen, press the Menu key and tap Settings, or tap the Settings shortcut.

2. On the Settings screen, tap Battery.

3. The summary that appears lists the features and applications that have been consuming the battery since the last time you charged the phone and shows the percentage of consumption attributable to each.

Refreshing the Data

While viewing the Battery screen, you can force a refresh to display up-to-date consumption figures.

4. *Optional:* Tap an entry to view additional information. Depending on the item, you may be able to alter its settings to reduce battery consumption or execute a force stop for it (in the case of an application).

3

Refresh

Battery

100% - Discharging

1m 7s on battery

Screen 39%

Android System 14%

Android OS 8%

4

Use details

Screen 39%

Battery used by display and backlight

Use details

Time on 1m 5s

Adjust power use

Reduce screen brightness and/or screen timeout

Display

Display Settings

It's Not All Good

About Force Stop

Android is responsible for handling memory management, halting applications and processes as needed. In general, you should avoid using the Force Stop button for items that present it. (In Task Manager, tapping End is the same as performing a Force Stop.) Don't assume that Force Stop is the equivalent of a computer program's Quit or Exit command. Similar to the capability to *force quit* a misbehaving Mac or PC application, Force Stop's main purpose is to give you a way to semi-gracefully shut down an app or feature that isn't responding.

When used as a means to temporarily halt battery consumption or free memory, the consequences may not always be what you intend. You may lose information; the phone, app, or feature may be left in an unstable state; or you might have difficulty restarting the application or feature.

Managing Talk Time and Data Usage

If you're on a limited talk, messaging, or data plan, the key to avoiding over-age charges is relatively simple: *Know your plan*.

Checking Current Usage

Each carrier generally offers several ways for you to check the current month's usage. For example, if T-Mobile is your carrier, usage data can be viewed in the Notifications panel. You can also check usage by tapping the Notifications panel entry to launch T-Mobile My Account (or by tapping its icon in Apps). Select the Account Info tab and tap Detailed Usage. Note that in a recent update, T-Mobile also provided widgets that display usage data on the Home screen.

Notifications panel (T-Mobile)

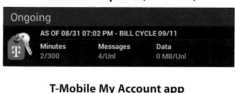

T-Mobile My Account app

Carriers also typically provide a phone number that you can call to check your minutes. If you use Sprint, for example, dial **#4** from your cell phone.

You can also check the carrier's website. At a minimum, you should be able to see your usage for the current billing cycle. In addition, there might be an option to automatically receive a notification if you come close to exceeding a plan limit. *Forewarned is forearmed.* (It has taken my entire life to come up with a decent reason for using that phrase.) For example, when you're precariously close to hitting your monthly data limit, you can take steps to ensure that additional data-intensive activities (such as streaming videos or music) occur only over Wi-Fi.

Managing Data Usage

If your data plan has a monthly limit, you can enable the Data Usage setting on the phone to automatically warn you when you come close to exceeding your data limit—ignoring data transmitted over Wi-Fi, which doesn't count toward usage. You can also manually disable *mobile data* (using the cell network to transmit data) if you're close to exceeding your plan limit.

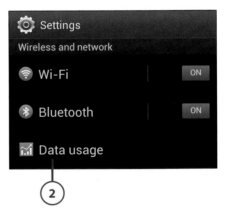

1. From the Home screen, press the Menu key and tap Settings, or tap the Settings shortcut.

2. In the Wireless and Network section of Settings, tap Data Usage.

3. The Data Usage screen appears. The position of the Mobile Data switch determines whether the cell network can be used to transfer data to and from the phone (On) or whether you're restricting it to Wi-Fi data transfers (Off). If you're close to or have exceeded your monthly limit, switch it to Off to prevent additional overage charges.

4. To instruct the phone to warn when you're approaching your monthly limit, tap the Set Mobile Data Limit check box. When the data limit (red line) is reached, mobile data is automatically disabled; you must do additional data transfers over Wi-Fi. Continue with the remaining steps.

5. Ensure that the Data Usage Cycle matches your monthly billing cycle and represents the current cycle. If the cycle is incorrect, tap it to select a different 30-day period. If the billing period is incorrect, tap it, tap Change Cycle, specify the date when the usage cycle resets, and tap Set.

6. Set the red slider to match your plan's data limit (in gigabytes), set the orange slider to reflect the usage amount at which you want to be warned, and set the white bars to the period that you want to monitor.

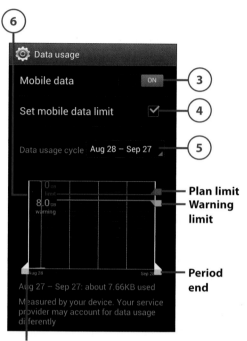

Plan limit
Warning limit
Period end
Period start

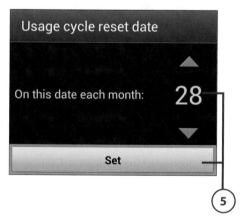

7. To set additional Data Usage
options, press the Menu key.
Enable Data Roaming to allow
your phone to use other networks
for data access when roaming.
Enable Restrict Background Data
to prevent background data
access. Enable Show Wi-Fi Usage
to add a separate Wi-Fi tab to the
Data Usage screen, showing the
last 30 days of Wi-Fi data usage
and the apps that contributed to
the usage.

What's Cheaper?

If you have unlimited or inexpensive text messaging, it may be advantageous
to send texts rather than make short calls. Conversely, if you're billed 25¢ per
message, it may be cheaper to call. Note that your carrier may allow you to
block incoming text messages (see the carrier's website for details). Received
text messages—including unwanted ones—may be billed to your account at
the same rate as texts that you send.

Can This Call Be Made Later?

The distinction between free and paid calls is typically determined by the
time of day at the location where you make the call. If your free minutes
begin at 7:00 p.m. each weeknight, try to reserve lengthy, chatty calls for eve-
nings and weekends.

If you're traveling and are in a different time zone, your daytime and evening
calling periods generally change to match the current time zone. Before
heading out, check your plan to be sure. Similarly, if you're leaving the country, ask how out-of-country minutes are billed. A friend didn't bother (thinking that he was covered or that the rate would at least be reasonable) and
returned to discover that his handful of calls resulted in a bill of several hun-
dred dollars.

Viewing and Expanding Storage

Although the Galaxy S III has 16GB of internal memory and 12GB of that is available for storage, you can exhaust it with a combination of photos, videos, apps, and other data. You can expand the available storage by inserting a *microSD* (Secure Digital) or *microSDHC* (Secure Digital High Capacity) card into the phone's internal slot, adding as much as an additional 64GB.

Viewing Used and Available Space

Consult the Storage section of Task Manager to view the total, used, and available storage on your phone.

1. Launch the Task Manager by pressing and holding the Home key, and then tapping the Task Manager button at the bottom of the screen.

2. Select the Storage tab at the top of the Task Manager screen.

3. Interpret the displayed information as follows:

   • *System Storage* is the phone's built-in storage.

   • If you've inserted a microSD or microSDHC card into the phone's internal slot, you'll see an *SD Card* entry.

   • The bright blue section of each bar represents the used space; the dark blue section is the unused/available space. Above each bar are two figures. The first represents used space; the second is the total space.

Storage Shrinkage

When viewing the Storage section of Task Manager, you may think that the total space listed is less than the stated specs. Don't be alarmed; the figures are correct. Although the Galaxy S III comes with 16GB of internal storage, part of it is used as system memory. And when formatted for use, an 8GB microSDHC card has only 7.48GB of usable space, for example.

Adding a Memory Card

The Galaxy S III can accommodate up to a 64GB memory card in its internal slot. When picking a card, take note of its *class* in the item description. The lower the class number (2, 4, 6, 8, or 10), the slower the card. Under current class specifications, the class indicates the card's minimum sustained write speed in megabytes per second. Thus, a Class 2 card should be capable of writing data to the card at 2 Mps (megabytes per second) or faster. (If a card's description or packaging doesn't mention a class, assume that it's Class 2 or slower. That frequently explains why some cards are so inexpensive.) Currently, you can purchase Class 10 cards for $0.75–$1 per megabyte. Unless you already have an older, slower card, there's little monetary incentive to go slower than Class 10.

Next, determine the amount of storage you need. An 8 or 16GB card suffices for most people. If you intend to pack it with videos and music or regularly shoot hundreds of photos or lengthy movies, go for the highest-capacity card you can afford—64GB is the max.

All Cards Aren't Equal

Even within a class, cards aren't identical. First, some Class 10 cards are able to sustain a minimum 10 MB/second *read* speed, as well as write speed. Second, the minimum speed on some of these cards is occasionally much faster than 10 MB/second. Third, based on user reviews and ratings on sites such as Amazon.com and NewEgg.com, some cards appear to be knockoffs that are slower than their stated class, fail quickly, or don't work at all.

When choosing a card from an online source, read the user comments, note the ratings, and check the seller's return policy. Amazon.com, for example, sells a card called AmazonBasics that's highly rated by purchasers and is inexpensive, too. Other sources for memory cards include pricewatch.com and crucial.com.

Although it isn't necessary, make a note of whether your chosen card includes a microSD to SD adapter. If it does, you can slip your tiny card into the postage stamp-sized adapter and use it in devices that require an SD card rather than a microSD card. (In the same vein, be sure that your chosen card is a *microSD* or *microSDHC*, not an SD or SDHC. Only a micro card will fit in the phone's slot.)

Inserting the Card

Whether the card is new or being moved from another phone or device, the first step is to insert it into your phone.

1. Shut down the phone by holding down the power button, tapping Power Off in the Device Options dialog box, and then tapping OK in the confirmation dialog box.

2. Remove the battery cover from the back of the phone by slipping your fingernail into the slot at the top of the phone (above the camera) and prying off the back.

3. Grasp the memory card by its edges and turn the card so that its gold contact strips are facing down. The labeled side of the card should face up.

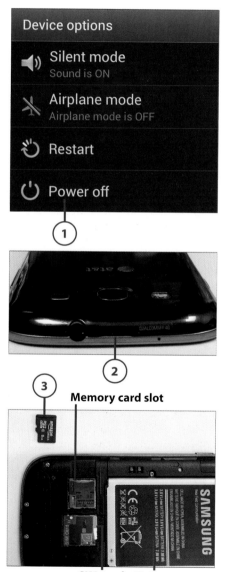

Memory card slot

SIM card   Battery

4. Carefully press the card into the
   slot until it clicks into place, and
   then replace the phone's back
   cover. Ensure that the back cover
   is sealed around all edges.

Formatting the Card

If the memory card contains
unwanted data from another phone
or device or isn't recognized by the
phone as formatted, you can format
the card.

1. On the Home screen, press the
   Menu key and tap Settings, or tap
   the Settings shortcut.

2. On the Settings screen, tap
   Storage.

3. On the Storage screen, scroll
   down to the SD Card section and
   tap Format SD Card.

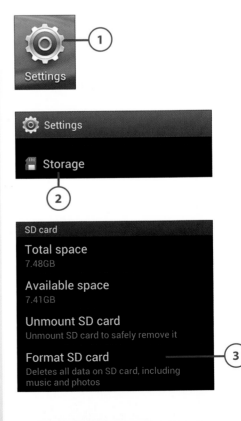

4. On the Format SD card screen, tap the Format SD Card button.

5. Tap the Delete All button.

6. The memory card is unmounted, erased, and remounted to enable the phone to see and use it.

⚙ Format SD card

Data cannot be recovered after SD card is cleared. Continue?

Format SD card

④

⚙ Format SD card

Formatting SD card will delete all data. Data cannot be recovered. Continue?

Delete all

⑤

Removing the Card

The following steps explain how to safely remove a memory card from the phone in order to replace it with a different card or move the card to another device. You begin by unmounting the card so that it can be safely removed.

1. Press the Menu key and tap Settings, Storage, Unmount SD Card. Tap OK in the confirmation dialog box.

SD card

Total space
7.48GB

Available space
7.41GB

Unmount SD card ————①
Unmount SD card to safely remove it

Format SD card
Deletes all data on SD card, including music and photos

2. Shut down the phone by holding down the power button, tapping Power Off in the Device Options dialog box, and then tapping OK in the confirmation dialog box.

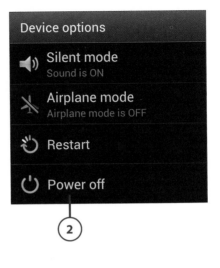

3. Remove the battery cover on the back of the phone by slipping your fingernail into the slot at the top of the phone (above the camera) and prying off the back. For photos relevant to this and the remaining steps, see "Inserting the Card," earlier in this section.

4. To free the SD card, press it into the slot. The card will spring free. Carefully slide the card out of the slot. (When handling the card, be sure to grasp it only by its edges.)

5. Replace the battery cover.

Using the Card as a USB Drive

By following the instructions in "Transferring Files over USB" in Chapter 13, you can mount your phone as an external drive on your Mac or PC (like a flash drive), enabling you to freely copy files in either direction. You can view and access the files on your phone by going to the Home screen and tapping Apps, My Files. The phone's built-in memory is displayed as sdcard. The extSdCard folder is your memory card.

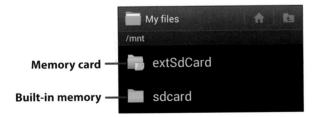

Checking for System Updates

It's a good idea to periodically check for system updates. You automatically receive a notice of a firmware update, for example, but you can still perform manual checks whenever you like.

Check the Battery First

Before performing any kind of system update—especially firmware and Android—be sure you have sufficient charge to complete the process. Interrupting updates can have dire consequences for the phone.

1. On the Home screen, press the Menu key and tap Settings, or tap the Settings shortcut.

2. On the Settings screen, tap About Device.

3. On the About Device screen, tap Software Update. From this point forward, each carrier handles the update process in its own way. For example, T-Mobile immediately checks for updates, whereas AT&T provides two additional confirmation screens to which you must agree.

What Version of Android Do I Have?

Halfway down the About Device screen, you can see the version of the Android operating system that's installed.

Troubleshooting

This section provides suggestions for correcting simple and complex problems that can arise with the phone.

General Troubleshooting

When trying to correct an app-related or OS-related problem, work from the least extreme to the most extreme solution. For example, depending on the type of problem, you might try the following—in order:

- Try appropriate button presses, such as pressing Home or Back to leave the current screen or pressing the Power button.

- Use the Task Manager to close unnecessary apps. (Press and hold the Home key, and then tap the Task Manager button.)

Task Manager button

- For app-related issues, check the app's settings (if it provides them) by pressing the Menu key and tapping Settings. You can also try uninstalling and reinstalling the app to see if the problem is corrected. If the issue continues, check the developer's website for an update and troubleshooting information, or consider uninstalling the offending app.

- For battery-drain issues, turn off services that you aren't currently using, such as GPS, Bluetooth, and Wi-Fi. Open the Notifications panel and tap icons to enable or disable services.

Active services (green)

- Restart or shut down the phone by pressing and holding the Power button, tapping Restart or Power Off, and then tapping OK in the confirmation dialog box.

- For a complete lock-up or similar issue, remove and replace the battery (as described in the next section).

- Perform a Factory Data Reset (as described in the section "Performing a Factory Data Reset"), but only if the phone is so messed up that no other solution remains. Call your carrier's customer service/technical support before performing this procedure or, if one of their stores is nearby, take the phone in to be checked out.

Fixing a "Lockup"

Yes, some apps have bugs, so what you *expect* to happen sometimes doesn't match what *actually* happens. When the worst occurs—the phone locks up so solidly that it ignores all taps, swipes, button presses, and attempts to power down, restart, or recharge—there's still something you can try. Remove the battery, wait two minutes, and reconnect the battery. Note that this is a solution of last resort. If you perform it while the phone is writing to memory, you can lose data.

Performing a Factory Data Reset

Using the Factory Data Reset procedure, you can restore your phone to its initial factory-default apps and settings. If you're planning to trade it in, sell it, or give it to a family member, performing a factory data reset also removes the applications you've installed and erases your personal data, such as contacts, photos, and music files. If this data is important to you, be sure to back it up to a microSD (Secure Digital) or microSDHC (Secure Digital High Capacity) memory card prior to performing the reset.

1. On the Home screen, press the Menu key and tap Settings, or tap the Settings shortcut.

2. On the Settings screen, scroll to the Personal section and tap Back Up and Reset.

3. On the Back Up and Reset screen, tap Factory Data Reset.

4. On the Factory Data Reset screen, review the explanation and then tap Reset Device.

Settings

1

↺ **Back up and reset**

3   **2**

Personal data

Factory data reset
Reset all settings and delete all data on device

⚙ Factory data reset

All data will be erased from USB storage, including your Google account, system and application data, settings, and downloaded applications
· Music
· Photos
· Other user data
· The key for decrypting files on the SD card. (You cannot use files on the SD card after a factory data reset)
You are currently signed in to the following accounts:

Ⓢ resident@hotmail.com

f resident@hotmail.com

🐦 ss

⌷ resident@hotmail.com

Reset device

4

5. To perform the factory reset, tap the Delete All button. If you've changed your mind, press the Back key.

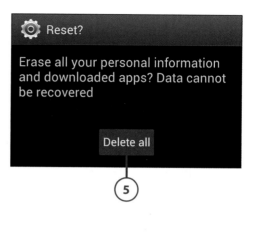

Index

Numerics

A

D

F

U

V